MURDER
IN THE
FOURTH CORNER

TRUE STORIES OF WHATCOM COUNTY'S EARLIEST HOMICIDES

1st edition.

Chuckanut Editions
Village Books
1200 11th St
Bellingham WA 98225
360-671-2626

research and writing by T. A. Warger
illustrations by Jake Reller
cover design by Vladimir Verano
page design by Brendan Clark
edited by Sara Stamey

ISBN 9780989289122

LCCN 2014953622

Printed in Bellingham WA, USA.

also by T. A. Warger

books

Mount Baker (with John D'Onofrio)

documentary films

The Mountain Runners (with Brian Young)

Shipyard (with David Lowrance)

Preface

Murder in the Fourth Corner is a collection of true stories, highlighting the more unsavory history of early Bellingham and Whatcom County. The title refers to the fourth corner of both the United States and Washington State. If the community finds this to be an entertaining and compelling read, I hope to continue with the subject; a potential series on Whatcom County murders and other seedy transactions would fill that gap in our history.

For several years I've collected and sorted through what early Bellingham and Whatcom County newspapers have colorfully referred to in their headlines as the most brutal "killings," "murders," "butchery," "slaughters," "massacres," "slayings," "carnage," "homicides," "bloodshed," "murder-suicides" and "crimes of passion" that have ever blotted our community. Several of these gruesome murders piqued my interest enough that I pulled their criminal case files to learn more. Other cases hit a dead-end, providing no further answers or clues, but lured me to ponder the same dilemmas that faced the original investigating authorities—was it murder or suicide?

My grandmother Viola Winn would have scolded me, saying, "These are our town's little secrets. Skeletons are best left in the closet. What would you drag them out for?" I always liked to poke my nose where it didn't belong. Perhaps it was because no one would answer my questions well enough to satisfy my curious mind. I had to search for the answers on my own.

I have no malicious intentions of dredging up sensitive crimes of Bellingham and Whatcom County's recent past. Those wounds are best left alone to heal for a few more decades. I'm more inclined to resurrect death and mayhem from the time of settlement, on through the desperate times of the Great Depression era. Nearly all these slayings have been long since forgotten. As in many other communities, the monstrous act of murder has become a part of our history, and a heinous slice at that.

Why would I resurrect these stories? Aside from being a bit of undiscovered local history, the topic interests me for several reasons. First, years of newspaper research spanning the dawn of the twentieth century have introduced me to a form of daily journalism that was far more dramatic, sensationalized, and morbid than anything we can imagine today. If you think the media is graphic now, read a newspaper from 1900. How does one beat headlines like "Killed with Axe After Struggle with Fiend: Nine Gashes in Head, Screw Driver Driven Into the Brain"?

Second, I grew up in a tiny hill-town in the northwestern corner of the Massachusetts' Berkshires. Of the ten small communities of western Franklin County, Shelburne Falls is the largest, with a population of about 1,500. During the fall of 1988, I was still living in this hamlet, alongside the beautifully quiet Deerfield River, when one of the most heinous murders to have ever taken place in that small town occurred. Needless to say, it was devastating for such a tight community. The horrendous affair came a week before Halloween. It involved twin, teenage sisters, a jilted maniac boyfriend wielding a butcher knife and wearing, yes, a hockey mask. Lots of blood was spilled that day. And that isn't even a tenth of the story. For nearly five weeks, we all lived in fear, in the most surreal environment imaginable. What I witnessed during those haunting days in my little hometown, together with family, friends and neighbors, resembled a classic scene of villagers carrying torches and pitchforks combing the woods, just like in the movies. The experience made me more acutely aware of human nature, its frailty of falling into paranoia, and the existence of our dormant fears when reacting under the stress of panic from the unknown.

Unfortunately, in the course of human existence, murder has been a reality, seemingly woven into our social fabric since the dawn of time. So ingrained is its evil presence that the act of killing holds a level of prominence in many religions. Maybe it's human nature for us to be obsessed with the macabre. Biblical history recorded that no sooner did Adam and Eve become evicted from the Garden of Eden, than in Genesis 4:1-8, we read about Cain's killing of his brother Abel. The first murder! Killing and slaying became the norm during biblical times, until I suppose, God decided he'd had enough, and put his foot down in Exodus 20:1-17, giving us Commandment number six of the Ten Commandments, "Thou Shalt Not Kill." This Commandment is oddly preceded by the obviously more important Commandments 1-4, which are reserved for God's own vanity, declaring himself the One and only, and taking precedence over the sin of killing.

But, like any good law, legal document or Congressional bill, there's always a little wiggle room, a loophole or an exemption. The Old Testament provided a few of these by making allowances for justified killing in the context of warfare (1 Kings 2:5-6), capital punishment (Leviticus 20:9-16), and self-defense (Exodus 22:2-3). So, not everything was written in Sinai stone.

Bellingham and Whatcom County have had a vivid history of such slayings, much like anywhere else. There were beheadings, shootings, stabbings, poisonings, hangings, stranglings, and bludgeonings. The stories within barely scratch the surface.

Author's Note

Murder in the Fourth Corner is not meant to be an academic work, with each sentence marked and marred with footnotes and citations. It is written purely for the purpose of entertainment and enjoyment, to be read while curled up in your favorite cushy chair, with the lights turned low, on a stormy night.

That said, I promise you that great pains were taken in researching each murder case or mysterious death to its fullest conclusions. I strove to obtain the facts of each, and not to delve into embellishment. I wanted to preserve the essence of the reporting of the day and give the reader a feel for the language used.

In some cases information was lacking, hampering my efforts. In other cases, I found an abundance. I was pleased when stumbling upon previously undisclosed information found in court records, and was annoyed by absurd dead ends in others. Nothing was more unacceptable and bewildering than to finally recover the court record of a notorious case, only to find the file contained nothing more than a detailed list of jury lunch expenses. Why were these receipts saved, but none of the record of the actual trial?

You may notice that in some cases I have dug up more questions than answers. Not all the answers exist, some so buried in legal archives that the whole story might still remain elusive. Because these are short stories of local murder and mayhem, a great depth of study is beyond the scope of this book. Possibly a reader will find one case intriguing enough to carry it further. My hope is to stimulate the reader's mind, in order to encourage formulation of your own conclusions.

Each story is accompanied by a list of sources and where they were obtained. At times, I tried to retain some of the flamboyant essence of journalistic reporting of the period, as I have a deep affection for the dramatic flair it offers. It is also a case study of how people of that era received their daily information.

My apologies to those who discover they now live in a "murder house." On the upside, you could make it as famous as the Lizzie Borden, Ma Barker, or the "Black Dahlia" homes.

T. A. Warger
Bellingham, Washington
2014

Acknowledgments

In the course of any project, so much is owed to those who contribute their time and knowledge, receiving little glory in return but a notation. They are truly the unsung heroes, as so little would be accomplished or discovered without their tireless efforts. To all those who contributed to the making of this book, I thank you dearly and cheer all your energetic efforts in the aid of preserving history.

I wish to thank local historian Candace Wellman for her permission to reprint "Murder in Happy Valley," first published in the *Journal of the Whatcom County Historical Society* in December 2012. I would never have been able to give the Padden/Clark tragedy the justice that she had already done so well.

The highest praise and my warmest thanks go to the talented artist Jake Reller. Many stories included in *Murder in the Fourth Corner* have no photographic record. His artistic renderings provide vivid, chilling images where actual photographs do not exist.

I owe much praise to Heather Britain, who pulled the old criminal case files from Whatcom Superior Courthouse. She had a horrified look when I produced a list of some 40 case files to be retrieved. Also, I want to thank Kirstie Massey and Kati Johnson for their assistance and patience in pulling records and fighting the new microfilm reader. They prevailed.

Alison Costanza from the Washington State Archives Northwest Regional Branch was, as always, fantastic in her knowledge of the holdings, and directed me to other potential sources.

I cannot omit Maggie Cogswell, assistant research assistant at the Washington State Archives in Olympia. Talk about undaunted heroism! With Maggie's support, in two days we pulled thirty prisoner records and scanned 200 files and photographs.

Jeff Jewell, Whatcom Museum photo archivist and historian, is a walking Wikipedia of local history. Thanks again, Jeff, for years of support, your vast knowledge, and unique capabilities of pulling photos and facts out of a hat.

Ruth Steele, thank you once again for the gracious support, which you and the Center for Pacific Northwest Studies have provided over the years.

Laura Nason Jacoby, thank you so much for opening your grandfather's image collection for my endeavors. The Galen Biery Collection is a wealth of images and knowledge collected over decades.

Thanks to Mike Impero, for his help with the murder at the Lone Jack mine.

Thanks once again to Brian Young for helping me out. You always have my back.

To Steve Pickens, who never asked questions, but gave up his photos to me anyway.

Special thanks to the glamorous Renee Sherrer for her support, editing skills, research abilities and factory-style talent at scanning images and documents.

And another special thank you to Brendan Clark, Chuck and Dee Robinson, and to all of the wonderful people at Village Books. What a gift to publish locally!

In memory of my nephew

Clinton Joseph Warger

November 29, 1985 to April 7, 1999

who I suspect was murdered

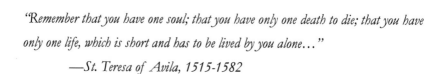

"Remember that you have one soul; that you have only one death to die; that you have only one life, which is short and has to be lived by you alone..."
        —St. Teresa of Avila, 1515-1582

"Man is the cruelest of animals."
        —Nietzsche

Table of Contents

PART I

Chapter 1: Murders on the Delta 19
Delta Precinct of Whatcom County, 1915

Chapter 2: Murder in Happy Valley 35
The 1880 Deaths of Michael Padden and Susan Clark
By Candace A. Wellman

Chapter 3: The Two Deaths of Snowball Wallace 51
Bellingham, 1907

Chapter 4: The Maple Falls Monster 75
Maple Falls, 1906-1911

Chapter 5: Who Butchered the Elk Street Butcher? 127
Bellingham, 1905

PART II

Chapter 6: Who is Charles Weatherford?...................................157
Bellingham, 1908

Chapter 7: Tunnel No. 21 167
South Bellingham, 1911

Chapter 8: The Cobbler 173
Blaine, 1918

Chapter 9: Sam Thompson 215
Maple Falls, 1910

Chapter 10: The Barber of Bellingham 231
Bellingham, 1933

Chapter 11: Headless in Bellingham 261
Bellingham, 1914

Chapter 12: Murder at the Lone Jack 285
Lone Jack Mine, Bear Mountain, 1915

Chapter 13: Foul Play at White Horn 301
White Horn, Birch Bay, 1927

MAPS 309

Part I

Chapter 1
Murders on the Delta

The first warning neighbors had of the tragedy was when eleven-year-old Darrel Thomson came running down the road and met a party of ranchers going to late evening church services at a nearby schoolhouse. The boy was clad only in his nightclothes, barefoot, and slathered in mud, having repeatedly fallen as he ran. His flight for assistance was hastened by a shot fired at him as he turned out of the yard-gate of his home. Samuel Thomson, having reloaded his gun, was determined to exterminate the whole family while about his bloody task. Releasing the boy to the women folk, the ranchers hurried to Thomson's home to see what horrors were unfolding.

Many Family Quarrels

Family quarrels were quite frequent at the Thomson residence. One neighbor claimed that Samuel's wife Josephine would take sinister delight in nagging her husband until one of his noted "tilts" would begin. Such occasions always ended with Thomson flying into a "rage of temper." One hired young man, who worked a season for Thomson, claimed he saw some real quarreling. More frequently, arguments regarding the management of the farm would take place in public. At such times "the most dramatic terms Thomson would use, would be to tell his wife to keep her mouth shut."

During the fall of 1914, Josephine, angered by her husband's temperament, left him for several months, returning to him in January. Just before her arrival, Thomson was in Bellingham displaying a letter from his wife, in which it appeared that whatever had come between them was all forgotten, and that he was glad for it. He seemed to take pleasure in telling his friends that his wife was coming home, and that she had written that he should take good care of himself. Thomson was excited, but friends of Josephine knew she was making a grave mistake.

Samuel Park Thomson was 64 years old in 1915. He was a native of Canada, although there is mention of him emigrating from Ireland. He came to Whatcom County from Montreal some twenty-eight years earlier, to establish a ranch for himself. The Thomson house stood on the crossroads leading from Haynie Corner to the city of Blaine. The plat today would cover three-quarters of road frontage from Sunrise Road, starting from W. Badger Road and extending north to Burk Road. To the south, from the corner of Sunrise and W. Badger, the property ran nearly half the length toward Delta Line Road. And to the north from Sunrise to Delta Line, the mid-section was Thomson property. It was a stunning piece of property by any stretch of the imagination.

Thomson was a hard worker, owning and building upon 232 acres of the finest farmland in the county. It was reputed to be worth at least $20,000. Mabel Young, Samuel's first wife, was born in Maine in 1878. She gave birth to Lynn, their only son, on March 25, 1896, in the Delta Precinct of Whatcom County near Custer. Mabel was eighteen years old to Samuel's forty-two at the time.

In 1899 Mabel ran away with a hired hand whose name was Osborne. Thomson is said to have taken a departing shot at the man as the couple fled. After a traumatic divorce for Samuel, Mabel married Osborne, but she died shortly after. Samuel, who was at first heartbroken, became very bitter from the experience. The 1900 census lists only him and his son Lynn living at the farm. The space for "marriage status" was left blank on the form.

Samuel remarried in 1908 to a Canadian woman named Josephine. The 1910 census listed a six-year-old lad named Darrel, who was taken in as a foster child and later adopted by the family.

Josephine Thomson was about 55 years old, "a comely looking woman and well preserved," said the *Bellingham Herald*. Neighbors knew her as a hard-working woman, self-reliant, fearless, and a friendly neighbor. Since their marriage, Thomson's health began to degrade. He had fierce headaches and mood swings that led them to fight often. She wasn't afraid of Samuel, and she wouldn't take his growing temper either. This led to further clashes between the couple and eventually to her leaving for a few months in 1914.

Reserved in their statements, Delta Precinct ranchers would later admit they began to stay clear of Samuel Thomson, citing several reasons. Family quarrels had intensified so that Samuel's hollering and temper could be heard from a distance. He would instigate violent encounters with his neighbors, or become irritated by them. It was thought that jealousy was behind his anger, as he still seethed from his former wife's running away. Hired hands came and left, but no one knew the reasons for their departure. Whether it was by his accord, or just to escape the family farm, Lynn left to join the Navy at an early age. Luckily, at the time of the tragedy, he was at sea serving aboard the USS *Maryland*.

But there may have been other reasons behind Thomson's behavioral change, his rages, and his increasing fits of anger. Thomson was compelled, it was discovered later, to consult his physician nearly every week. His doctor visits were increasing, and it was believed that failing health had much to do with the coming tragedy. Thomson had been ill, and his mounting pain most likely resulted in an increasing dependence on opiates, including laudanum. These drugs, coupled with the severity of his pain, likely contributed to his irrational mental state, delusions, paranoia, and rage, making the farmer increasingly unpredictable.

Josephine's return home in January may have been her last attempt to reconcile their relationship. The neighbors had already made their decision long ago, as one would later state: "At times he was hard to get on with… and it was the policy of the nearby ranchers to have as little to do with him as possible."

A Dark Day, Followed by a Dark Night

Weeks after returning home, Josephine Thomson apparently had enough of her husband. Samuel may have been ailing, but he was also becoming dangerously abusive. Josephine was a sharp, intelligent woman, with little fear of her husband. That was a perilous mistake on her part. She underestimated the effect of Samuel's history with his first wife Mabel, when she threatened divorce. Josephine had consulted Bellingham attorney S. M. Bruce the previous week concerning her legal grounds for obtaining a divorce, but had made no definite move to start proceedings.

Sunday March 14 was another dark day in the Thomson home. It was also a dreary and wet day outside, which didn't help the mood at the ranch. Samuel was in excruciating pain again, and had heavily medicated himself. He must have been particularly foul and cruel that day, as Josephine told Samuel she'd had it with him, and would be seeking a divorce. We know this conversation occurred due to the tragic events that unfolded, and from witness testimony. There is no doubt that Samuel Thomson dwelled on the conversation, and his mind may have harkened back to his former true love Mabel, who had left him for their hired hand. As it happened, Thomson had just recently hired a new man weeks earlier. In his delusional state, did Thomson see the new, young hired man as a rival?

Hugh Boyd was a strapping, twenty-eight-year-old, finely built fellow, who had once been a cowpuncher in western Canada. Ranchers say he appeared in the area about two months prior, looking for work. But, in the dead of winter there was little work to offer. Thomson hired the man possibly due to his own failing health and the fact that Hugh was a fellow Canadian. There was certainly work to be done. If Samuel had been ailing and found his daily chores burdensome, he would have needed the help. Thomson had over a hundred chickens, twenty-five head of cattle, at least fourteen horses and a pen of hogs to feed. Besides the usual farm chores, Samuel had Hugh repairing field equipment in the barn, as spring was fast approaching. Hugh was offered modest pay, meals and a room in the main house.

Had Thomson tried to pick a more appropriate night for his sinful deed, he could not have done better. It was a dark, disagreeable night with curtains of falling rain. Few people were out, and those who were hardy enough were on their way to evening church services. Around 7:00 pm Josephine settled young Darrel into bed for the evening, after which she told Samuel she had to run over to the neighbor's for a bit. It's possible that while visiting she shared her news of leaving Thomson for good. She may have even been saying goodbye to her neighbors. Between the time she left to go to the neighbor's and her return, events are uncertain, but we know their fatal results.

Hugh Boyd came into the house soon after Josephine had left. Working all afternoon in the chilly barn, Boyd was tired. He would have washed up first, and then, for some reason, sat down at the dining room table on a hard wooden chair. As uncomfortable as it may seem, Hugh seemed to have nodded off with his bare feet resting on the rungs of the table.

Samuel Thomson heard Boyd come indoors, and waited patiently from his bedroom for him to settle in. With his 12-gauge shotgun in hand, the rancher slowly maneuvered from his hiding place and crept down the hallway. Turning the corner into the undivided kitchen-dining room, he could see the back of the sleeping man's head. The rancher moved stealthily behind him, as if stalking prey in the wild, lowered the barrel of his gun, and pulled the trigger.

From all indications, the man never knew what hit him. As described later, the impact of the round took half of Hugh's head clean off, spreading skull, bone, and brain matter straight out across the table, onto the floor, and against the wall. Blood splattered one side of the room and dripped from the ceiling.

At that very moment, Josephine Thomson stepped into the house through the kitchen door. At first, the shudder of the blast in such a confined space must have shaken her senseless. Just a few feet to her right were the backs of the dining room chairs and the profile of her husband. Hugh was still sitting upright at the table with what little there was left of his head, attached to the stump of his neck. The room was peppered in red. Josephine must have been thunderstruck by the horrific sight. Samuel just stood there for a few moments looking at Josephine, his shotgun in hand. He made no effort of quick movement toward her. This theory is borne out by the following events.

Josephine must have offered some plea or attempted dialog with her husband as she moved in the direction of the kitchen wall telephone. Whatever defense she exhibited soon vanished. Quite possibly, her husband's vacant expression and blazing stare in those last moments must have indicated that Samuel had totally lost his senses.

She picked up the receiver and started hollering for help to the switchboard operator in nearby Custer. A verbal exchange of sorts soon began with Ida Flint, but Samuel didn't seem worried in the least. He didn't even attempt to intercede in his wife's efforts to get help. Slowly and methodically, Thomson opened the breach of the shotgun, extracted the empty shell casing, and replaced it with another shell from his pocket. With a clap, the breach closed and the farmer turned the barrel toward his wife. As Josephine screamed into the mouthpiece, a piercing bang erupted in the confined kitchen space, as Thomson pulled the trigger once again.

The most startling, and without doubt, the only real insight into the tragedy is what Ida Flint, switchboard operator in Custer, heard as Josephine jerked down the receiver and cried for help:

"I was at the switchboard," said Ida in recounting her experience, "at just 8 o'clock last night, when the board signal from the Thomson house lit up before me. Before I could think twice came a scream of 'Help,' and this was repeated several times in a frantic voice. In between the cries of 'Help' she shrieked, 'I'm Shot,' then I heard her say in a voice more subdued, 'Sam Thomson, how could you do it?' She said no more. But at this point Mr. Thomson said, and he must have been speaking in a pitched voice or else close to the receiver, as I could hear him quite as well as I could Mrs. Thomson, 'Put that down.' Then the receiver clanked against the wall and I heard footsteps. The next minute I heard a shot. I could not be sure about hearing a second shot, as the telephones were busy and I was making other connections. I should say that the entire scene took place in the space of two minutes from the time the signal flashed until I heard the shot after the conversation at the phone."

TELEPHONE GIRL HEARS WIFE CALL FOR HELP OVER WIRE AS CRAZED HUSBAND FIRES SHOT

Samuel Thompson, Reputed to Be Worth $50,000 and Owner of 200-Acre Farm at Haynie Corner, Kills Hugh Boyd, Hired Man, as Latter Sits at Table and Fires at Wife When She Calls Frantically for Aid Over Telephone—Shoots Her Second Time as She Begs for Mercy Lying Prostrate on Ground—Shoots at Adopted Son, Who Notifies Neighbors.

The shot that Ida Flint heard struck Josephine's shoulder, shattering that side of her body. She bled profusely from a gaping wound that tore out a portion of her torso, as was evidenced by her body parts embedded in the wall by the wall phone. She dropped the receiver and drew her body along the wall for support, struggling to reach the kitchen door, hoping to escape while her husband reloaded. The wound was a mortal hit, but Josephine managed to stagger outside into the front yard. Samuel walked slowly behind, watching her every slowing step. That she stumbled from the house and was shot a second time in the front yard, is borne out by young Darrel.

The only witness to the any part of the shooting was the eleven-year-old adopted son, Darrel, who was asleep upstairs when he heard the shot that struck his mother. Shut off from the lower part of the house, Darrel did not hear the shot that killed Boyd, or if he did, he made no mention of it later. He was awakened by the shot that was fired at his adopted mother, as she stood at the telephone. Darrel ran downstairs to the bloody kitchen. He was barefoot and wearing only his lightweight nightclothes. He looked out the door and saw his parents outside. His crying mother was lying on the ground, the boy said, "moaning and begging for mercy."

Darrel stood in the doorway while his mother frantically called out for help. She lay prostrate in the yard near the fence bushes, begging her husband not to shoot again. As Darrel came out onto the porch he heard his father yell, "You'll get a divorce, damn you, you will!" The second shot was fired, flame leaping from the muzzle of the barrel. The boy wasted no time getting away. He leaped from the porch and started running for the gate, some twenty yards from the house, turning onto the muddy road. He ran along the frontage length of the house, past his father. As Darrel ran with all his might in the darkness, Thomson watched his son escaping. Fishing in his pockets for another shell, the rancher extracted the empty carriage that just killed his wife. Reloading, he took aim and fired a shot toward his running son, missing him.

WOMAN SEEKS DIVORCE AND HUSBAND IS INSANE

"You Will Get a Divorce, D—n You!" He Cries as He Fires— Goes to Clump of Woods Half Mile From House and Kills Himself, Pulling Trigger of Shotgun With Foot—Motive for Killing Boyd Not Known.

A minute or two later, Darrel reached a party of ranchers on their way to the schoolhouse for late church services. He could see their lanterns in the distance to guide him, and he made straight toward their glow.

Darrel was petrified and stammered his words with mixed tears as he told his story. Perhaps the ranchers wouldn't have believed the heinous tale, except that the farmer in question was Samuel Thomson. After securing the boy, the men decided to investigate their neighbor's farm. The sight that met their eyes was almost too horrifying for description. In the front yard, partly under a shrub, lay the mangled, bloody body of Mrs. Thomson. At first they thought that her life was not extinguished, and a runner was sent to Custer for a physician. Her limp body was then gently lifted and placed on the porch, where it was determined she had passed.

The ranchers looked just inside at the kitchen door, but probably missed seeing Hugh Boyd, as no mention is made of finding him that night. Chances are they never entered the house for fear of being shot themselves. Not being equipped to meet up with a raging maniac with a shotgun, the ranchers fled, leaving Mrs. Thomson's corpse resting on the porch. With half a dozen lanterns in the party, Thomson, if he so desired, could have had a well-lit target for his murderous shotgun.

The Next Morning

Sheriff Wilson Stewart first received notice of the murders from Fred Flint of Custer, as relayed by his wife, Ida. Summoning two of his deputies, Sheriff Stewart started for the Thomson ranch. Going by way of Custer, the party arrived at the ranch about 10:15 pm. A dozen or more ranchers joined the sheriff's party on the road, and the hunt for Thomson began.

The odds were in favor of Thomson if he were in his own home waiting with a loaded shotgun. Sheriff Stewart went around the side of the house with his deputies, Ernest R. Nunamaker and David H. Dunkle, to peek through the windows. They looked for any sign of movement before entering, but Thomson's dog was soon heard barking at the barn. Thinking they had their man, Stewart and his deputies and the ranchers charged from the house to surround the barn. Dark and rainy, the officers rushed the entrance, threw open the large doors, and hastily crossed the threshold not knowing what would happen next. Fortunately, no one was shot at, and Thomson was not to be found. Realizing they were being reckless, Stewart put a stop to their foolhardiness.

Stewart knew that Thomson was ill, both mentally and physically, and possibly suicidal at this point, not caring who he took with him. He figured his fugitive was holed up and if they started poking around in the darkness, someone would get shot by accident, or on purpose. The sheriff posted a deputy to be hidden on the road, and another near the barn, and then pulled back the rest of his men until morning.

Josephine's body was gathered in a blanket and hastily retrieved from the porch. Closer examination in better light revealed that she was killed instantly in the final savage attack. The left lower side of her head was torn away, and it was "that shot as she lay in the yard, undoubtedly, that accomplished the enraged husband's desire."

During the night, Stewart interviewed the Flints, Thomson's neighbors, and young Darrel, to piece together the events leading up to the shooting, and to glean any new information previously overlooked. The neighbors knew Thomson was very ill. Whether it was entirely physical or mental, they were not sure. It was common knowledge, through the wife and son, that the rancher was taking heavy doses of opiates for the problem. Many believed he was going insane. During the week previous, Josephine was telling close friends of her intentions to divorce Samuel, which no doubt would have set the rancher off. These facts, coupled with what the boy had heard during the shooting, gave Stewart a better understanding of the tragedy.

Darrel again mentioned talk of divorce. It occurred to Stewart that Thomson's unbalanced mind may have been "tilted" by recollections of his previous wife running away with the hired man. If that were so, the one question remaining was, where was Hugh Boyd? Stewart suspected he would discover that answer in the morning.

When daylight finally arrived, a search party was organized to make a thorough search of the property. The barn and house were searched first, but there were no signs that Thomson had entered the barn during the night. Daylight revealed a scene of carnage in the front yard. On the ground a large patch of blood lay thick, with remains of brain matter, flesh, and shattered bone. It was with trepidation of what they might find in the house that the men hesitantly moved forward. On the porch, officers paused to see where Mrs. Thomson had been laid before she was retrieved. Blood still seeped through the floorboards.

If the scene in the yard turned the men's blood cold, the inside of the house was even worse. On the threshold, where Mrs. Thomson had stood shouting into the telephone, a large pool of blood indicated that the first shot had struck her vitally.

Upon entering the open dining room just feet away and with his back to the front door, they found Hugh Boyd, who sat in the chair as if asleep.

As officers and ranchers walked in, they could see what little remained of his scalp, right ear, and neck, which rested lightly across his folded arms. From the body's position, thought Stewart, there was no doubt that Boyd was shot while asleep, or as he sat resting his head. The right side of his head was missing and his brains lay scattered on the table. So sudden was his death that his bare feet still rested on the lower rungs of the table. Boyd was killed instantly, evidently caught unaware by his assailant.

A close inspection of the house, the blood splatter, and the position of the bodies indicated to Stewart that Boyd was shot first. He surmised that Josephine only had time to contact the switchboard operator in Custer before Thomson had reloaded the gun and turned it on her. The telephone receiver was still dangling when Sheriff Stewart reached for it and set it back on its cradle. The wall surrounding the telephone was splattered with Josephine's blood. A wide bloody smear snaked along the wall heading toward the door, resembling a wandering paintbrush, obviously made as Mrs. Thomson attempted to flee.

On the floor, Stewart could see exactly where Thomson had stood when he shot his wife. There was a shotgun shell casing on the floor next to a partial bloody outline of Thomson's shoe. Directly behind him was the chair where the body of Boyd sat in repose. Below the hired hand, Josephine's blood pool extended almost to his chair. Bloodstains were found in other parts of the house, most noticeably in Thomson's bedroom. It was thought that Thomson went back into the house for more shells after firing the shots in the yard.

Now it was time to find their killer. Neighbors claimed Thomson never would permit himself to live after going on such a murderous rampage. Searchers fanned out and began a systematic hunt about the farm. Finding nothing, they searched the fields and headed toward a stretch of woods a half-mile in the distance. Their hunt was rewarded at about 10 am, finding the body of Samuel Thomson beside a large log under a tree grove. Thomson had apparently gone as far into the woods as his strength allowed, then placed a final shell in the shotgun.

It was Sheriff Stewart's theory that Thomson killed himself that evening, soon after slaying the others. Thomson had tied a string to the trigger of the shotgun, put his foot into a loop at the other end, placed the muzzle of the shotgun against his left breast, and pulled the trigger with his toe. Death was instantaneous as the entire load of shot passed through his heart and out his back, leaving a hole larger than a man's fist.

If Samuel Thomson planned the murders with any degree of care or certainty, he left no evidence that Sheriff Stewart could find. The rancher left behind no letters or notes of any kind indicating his intentions. No one will know the exact moment when Thomson's mind turned and set forth his determination to exterminate his family. Whether or not Hugh Boyd mixed into the "family tilts" could not be known, but it is certain that Boyd wholly unexpected the attack on him.

In his last Will and Testament, admitted into Probate by Judge William Pemberton, Samuel Park Thomson left one-third of his estate to his wife Josephine and the remainder to his son Lynn. The will was made in November 1912, and Clifford K. McMillin, who was named as friend and executor, was confirmed as the Executor. Having been murdered by her husband, Josephine's inheritance passed to their son Lynn who was considered a minor at nineteen. To release Lynn from naval duty, $238.00 was posted for early discharge. The court would so order attorney Charles B. Sampley as Lynn Thomson's guardian until he became of age.

As McMillin was settling outstanding debts, it was noted that $78.00 was owed on medical expenses, indicating that Thomson was having serious medical issues at the time of his rampage. Those asking for their debts to be paid included Dr. Carl C. Hills of Bellingham, Dr. Victor B. Mounter of Bellingham, and Dr. William C. Keyes of Ferndale.

A curious notation in Thomson's Will was that Lynn was his "sole and only child." However, a photograph of two young men in the possession of Judge E. M. Day, who held an official inquiry into the double murder, indicated two sons. The photograph's cover bears this inscription: "From your two sons; to Mr. and Mrs. Thomson." This led Judge Day to suspect that there was another son, but Thomson's Will refutes this possibility. Adopted eleven-year-old son Darrel wasn't even mentioned, nor was there any reference whatsoever as to what became of him.

Lynn Thomson returned from the navy and married his sweetheart, Violet C. McLeod on January 4, 1916. It took several years to settle his father's estate, paying off outstanding debts and settling accounts that he had let fall behind due to his illness. It would seem from all indications that Lynn had the estate settled, but for whatever reason he and Violet started selling off sections of land in April 1917. By February 26, 1919, the last of nine portions were gone. Maybe the farm was just too big for them. Or maybe the memory of that horrible night was too unbearable. Regardless, the young couple moved into Bellingham, where Lynn became a truck driver.

Samuel and Josephine Thomson, along with Hugh Boyd, were all buried side by side in unmarked graves in Lynden. In February 1964, Lynn Thomson passed away and is buried in Burlington, Skagit County.

SOURCES

American Reveille: 3/16/1915.

www.ancestry.com

Bellingham Directory: 1914, 1915, and 1916.

Bellingham Herald: 3/15/1915, 3/17/15, and 3/18/15.

Heritage Quest

www.geneologybank.com

U.S. Census. Whatcom County, Washington: 1890, 1900, 1910.

Washington State Digital Archives.

Washington Superior Court for Whatcom County, Probate No. 2881, 1915.

Whatcom County Assessor & Treasurer – Property Details.

Whatcom County Auditor Grantor Indirect and Grantee Direct Records, 1914-1926.

Whatcom Sheriff's records 1915, Washington State Regional Archives.

Chapter 2
Murder in Happy Valley

The 1880 Deaths of Michael Padden and Susan Clark
by Candace A. Wellman

An earlier version of this chapter was published in the 2012 Whatcom County Historical Society Journal.

Few Bellingham residents familiar with Lake Padden, Padden Creek, or Padden Lagoon know anything about the "Happy Valley" neighborhood's first settler, who discovered the lake and became the namesake for all three. Fewer still know of the tragedy that enveloped the first two families who staked homesteads on the natural prairie south of today's Sehome Arboretum and South Hill, which is now neatly sliced in two by Old Fairhaven Parkway.

While the fortunes of Whatcom County's 1854 Sehome Coal Mine beside Bellingham Bay slowly declined from fires and floods until its operation was constantly troublesome by the 1870s, many coal miners migrated in and out of the community around it. Experienced men came from the British and Pennsylvania mines, while others went into the tunnels under the bay for the first time. Many employees moved on to the newer and larger coalmines near Seattle, while others with their Lummi Indian wives started the first homesteads in the county on the lower Nooksack River. In 1870, miner Michael Padden decided to try his luck on the prairie only three miles around the bay from the mine. Thomas Clark followed him and staked a claim next to Padden's. Both families being good-humored Irish immigrants, their prairie soon took on the name "Happy Valley."

Probable wedding portrait of Michael and Anna Padden, 1877. Laura Jacoby, Galen Biery Collection.

Thomas and Susan Clark

Thomas Clark, another Irishman, served in Her Britannic Majesty Queen Victoria's army from the age of 19. After his stints in India and China, the army posted him to Esquimalt near Victoria, B.C., where he left the service when his term expired. He and his Irish wife Susan and three small children joined the Sehome Mine community. When they moved to Happy Valley after Michael Padden had staked out the best soil, Clark had to take a homestead that was swampy, hilly, and full of creek flood debris, which made quick income a problem. He worked days at the mine and then alone into the dark evenings on his farm. The Clarks built a home atop a bowl-shaped knoll that afforded the family a view across the valley. In 1877, the local paper reported that Thomas narrowly escaped death when a coal room deep underground collapsed. Following the close call at a dying mine, he began to work at the newly discovered coal seams across Lake Washington from Seattle, chiefly the Newcastle mine. Except for working visits home, he had to leave Susan and the older children to tend the garden and orchard. After eight years, the family had wrestled barely eight acres into cultivation.

The Padden home. Circa late 1880s – 1890s. Laura Jacoby, Galen Biery Collection.

Michael and Anna Padden

Michael Padden's history was very different, and while the general facts are clear, some dates and events are not consistent across researchers or documents. He was apparently a young teenager when his family emigrated in 1848 from famine-devastated County Mayo, Ireland. The older males found mining jobs in Mauch Chunk, an eastern Pennsylvania coal town in the Lehigh Valley. After coal was discovered in Washington Territory in the 1850s, Michael migrated with his brothers and their families, followed by the senior Paddens who left mining and settled on a homestead near Fort Vancouver, Washington. About 1858, Michael married a Pennsylvania friend's young widow, Mary Shearing, and had two children with her. At first, his brothers Dominick and Patrick worked at Sehome while Michael labored in the new Seattle-area mines. Sehome Mine management recruited Michael to be the foreman of their operation in 1863, but he was unhappy with the place and returned to the King County mines. In a community and family tragedy, Dominick Padden died in a Sehome Mine accident four years later, leaving behind his widow and two children. Not long after, Michael brought Mary and his children to Sehome, probably to help support Dominick's family if they hadn't left.

Three years later, in 1870, Padden filed the first homestead on the prairie that became Happy Valley. By that time, he and Mary had three children, one still an infant. When Mary gave birth to their fourth baby on the homestead, she died. In 1877, Michael married much-younger Anna Connelly, whom he had met at Renton's Talbot Mine. His Irish bride suddenly had four children to mother before she had two of her own. The Paddens increased their holdings before Anna's parents, Edward and Bridget Connelly, and their four other children, moved to Happy Valley onto land Connelly bought from Padden.

Both the Clarks and the Paddens worked hard to establish their adjoining farms while the men continued to work at the mines. Though they had different histories, the Irish miners became friendly and supportive neighbors in Happy Valley. Their houses were at most 1500 feet apart, Connelly was a male presence during the long hours the men were miles away, their wives had company, and the numerous children had playmates.

A Boundary Dispute

Two years after the wedding and the Connelly move to neighboring land, it became apparent that there might have been a surveying error in a 3 acre wedge of land that held four of the Clark's apple trees and some of their garden, so the men had County Surveyor John Cornelius re-survey the lines. Both owners agreed with Cornelius that the piece of land was properly Padden's before Thomas Clark returned to the Newcastle Mine. Though Clark publicly agreed to the partition, his wife and children still felt entitled to the apple trees that had been nurtured in the swampy and rocky soil with such difficulty. They continued to resent the loss of nearly half of their cleared ground while Padden had the better soil easier to turn into a profitable farm. The Clark family continued to use the land in question without asking permission. With seven children under sixteen, the Clarks needed every possible bit of income and food production they could manage. Though Padden was annoyed, he did not make an issue of it at first.

In late winter 1880, Padden and Connelly eagerly used every decent day to build and repair fences around their fields before planting season began. On Monday, March 8, Padden, his son Anthony (13), Ed Connelly, and his son Bernard (18) worked on several fences; these included the new fence that would clearly demarcate the boundary of the disputed acreage, and the job carried on after their noon dinner. Anthony carried posts and rails to his father, while Michael staked the new fence between his land and Clark's. Strangely, they found stakes placed earlier to mark the line had been knocked down. Had the Clark's plow accidentally hit them? Padden couldn't tell before he repositioned them. Connelly and Bernard drove posts at the edge of one of his adjoining fields some distance away. About one o'clock, Anna Padden walked the brushy and tangled path to the distant creek to bring home a bucket of water, probably to wash the dinner dishes or to do more Monday laundry.

This twentieth century photograph showing the proximity of the Padden (arrow on left) and Clark homes, (arrow on right) both just east of 23rd Street in Happy Valley. Photo by Leslie Corbett; Gordon Tweit Collection, Whatcom Museum.

Growing Resentment

From her front porch at the top of the knoll, Susan Clark watched the Padden and Connelly men work while two of her older children labored in the vegetable garden below, not far from the fence. She had been left alone with her seven children and the farm for the past fifteen months, her husband only intermittently home. The eldest was only sixteen and her youngest, two-year-old Mary, had special needs and required much extra care. At night, Susan and the children could hear bears prowling around the house and beneath their windows. She was exhausted, she was probably deeply depressed, and she was defensive about the loss of the soil she had worked so hard to clear and the apple trees she had coaxed into maturity. Only days before, Susan had walked down to where Padden worked on the new fence and shouted that she would shoot him if he didn't stay away. Padden did not take the overwrought woman seriously and ignored her. She thought he was laughing at her.

Now, seeing Padden working on the fence again and ignoring her warning, Susan told her eleven-year-old son Tommy to fetch the double-barreled shotgun kept handy for protection against the bears and for duck hunting. Just that morning, Tommy had walked two miles to the store to buy ammunition. One barrel of the gun now held buckshot and the other held two home-molded bullets from his father's stash. Susan told Tommy to come with her. The big gun over his shoulder, Tommy followed his mother down the slope toward where Michael Padden was placing fence posts.

A Warning Shot, or Worse?

Tommy later said that he just took the shotgun to frighten Padden. When he used the gun for hunting, he said, he braced it on his brother's shoulder. Not this time. Susan told her son to shoot Padden, who was turned away from them. Tommy Clark fired at Michael Padden with both barrels from only 40 feet away. Padden screamed and ran about 60 feet before he collapsed on his shattered right arm. His father-in-law ran to him and cradled his head.

Susan shouted at Tommy over and over to shoot Connelly too. Connelly ran for his life and leapt over the nearest fence, yelling at Anthony and Bernard to run for the house and get the guns.

Tromping home through the mud and brush, Anna heard the scream and saw the Clarks ahead beside the trail, then the smoke from the gun. She dropped her bucket of water and ran toward the field. Anna collided with her father who held her back until the boys could return with the guns that would hold the Clarks at bay. When Susan saw Happy Valley's other young mother, she shouted at Anna to stay away from her wounded husband. She taunted the pair for being too afraid to go to Padden's aid. The two other nearby Clark children watched the deadly confrontation.

Tommy may or may not have reloaded in the chaos. Though Anna and her father stood their ground near the fallen man, Tommy never fired his father's big gun again. He was crying too hard. The young boy was never able to admit to authorities, or perhaps even to himself, that his mother had commanded him to kill Padden. He said the gun just went off when he thought it was pointed skyward.

Anthony and Bernard arrived with the guns fifteen minutes later, and the Clarks retreated up the hill to the house. Ed Connelly and the boys lifted the badly bleeding Michael into the wheelbarrow and started for home. Only then did Anna finally look up at the Clark home. She saw the family nailing boards over the windows, as if preparing for the Padden clan to come after them with guns blazing.

Michael Padden died less than 30 minutes after he was shot, before the family could even get him home. He was peppered with buckshot. The bullet that had pierced his shoulder and chest was not a fatal injury, but another bullet had broken his arm and severed two arteries.

No one saw the Clark family go out the back door of their house into the towering cedar forest. They walked down to the bay and around to Whatcom, a mile past Sehome. They registered at the Whatcom Hotel.

Justice of the Peace A.C. Marston held a coroner's inquest that very night at the Padden home. The hastily called jury and local coroner "Dr." T.D. Hunter examined Padden's body by candlelight, visited the crime scene, and heard witnesses. Hunter later confessed that he was a "scientist," not a trained doctor, but he did the best he could. About 9 pm, the jury ruled that Michael Padden died from "gunshot wounds fired by the hands of Thomas Clark, Jr., aided and abetted by his mother Susan Clark."[1]

There was nothing in local experience that told the sheriff how to incarcerate an eleven-year-old murder suspect. He and advisors decided to leave mother and son at the hotel under Constable William Utter's guard, and pay Mrs. Jenkins $1.00 per day for each of them. By then, pioneer settler Utter was up in years, so no one must have deemed the pair a flight or violence risk in the aftermath. Justice Marston issued a formal warrant of arrest for premeditated murder on the 11th, but it was another five days before Utter arrested the pair on the 16th, when a preliminary hearing was held. During the gap, the officials may have also deliberated on what to do with Tommy, and with little Mary whose extra needs her harried and distraught father was unable to handle. The solution was to jail the toddler too. Utter and the prisoners took the steamer Dispatch for the Port Townsend jail on the Olympic Peninsula, the location of the district court.

Preparation for Trial

Thomas Clark, Sr. had hurried home as soon as word of the tragedy reached him. He mortgaged his homestead to pay for an attorney capable of defending against a premeditated murder charge that could bring his wife the death penalty. If Susan was lucky, she would join Mary Fitzhugh Lear Phillips of Orcas Island at Seatco, the two-year-old territorial prison. The previous September, a jury convicted Mary of killing her alcoholic abusive husband. The S'Klallam Indian woman garnered community sympathy and pleas for mercy because of the deceased's character, plus two of her children had died in a horrific accident, and she seemed never to be mentally the same after. She had also once been married to Territorial Justice and Sehome Mine manager E.C. Fitzhugh, and then to Wrangell, Alaska, founder William King Lear. Still, after Mary's conviction for manslaughter instead of murder, the judge sent her to the prison for two years, the territory's first woman so sentenced. She took her two small children with her. Perhaps a good lawyer could get Susan Clark a similar sentence.

Clark hired University of Michigan-trained Orange Jacobs to defend his wife and child. Jacobs had been Chief Justice of the Territorial Supreme Court from 1871-75, and after serving in Congress for two terms, had resumed his law practice in Seattle.

Opposing the venerable Jacobs would be Irving Ballard, the young son of the town of Auburn's founder. The self-taught prosecutor had obtained a manslaughter conviction of Mary Phillips despite obvious elements of self-defense. There were no such circumstances in the crime the Clarks had committed. Ballard meant to hang Susan.

While the Clarks awaited trial in the Port Townsend jail, the editor of Whatcom County's only newspaper, *The Puget Sound Mail*, decided to investigate the living conditions for the accused and the little girl with them. He found that former Whatcom resident J.A. Chapman kept a clean and tidy jail. Susan and Tommy told him that both Jailer Chapman and Sheriff B.S. Miller were treating them with kindness, and their quarters were more comfortable than they could have expected.

The men told the editor that the special needs little girl was the only problem, as Whatcom County had disallowed extra payment for her care. With five children at home, Thomas Clark had no more money to pay for it. Both men thought that Susan was so emotionally fragile that she would probably kill herself if little Mary was taken away. Young Tommy kept a constant watch over his mother. The conditions of the case were extraordinary in the editor's opinion, and he left ready to recommend that the County Commissioners get involved to find a solution.

The Trial

When the August trial began, Territorial Chief Justice Roger Sherman Greene was on the bench. Grandson of a Declaration of Independence signer, and a wounded Civil War veteran, Greene was both a devout Sunday school teacher and an advocate of equal rights for women. Entering the law profession in a way different from either Ballard or Jacobs, the talented jurist graduated from Dartmouth College and received his legal training in a prestigious New York firm.

Prosecutor Ballard called many witnesses in addition to the Padden and Connelly families. He depended on the overwhelming testimony about the events; Tommy's purchase of ammunition the same day, and the condition of Padden's body. He used only about an hour to argue that the defendants went down the hill planning to kill Padden.

Defense attorney Jacobs called only Tommy, his father, and his sister Jenny who had been working in the garden when the shooting occurred. Jacobs gave an impassioned two-hour plea for acquittal after his associate's impressive attempt to explain away evidence presented by Ballard. Jacobs asserted that the Clarks only went to protest Padden's work on the fence and an accident happened.

The jury retired with exhaustive instructions about the conditions for finding one defendant or the other, or both, guilty of murder. The men returned once to tell Greene they could not reach a verdict because two members said their minds could not be changed. The justice sent them back to the jury room. They deliberated a total of ten hours over two days before finding Susan and Tommy guilty of the reduced charge of manslaughter. Minutes after sending out their verdict, they sent a second note to Greene to add "and not guilty of murder as charged." It was the same verdict Mary Phillips had received in the Port Townsend courtroom. The all-male juries across the West were finding it difficult to find a "respectable" woman guilty of premeditated murder with the possible sentence of hanging. It didn't fit 19th century idealistic assumptions about wives and mothers. Third district jurors followed the same pattern.

A New Trial for Tommy

Orange Jacobs filed a motion for a new trial for Tommy immediately after Justice Greene rejected his petition to dismiss the entire case for want of evidence to fit the charge. After due consideration, Greene granted the petition. The boy was under twelve, and the law assumed that children under fourteen were incapable of committing a crime. Ballard had shown no proof of criminal knowledge or capacity. Greene said he saw the boy only as a means of the crime, not the instigator. Plus, if the killing had perhaps been involuntary as Tommy said, there was no common intent with his mother's. Greene sent Tommy back to the jail to wait for his new trial at the next term of court in four months.

The pious Justice Greene was known both for his faith-based sympathy for transgressors gone wrong, but also for his severe sentences. He gave Susan five years at hard labor in the territorial prison, three more than Mary Phillips. If the bailiff followed standard procedures, he immediately placed her in wrist and leg irons. Little Mary went home with her father.

Seatco Territorial Prison

Susan Clark thus became the second woman to walk through Seatco's log stockade gates into the contract prison's profit-based system. It had been devised by men for men to support the owners' lumber mill. They made no provision for women in the iron bar-laced wooden barracks. They hired no female guards. Unlike Mary Phillips for whom a shanty to house her little family was built, Susan was confined upstairs from the men's cellblock in the small shoe and tailor shop which doubled as a "hospital." No record says if the women were given more gender-defined "hard labor" than what the men did.

Women who had always lived as part of the "respectable" community were ill-equipped to deal with the realities of a men's 19th century territorial prison. No glass covered the prison's windows. No heat went to individual cells whose only furnishings were a mattress and a straw-stuffed grain sack for a pillow. A bucket served as a toilet. The owners did not allow friends and family to visit the prisoners. Nor did they allow a minister or doctor in for several more years. Susan may have worn leg irons at all times as the men did.

Neither Mary Phillips in her shack nor Susan Clark in her cell was safe in the prison, particularly after dark. Both had lost their right to be treated with respect. A male inmate who was there with them later called it "a pilgrimage through hell." [2]

Like Mary Phillips had, Susan Clark had responded with violence when she was overwhelmed by events in her life, and instantly lost all social status. Unlike Mary, she did not possess the inner strength to endure her new conditions and the separation from her family. Susan began to exhibit symptoms of a total emotional breakdown. The inmates in cells below could hear her walking the boards night and day in a "frenzy of grief and despair."[3]

About a week after she entered the prison, the distraught mother received word that a cow had nearly gored little Mary to death. Thomas, Sr. and the other children could not provide the level of supervision that Susan had.

Just days later, when no one was looking, Susan Clark took a towel and hung herself from a post.

A Very Sad Affair

The Puget Sound Mail published both the account of the trial and the news of the suicide in the same issue. Reflecting the community's feelings, the editor added that the case was "a very sad affair from beginning to end, and both families have our deepest sympathy in their affliction."[4]

By January 1881, Irving Ballard was dead and the acting prosecutor petitioned the court to release Tommy. He believed that no public interest would be served by another trial. Justice Greene agreed that Tommy could not be held responsible for an act he committed at the command of his late mother and released the boy (now 13) immediately. Orange Jacobs was there to see his young client released before he returned to his new position as Seattle's mayor.

The Paddens, Connellys, and Clarks stayed on their neighboring farms. Over the years, the kind and generous Anna Padden became known as the Mother of Happy Valley. She remarried and had more children by German immigrant Henry Oeser, one of whom founded a local cedar company that lasted nearly a century. Michael Padden's children later donated Lake Padden's water rights to the city for its municipal water supply.

Tommy Clark became a coal miner like his father, and moved to Newcastle. His father's 1904 obituary said only that "Mrs. Clark died in 1880."[5]

[1] Coroner's Jury verdict, 3/8/1880. In Territory v Thomas Clark, Jr. and Susan Clark, #127 (1880). 3rd District Territorial Court, Washington Territory.

[2] George France, The Struggles for Life and Home in the Northwest.1890.

[3] France, p. 279-280.

[4] Puget Sound Mail, 9/4/1880.

[5] Thomas Clark obituary, *Bellingham Herald*, 10/10/1904.

I felt honored and privileged when Candace accepted my invitation to reprint her "Murder in Happy Valley," which first appeared in the Whatcom County Historical Society Journal. I found it an exciting read, and knew immediately her story would fit in nicely with the other Whatcom County murders.

SOURCES

Atkinson, Cathy Padden. Family Genealogical Research.

Bellingham Bay Mail. 4/28/1877.

Bellingham Herald. 10/10/1904.

Biographical Dictionary of Congress, online. "Orange Jacobs."

Bureau of Land Management, General Land Office records. Online.

Butler, Anne M., *Gendered Justice in the American West: Women Prisoners in Men's Penitentiaries.* University of Chicago Press, 1997.

Corcoran, Neil B. Bucoda, *A Heritage of Sawdust and Leg Irons.* Bucoda Improvement Club, 1976.

Edson, Lelah Jackson. *The Fourth Corner.* Whatcom Museum, 1968.

France, George. *The Struggles for Life and Home in the Northwest.* New York: I. Goldman, 1890.

Nix, Alma and John, editors. *The History of Lewis County, Washington.* Lewis County Historical Society, 1985.

O Donnabhain, Tomas Sean. Padden family research in Ireland, online and via Cathy Atkinson.

Puget Sound Mail. 3/16/1880, 3/20/1880, 6/19/1880, 8/14/1880, 9/4/1880, 1/15/1881.

Puget Sound Weekly Argus 9/10/1880.

U.S. Census. Whatcom County, Washington. 1860, 1870, 1880.

U.S. Department of the Interior, National Park Service. National Register nomination form for Seatco Territorial Prison, 1975.

Vedder, O.F. and Lyman, H.S. History of Seattle, Washington. 1891. Online.

Wahl, Tim. Composite map of Happy Valley, 2012.

Washington Territory v Thomas Clark, Jr. and Susan Clark. #127 Series 2 (1880). 3rd District Territorial Court, Washington State Archives, Northwest Region.

Washington Territory v Mary Phillips, #1070/#45 Series 2 (1879). 3rd District Territorial Court. Washington State Archives, Northwest Region.

Whatcom Museum. Photos of Happy Valley and of Michael and Anna Padden.

Chapter 3
The Two Deaths of Snowball Wallace

In researching the murder of Odia Briscoe, aka "Snowball Wallace," I found myself once again going down the rabbit hole seeking the truth. It was particularly disturbing to find such a tragic slaying superficially recorded on page seven of the local newspaper. That is, until I learned the murder involved a drunken foreign sailor and a prostitute of the ill-reputed "Restricted District." The fact that there was any trail to follow surprised me; I was even more stunned to discover two completely different conclusions to the murder. For that reason, I call this chapter "The Two Deaths of Snowball Wallace."

Wood of Gold

The timber mills on Bellingham Bay were witnessing a boom in business, related to the increased sales of lumber and wood products. This increase was reflected in the harbormaster's marine traffic reports for summer and fall months of 1907. The E. K. Wood Company mill's output in October alone nearly equaled those of the previous month from all the waterfront mills. Combined, lumber hoisted and loaded into ship hulls doubled on the bay from September to October. The September totals alone were 10,847,490 feet of cut lumber, and 5,000,000 shingles. The harbormaster credited the increase of exported wood products primarily to excellent low freight rates, and the high demand coming from the San Francisco market.

The sudden boom in exports found far-off destinations in such markets as Asia, South America and colonies throughout the British Empire. There were dozens of vessels of all sizes and kinds in the harbor: schooners, sloops, windjammers, and barquentines harkening back to the ancient mariner days of sail-power. At all times, there were ships in one of the three stages: at the wharves and docks loading, anchored in the bay awaiting a berth to enter and load, and arriving daily, getting in queue for a berth to open.

By the turn of the twentieth-century, the Bellingham Bay waterfront was bustling with waterborne traffic. Lumber products were being shipped all over the globe. The wharves were lined with a mix of cargo steamers and sailing ships. Circa: 1900s. Laura Jacoby, Galen Biery Collection.

One of these many lumber carriers was the large, steel-hulled British steamer *Hatasu*, mastered by a Captain Calder. The *Hatasu* was a typical steamer of the day, launched in 1899 by Furness Withy & Co., Ltd., of England. It was 337 feet in length, 45 feet in berth, and had a displacement of 3358 tons.

Sometime during the last weeks of August, as longshoremen in Bellingham were working night and day loading timber, steamer *Hatasu* untied from a dock in Calcutta, India. Laden with East Indian products, she was bound for a seventy-plus-day voyage to Bellingham. It is speculated that *Hatasu* may have stopped en route at the ports of Burma, Singapore, Borneo, or Hong Kong, all possessions of the British Empire. We know for a fact that the steamer docked in Australia, the last port of call before reaching Bellingham.

Merchant crews were diverse the world over, joining the service for many reasons. Mariners were seldom asked why they joined, and for good reason. Many were adventurers, some sought their fortune, and others wanted nothing underfoot except for the sea. Others, of course, represented the worst elements society had to offer. Some were criminals running from the law. Some would sign aboard at one port, only to disembark or jump ship at another. It was one way of getting from point A to point B, without having to pay steerage.

A crew on a merchant ship could represent a host of nations, and contain as many languages. It wasn't unusual for a seaman not to speak the language of his fellow shipmates. On the crew manifest of the *Hatasu* sailing out of Calcutta were two such ruffians, both of Russian origin. One was August Friedberg (or Friedburg), and the other his friend W. Lindbare.

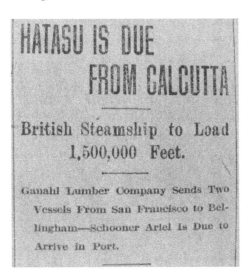

HATASU IS DUE
FROM CALCUTTA

British Steamship to Load 1,500,000 Feet.

Ganahl Lumber Company Sends Two Vessels From San Francisco to Bellingham—Schooner Ariel Is Due to Arrive in Port.

Friedberg was a locksmith by profession. He turned sailor, serving two years at sea on at least two other vessels—a schooner and another steamer. After the fifth grade, he left school to go to work, although it's claimed he came from wealth. Records describe Friedberg as being five foot four inches, or five-foot six inches in height, depending on reportage. He was 23 years old, 157 pounds; he had dark brown hair with grey-blue eyes and a swarthy complexion. At some point in his world travels, he got a tattoo of an anchor on the first digit of his right hand.

Of his buddy, Lindbare, there is less known. It is believed that he was Russian, but one account suggests Swedish. He was 25 years old, five foot eight inches tall, with light brown hair and blue eyes. They were cargo deck hands, and very likely bound by language and culture.

During the first week of November, Bellingham Bay was bustling with activity. The harbormaster kept a register of daily activities and maritime traffic on the bay, providing harbor dispatches of the goings-on to the newspaper. That week he reported the first vessels expected to reach the port that month to be the steamers *Hatasu* and *Beckenham*. Each was expected to take on half-cargo loads. *Hatasu*, 1,5000,000 board feet from the Bellingham Bay Lumber Mill, bound for Calcutta, and the same for *Beckenham*, bound for Australia. The E. K. Wood steam schooner *Olympic* was due any day.

The large Norwegian steamer *Thode Fagelund*, the barquentine *John Smith*, and the schooners *Sanders* and *Sehome* were presently loading. The harbormaster's end-of-month figures for October indicated Whatcom County timber was heading for San Francisco, Los Angeles, San Pedro, Mexico, France, Japan, and Australia.

On the afternoon of November 6, *Hatasu* arrived, dropped anchor and awaited a berth to come available. She would wait only overnight. The *Beckenham* arrived soon after, followed by *Ariel* and *A. M. Baxter*. On Friday, November 8, "with their masts and decks fairly glistening in the sun, and huge bundles of clean, yellow lumber rapidly disappearing into the hold, the vessels at the mill docks present a picture of industry…the deck hands and longshoremen welcomed the sunshine, and the *Beckenham* and *Hatasu* were now lined up at the end of the wharf," so said the *Bellingham Herald*. For the next two weeks timber was hoisted aboard, and the British steamer was replenished with stores for the long voyage home. As the days ticked by, the destiny of Friedberg and "Snowball Wallace" was fast approaching.

The Restricted District

As the nineteenth century came to a close, it was hoped that it would open to a more prosperous new century. However, many remnants of the county's disreputable past carried over. The most lucrative and least tolerable was the world's oldest profession. Vice and prostitution, interlocked with their two bad brothers, drinking and gambling—powerful evils that had become less and less acceptable in the developing American West.

Many communities after 1900 tried to shake this tarnished vestige from their growing townships. As "cultivated civilization" took root and pushed back the wilds of frontier life, such vices were no longer welcome. West coast businessmen wished to be taken seriously, and respected by their Eastern counterparts. Ruffians were removed and law and order established. Christians were trying to save souls from temptation, establishing safe havens for families. Schools were now desired.

Thriving townships experienced the growing pains of change brought on by Temperance. Some communities, including Bellingham, had relied on proceeds derived from establishments that promoted vice. These included licenses, taxes, and fines. Until a satisfactory transition to a more "respectable" tax base could take place, many restricted districts, (aka Red Light Districts or Sporting Districts) had to be tolerated. One of the finest descriptions of this issue, comes from an "Opinion" written in the Wednesday, October 24, 1906 edition of the *Bellingham Herald*:

> "There are hundreds of good citizens who, while they believe that
> a restricted district is to be preferred to the general dissemination

of vice throughout the city, are convinced that the present restricted district is too centrally located, and too conspicuous. It occupies the most prominent place on the city waterfront. It is in plain view of the principal railroad station of the city. The deadline that has been established is on the principal thoroughfare from east to west, and through which thousands of men, women and children pass daily."

"We have no courage to suggest where the restricted district should be, but we are convinced that it should not be allowed to remain where it is. If the law is enforced for a time the place may be abandoned and the city officials may then decide upon a place in which the creatures of the underworld can be conveniently corralled."

A footnote to this writing comes later in 1908: "Almost one-half of the city's revenue is derived from the sale of liquor licenses and receipts from the restricted district. The cost of running the city in 1907 was approximately $120,000. There are 59 saloons in the city." The issue of the restricted district was a dilemma for the citizens of Bellingham.

Brothels dotted numerous areas of Bellingham and Fairhaven, behind restricted districts, or "Devil's Rows." Bellingham's most heavily concentrated houses of ill fame were located just beyond the "deadline," an invisible boundary that separated the restricted district from the more pleasing parts of downtown. In Bellingham, the demarcation of the "deadline" was entered according to Ordinance 18, City of Whatcom, 1903: "Thence along the outer harbor line to F Street; thence in a northeasterly direction along the west side of F Street and Twelfth Street; thence along the south line of Twelfth Street to its intersection with Whatcom creek waterway: thence along the west side of Whatcom creek waterway to its intersection with the outer harbor line; thence following a direct line to the place beginning…"

Looking down at Colony Wharf and Whatcom Creek Waterway. Behind the sailboats, toward the large warehouse would have been the stilted pilings, elevated planked roads and rickety structures of the "Restricted District" Bellingham's red-light quarter. To the left of the smaller red roof was the approximate location of the Paris House, at 1121 B Street in 1907. Photo taken by the author.

Today's vicinity of the old restricted district is nonexistent. It would have stretched along the length of Roeder Avenue from B to F Streets, and would then extend outward over the outer harbor. Today this area is entirely land-filled, but at the turn of the century, it was a series of extended pilings and boardwalks, essentially a city district built on stilts. The last of these stilted structures, the Waterfront Tavern at Whatcom Creek Waterway, can still be seen at the time of this writing. Another remnant of those bygone days is the T. G. Richards building, or the Whatcom County territorial courthouse at 1308 E Street. The fill brought the level of E Street up to the second floor of that building, making that floor today's first floor.

Hatasu Causes Police No End of Trouble

On Thursday, November 21, three vessels were cleared from the docks with heavy loads of E. K. Wood cargo – the *Strathearn*, *Resolute*, and the

Garden City. The *Strathearn's* hold alone was filled with 250,000 feet of lumber, bound for the west coast of South America. The other two vessels were in route for San Pedro, California. The *Tallac* was awaiting a berth to open, while the overworked little tug *Tyee* was rushing about, pushing-and-pulling vessels. Further down the dock the British steamer *Hatasu* had been loading for the past week, and suffering from a few delays. Captain Calder wasn't happy about a late departure, as he wanted to beat the early December weather coming out of the north Pacific.

With *Hatasu* readying for the long sea voyage to Calcutta, Captain Calder had to contend with the bane of all captains, shore leave. The crew had been cooped up for months at sea. Except for those jumping ship, the rest of the crew remained aboard loading the hold. If they didn't, they wouldn't have fulfilled their contracts and wouldn't be paid. For a few, their contracts were up once the vessel docked and they were free to leave the ship. These sailors usually re-upped or signed on to a different ship once their money ran out. Regardless, those remaining on board expected to be paid and take their much-needed shore leave.

In port communities like Bellingham, the citizen rapport with sailors was usually a love-hate relationship. Most businesses, such as saloons and brothels, loved a sailor's money—once his cash was gone, he becomes a nuisance. Port cities the world over can attest there is nothing worse than a drunken sailor… except for many drunken sailors. After long months at sea, the sailors just wanted to cut loose, have fun, and sow some wild oats. Under most circumstances "fun" was loud, abrasive, unruly, obnoxious, rude, offensive, vulgar, destructive, and sometimes downright violent! With shore leave coming to every ship's company, communities like Bellingham cringed.

It wasn't long before the crew of the *Hatasu* were on shore leave and on the loose, terrifying the city and making headlines: "Hatasu's Crew Is Made Up Of Bold, Bad Men" and "Negro Sailor Tries To Shoot An Officer."

The first encounter occurred one evening when three sailors started to celebrate and landed in jail, answering to charges of breaking out the widows of the Diamond Bar on Elk Street (State Street). A few days later, a fistfight broke out between the second and fourth engineer ratings in a saloon, resulting in the superior officer having the subordinate arrested on assault and battery charges, for which the offense resulted in a $15.00 fine (and costs).

He was drunk.

Another night, seaman Jimmy Malone, described as a "negro" standing at six foot four inches started out his shore leave by "terrorizing the saloon keepers" on Elk Street. Malone ordered drinks at several saloons and refused to pay. In one establishment he took the $3.00 change of a patron. Soon Malone found himself in a heated battle with the owner of "The Coin" when foot patrolman James E. Lee wandered by and heard the commotion inside.

After a lengthy scuffle, Lee managed to get the "darbies" (handcuffs) on Malone's wrists. Despite the metal bracelets, Malone attempted to take Lee's pistol as they were walking to the jail. Rather than deal with the drunken troublemaker, police decided to just get Malone out of their hair. Under heavy escort, they returned the crewman to the *Hatasu*. Captain Calder was asked to restrain the man until they were out to sea and heading to Calcutta.

Celebrating their shore leave, August Friedberg and W. Lindbare walked down the gangway onto the Bellingham Bay Lumber mill dock about 9 am on Saturday, November 23. Each had a fist full of cash to spend. Undoubtedly they heard from fellow shipmates, who had been out earlier, where to go. The saloons along Elk Street were hardened to their type, and the restricted district just north of the enormous brick city hall building was reputed to have fine women and drink.

Walking along Elk, the men encountered the boarded-up windows of the Diamond Bar, The Coin, and other fine establishments that served their kind. After swapping sea stories with other sailors and getting well liquored up, they wondered down to Holly Street, eventually reaching the "resorts" as they were known, located over the deadline on the far side of Whatcom Creek. At midday, there may not have been many clients in the restricted district; yet again, there were many ships on the bay. As it was the weekend, loggers and lumberjacks were also in town spending their own paychecks. The gold mines on Mount Baker were closing down for the winter and many prospectors, with their precious few nuggets and gold dust, hadn't seen a woman since spring.

August Friedberg and Lindbare would have walked down this stretch of Holly Street and over the Whatcom Creek waterway on their way to the Restricted District the day "Snowball Wallace" was killed. Circa: 1900s. Laura Jacoby, Galen Biery Collection.

Friedberg and Lindbare eventually found their establishment, the Paris House, at 1121 B Street and walked inside at about one-o'clock in the afternoon. Their choice of preference was known as a "colored resort." The men took a table, ordered rounds of beer and drank for some time. Friedberg wasn't an unattractive man, and being a young robust sailor, he must have acquired a sharp physique in the two years of his work as a sailor. Certainly, they must have caught the attention of three of the working girls: Dolly Belmont, Lizzie Lee and Mary Davis. However, the men's attention was on a full-figured "negress" who went by the name "Snowball Wallace." Unfortunately, due to the nature of her profession, we know little about Snowball, except that her true name may have been Odia Briscoe. Odia was 33 years old, and may have come from Chicago.

August Friedberg's mug shot taken when he entered the state penitentiary at Walla Walla, February 5, 1908. Washington State Archives, Olympia.

The two Russians may have even seemed exotic to the women; many sailors were Scandinavian, English, Irish, and Dutch, with some French, Italian, and German. Soon the Russians had Snowball dancing for them. She twirled for about an hour and was becoming exhausted. By two o'clock in the afternoon, both men were intoxicated; even so, they ordered more liquor.

Friedberg kept telling Snowball to keep dancing for him and not slow down. She eventually had to stop, out of breath and unable to continue.

Friedberg demanded that the woman dance. When she refused, after having accommodated him several times, Friedberg was said to have muttered a vile oath, then shouted so that the women throughout the establishment heard, "I'll teach you to dance, you black ----." He pulled out a gun from his coat. Two revolver shots rang out. The first bullet crashed through the window in the rear of the resort, and the second passed through Snowball's abdomen. The women screamed as Snowball hit the floor, which added to the mayhem, quickly attracting a morbid crowd.

While walking his beat, patrolman B. F. Borsheim was attracted to the "colored resort" by the sound of the shots. Meanwhile, police were notified at once, and detective Clarence Logsdon and patrolman Michael Nugent rushed to the scene. On their way they met Borsheim, who was on foot with his two drunken prisoners, Friedberg and Lindbare.

Borsheim related the story of the shooting to Logsdon and then continued on his way to deliver his prisoners to lockup. Meanwhile the officers entered the resort to investigate the crime. When they reached Snowball she was still conscious, but unable to speak coherently, and refused to give her true name. Her pain was extreme. She was rushed to St. Joseph's hospital, where all attempts to save her life by Dr. William H. Axtell proved futile. Axtell did all he could to stop Snowball's bleeding, but the damage was too extensive. He then did what he could to make her comfortable with painkillers, but even his strongest narcotics couldn't stop her pain.

From the time she was injured until her death, she suffered intensely. Snowball died at 8 pm, just before she told the sisters at the hospital her true name was Odia Briscoe, that she was from Chicago, and that her father still lived there. The nuns assured her that he would be notified of her passing. Odia made no statement as to how the shooting occurred. The report of her death was telephoned to the police, and charges against the sailors were changed from assault to murder.

Office Hours—
11 to 12 a. m.
2 to 5 p. m.

Telephone—
Office—M. 2061
Res.—M. 2062

W. H. AXTELL

PHYSICIAN AND SURGEON

Pike Block, Cor. Elk and Holly

Top left: Dr. William H. Axtell worked valiantly over Briscoe trying to save her life. Laura Jacoby, Galen Biery Collection. Top right: Saint Joseph's Hospital; Odia Briscoe was rushed here, only to die painfully hours later. Lower left: A primitive operating room at Saint Joseph's Hospital. Circa: 1910. Laura Jacoby's Galen Biery Collection.

Borsheim's two prisoners stumbled and fell all the way to the police station, making quite the spectacle of themselves. Both men fell to the floor of their cells in a drunken stupor, unable to make a statement to the police.

The man who possessed the gun claimed to Officer Borsheim that his name was Friedberg. However, a search of his effects disclosed naturalization papers made out for a Karl Johnson, even though he had signed the papers as Karl Tabor, dated at Boston, October 1906. In Friedberg's possession, there was also a draft made out by the First National Bank of Bellingham, dated November 1, in the amount of $49.00 and sent to Russia. At the time of his arrest, Friedberg had $25.00 in cash on his person along with cards and letters addressed to Karl Johnson.

The next morning, when questioned by Detective Logsdon, Friedberg admitted to the shooting and said he killed the woman. He gave no reason other than that he was drunk. When first placed under arrest, he did not realize what he had done, and it was not until told that the woman was dead that he showed any signs of concern. After the prisoner's statements were taken, Friedberg and Lindbare were transferred to the county jail and placed in the custody of Sheriff Andrew Williams. They would be held until the January court term, when Friedberg would be tried for murder, and until that time his companion Lindbare would be detained as a witness. Coroner Henry Thompson said that in view of the strong case against the prisoner and his own admission of guilt, an inquest would be unnecessary, and no post-mortem would be held over the remains of the victim. Undertaker A. R. Maulsby retrieved Briscoe's body.

Captain Calder on the *Hatasu* was notified that two of his crew would be detained for a murder. Being an experienced ship captain, Calder was far from surprised. He knew the trouble sailors were capable of getting into during shore leave after weeks or months at sea. Once they had cash in their pockets and were let loose, they became unleashed savages. Deckhands were easily obtainable, and Calder ordered the third officer to send the first mate to scour the docks and sign on replacements before *Hatasu* set sail.

Woman Killed by Drunken Sailor

On Tuesday, November 26, Whatcom County Prosecuting Attorney Virgil Peringer filed in the Superior Court a formal charge of murder in the first degree against August Friedberg, alias Karl Johnson, alias Karl Tabor, and W. Lindbare, for the slaying of one Odia Briscoe, "an inmate and colored resident" of the restricted district. The men would be arraigned at a later date. The murder charge against both men came as a surprise. It was thought that Lindbare was being held only as a witness. However, it was determined that he was in the room at the time of the shooting, and was therefore in the company of a confessed killer; therefore, he also must stand trial.

On Wednesday morning, prosecutor Peringer filed affidavit No. 781 with the offices of Deputy-Clerk of Superior Court of Whatcom County, Samuel E. Leitch. He swore on his oath that Dolly Belmont, Lizzie Lee and Mary Davis were important State witnesses and that there "was danger of their going to parts unknown to the officers charged with calling them as witnesses to trial." [sic] Therefore, Peringer requested that the court hold a reasonable sum from each of the three women until their appearance as witnesses for the State were provided. That same day, Superior Court Judge Jeremiah Neterer approved the prosecutor's request and ordered a sum of $300.00 bond from each of the "inmates" be obtained until their appearance obligations to the State had been fulfilled.

WOMAN KILLED BY DRUNKEN SAILOR

Ada Bristol, Known In Restricted District As "Snowball" Wallace, Is Shot Because She Refuses To Dance for Entertainment of Visitors.

The breaking story in local newspapers was printed in cavalier style, with callous disregard for the victim. The first series of articles in the *Bellingham*

Herald were buried as far back as page seven; follow-ups stayed buried until the trial made it to the front page. "Owing to the place where the killing took place; the fact that the woman was a negro and an inhabitant of the restricted district, and that the men are unknown here, but little interest has been taken in the case," said the *Herald* at one point in its own lack of coverage. The other leading newspaper in town, the *Reveille*, chose to ignore the slaying after burying it in the November 24 issue.

The court engaged Attorney James B. Abrams as counsel for the defense. Abrams learned that the men were fairly well connected in Russia; in fact Friedberg had wealthy relatives there and in the Baltic. Abrams hoped for his pockets' sake that these rich relations would come to his client's aid.

Abrams immediately contacted Oscar Klock, the British vice-consul in Port Townsend, who came directly over to Bellingham to look after the interests of the two men, being sailors of a British-registered ship of a crown colony. No doubt, "Vice-Consul" Klock couldn't have been all too pleased taking a cold December ferry over for two criminals, whose actions had tarnished the reputation of the empire. But, it was his official duty to visit the men and see that they were treated well and not abused by a foreign power. Klock took custody of their personal effects, posted letters for the prisoners, and filed a report. His other duties required him to assist Attorney Abrams in defending the pair, if requested.

Whisky Fumes Cause of Murder

On Monday, Dec 16, the Russians were brought before a Superior Court judge for arraignment. Friedberg and Lindbare pled "not guilty." Friedberg's trial was set for Saturday, January 18, 1908, and would conclude in a day, as only a few witnesses were to be called for each side. It was decided that Lindbare would be tried later.

Jury selection proceeded during the early evening hours of January 17, in preparation for an 11 am session. The twelve men chosen to decide the fate of prisoner Friedberg were: L. J. Ford, Lars Barbo, John Siegfried, W. B. Hart, C. B. Willyard, W. M. Hazen, C. R. Axling, F. A. Burns, G. Vander Linder, W. E. Dement, W. R. Kline and J. F. Newberry. Neither attorney took exception to the men who would sit in the box. Late Saturday morning, County Prosecutor Virgil Peringer read the State's facts regarding the case to the jury. He stated that Friedberg and Lindbare, who was with him at the time, were charged with murder in the first degree, but that today they would only hear from the man who fired the gun, August Friedberg.

Attorney James Abrams, with very little evidence to display, or even a good defense to offer, decided to use the circumstances to his advantage. "Mental irresponsibility of mind due to excessive drink" was offered to the jury in the defense of August Friedberg. "The said defendant, being then and there intoxicated to such an extent [that he was] unable to form an intent, malice, or premeditation and deliberation…" according to counsel. "The defense will not attempt to show that Friedberg did not kill the woman," said Abrams, "but will strive to convince the jury that he was not responsible for his actions at the time owing to hard drink." Abrams called only the accused and Lindbare as witnesses, posited this defense and then rested his case.

For the prosecution, first on the witness stand was officer B. F. Borsheim, who arrested August Friedberg and W. Lindbare. He testified that Friedberg offered him $50.00 to permit him to escape. In denial of this, Lindbare was put to the stand and said that no such offer had been made, as he was with the two men the whole time, and heard all that was said. Lindbare next told the details as he remembered them. He said that they left the ship early in the day, made the rounds of various saloons, and in the course of their travels, Friedberg got very drunk and that he himself was not sober either.

"We wandered into the resort about one o'clock, Saturday afternoon, purchased several rounds of drinks and, as we both were under the influence of liquor when entering, and were soon hilariously drunk."

He then spoke of the events that led up to the shooting and claimed innocence insofar as he was concerned, and that he had started to hunt for the police when one arrived on the scene. Prosecutor Peringer summarized for the court how the Russians persuaded Snowball to dance for them, which she did for some time. Finally, declining to perform any longer, as she had tired out, Snowball sat down. Friedberg, in a fit of rage, ordered her to continue dancing. When she refused, he pulled his revolver and, with an oath, fired, the bullet going out through the side of the house, and then, as the woman started to run out of the room, he shot at her again. The leaden missile struck the woman just above the left hip and passed clear through her body, coming out her right side and hitting against the wall of the room.

Then, claimed Lindbare, Odia Briscoe grabbed up a stick of firewood from the box near the stove and smashed out a window, calling out wildly for help. The shot, the broken glass and the woman's screams attracted the attention of the residents of the district and Officer Borsheim, who was nearby.

Other witnesses for the prosecution were "house-inmates" Dolly Belmont, Lizzie Lee and Mary Davis; police officers Michael Nugent and Clarence Logsdon; doctors William H. Axtell, Max Mehlig, George F. Cook, John W. Goodheart; and undertaker A. R. Maulsby.

The prosecution rested its case.

Jury's Verdict

The jury didn't take long to decide, and August Friedberg was called back upstairs from his cell to receive his sentence on Sunday, January 19. The

Russian had a hard time comprehending what the court meant when he was asked if he had anything to say. He replied with a simple "No," after which Attorney Abrams had to explain the situation to him.

August Friedberg, charged with murder in the first degree for the killing of Odia Briscoe, was instead found guilty of manslaughter. For whatever reason, Friedberg's sentencing wasn't made until Saturday, January 25. The court first fined Friedberg $100 and then sentenced him to serve from five to twenty years in the state penitentiary at Walla Walla. Attorney Abrams objected, holding that the court had no right to fix the minimum sentence, as that had already been done by the legislature. After looking up the new law, Judge Neterer withdrew the first sentence to hand down a corrected one, which was for Friedberg to serve from one to twenty years of hard labor in the state penitentiary. Attorney Abrams offered no objection to the new sentence.

The case against Lindbare was dropped, as a result of the testimony presented at the Friedberg's trial.

Author's Note

The story of Odia Briscoe, aka "Snowball Wallace" would have ended right here and been chalked up to being a tragic death during the notorious days when towns and cities had such open places as restricted districts, red light districts, brothels and deadlines.

Normally in 1907, this story wouldn't have garnered much attention, unless there was a movement afoot to close a particular restricted district, or opponents were looking for ammunition to support their opposition to the evils of their continued existence. Or possibly it was just a slow news day. I was about to close the books on this murder case when I discovered within the few trial records an "alternative" ending to the death of Odia Briscoe.

In a file titled "The State of Washington vs. August Friedberg," dated 25 January 1908, signed by Prosecuting Attorney Virgil Peringer and presiding Judge Jeremiah Neterer was the following statement:

"On the 23rd day of November, 1907, while ashore on leave, August Friedberg, with a shipmate, W. Lindbare went to the room of the deceased, Odia Briscoe, in the restricted district of the city of Bellingham according to the evidence at the trial. The evidence further showed that while in the room of the deceased she invited first the defendant into her room, and later his shipmate; that they were intoxicated, and she told them they had better come back later. The defendant commanded the deceased to stay in bed until his shipmate had finished, and, as testified, a very short interval after he made such a demand he fired at the deceased; she was taken to the hospital and within three hours died."

It appears that the story of the death of Snowball Wallace differs to the one released in all other records. Why? It certainly couldn't have been a surprise that adults were having solicited, paid sex behind the deadline of the restricted district, inside a "house of color." There is no explanation. The killing didn't occur on the main floor, as the Russians sat around a table drinking, watching Briscoe dance, unless these events occurred earlier. Also, Dolly Belmont, Lizzie Lee, and Mary Davis would not have been witness to the shooting.

Rather, Odia Briscoe invited Friedberg (who paid) for some pleasure into her small bedroom. He either performed or was too drunk to be aroused. Possibly, Lindbare joined in with them, or as Briscoe was already paid for, Friedberg may have passed her on to his shipmate. Apparently Briscoe suggested they come back later as they were too intoxicated, which implied Lindbare was also having a little difficulty in getting his machinery operating. Briscoe may have been getting out of bed to leave, or attempting to lead the men out, as Friedberg ordered her to remain in the bed and finish with Lindbare. The situation amongst the trio may have even been humorous at first. Maybe Friedberg felt they were getting hustled, or possibly Briscoe made a threat or a joke about Friedberg's manhood? Regardless of the chain of events, the Russian took a mean turn and gunned down poor Odia Briscoe. At this point, Dolly Belmont, Lizzie Lee, and Mary Davis may have entered the room to witness the aftermath.

All the sworn statements as to Odia Briscoe being told to continue dancing may have been a metaphor for what was really happening behind the resort's closed doors.

August Friedberg entered the state penitentiary at Walla Walla on February 5, 1908, becoming prisoner No. 4793. His mental examination said, "Perception was – absence of illusions and hallucinations. Thought – coherent in its duration and intensity, Emotions – normal excitability. Able to do hard work."

Twenty-four months later Friedberg, campaigning for early parole sent a letter to Judge Jeremiah Neterer asking for a letter of support on his behalf. Neterer readily replied sending a letter to prison warden, C. S. Reed, dated October 14, 1909. Neterer wrote:

"I remember the circumstances surrounding the commission of the offense for which this man was sentenced and I am satisfied from the circumstances surrounding the place in which the offense was committed, that it was conditions that were responsible for what was done more than any criminal intent...so far as I am concerned and I believe so far as this community is concerned, the desires of justice have been served by the incarceration of this young man...I, therefore recommend that he be paroled..."

Hand-written at the bottom of the letter is a statement by Whatcom County Prosecuting Attorney Virgil Peringer, affirming that he joined Judge Neterer in the statements above and recommendation.

On November 26, 1910, prisoner No. 4793 was paroled; on December 12, he received a final discharge from the prison by Governor Marion Hay. The prison board stating their reasoning was based on Friedberg's good conduct and further reasons being:

> "That the said August Friedberg has performed faithful services at State Road Camp #3 for a period of nine months; that the superintendent of said camp recommends that a final discharge be granted to said August Friedberg on account of faithful service rendered and exemplary conduct during the time he has been employed on state road work."

So ends the sad and tragic death of Odia Briscoe.

SOURCES

Affidavit: Prosecutor Virgil Peringer to the Superior Court Judge Jeremiah Neterer.

American Reveille: 11/24/1907

Bellingham Herald: 10/24/1906, 11/1/1907, 11/5/07, 11/6/07, 11/7/07, 11/8/07, 11/21/07, 11/25/07, 11/27/07, 12/16/07, 1/17/1908, 1/18/08, 1/20/08, 1/25/08.

Bellingham Police Records, Washington State Regional Archives.

Plea for Mental Irresponsibility.

Smith, Curtis F. D.D.S., *The Brothels of Bellingham: A Short History of Prostitution in Bellingham.* WA. Whatcom County Historical Society, 2004.

State of Washington, VS. August Friedberg, Judgment and Sentence Case Files.

Washington State Archives #4793 1908 Inmate box 140.

Washington State Bureau of Vital Statistics.

Washington State Digital Archives.

Washington State Penitentiary, Biographical Statement of Convict.

Washington State Penitentiary, Convict Entrance Medical Examination.

Washington State Penitentiary, Penitentiary Inmate Register.

Washington State Penitentiary, Prison Board of Pardon.

Whatcom Criminal Index: No. 781 11/27/07 Book 3.

Chapter 4
The Maple Falls Monster

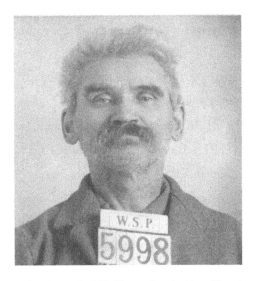

Frank E. Romandorf. Washington State Archives, Olympia.

The name William Frederick Jahns, otherwise known as, Frank E. Romandorf, has become a legend of local lore for those who remember his name. It wasn't until November 1909 that his name reappeared in local newspapers, and that the populace of Whatcom County realized they had a serial-killing psychopath living amongst them only three years before.

Romandorf surfaced in Stevens County, where he was on trial for the brutal slaying of Agnes Janson, his housekeeper and prospective wife. What emerged during his trial was a list of diabolical murders committed by Romandorf, and further slayings that he was suspected of committing. If he were found guilty in the Janson murder, he would be sentenced to hang by the neck until dead. The downside of such a verdict would give authorities little reason to investigate or try Romandorf for his other deeds. After all, you can only kill a man once, yet by neglecting so many cold cases, the full extent of Romandorf's killing spree will never be known.

So convoluted is the Romandorf case, that even today we can only speculate as to its full extent and death toll. His life, what little we know of it, resembles the jumbling of various jigsaw puzzles, tossed together with the absence of many key pieces. The players involved are every bit as confusing and complicated as the killer himself, often changing names, relationships and nearly every other aspect of their lives. Who was killed will always remain the question. When were they killed and where are the bodies? The madman refused to answer most of the questions put forth to him, but answered others in a roundabout manner and only divulged some of his slayings. Admitting he was a killer, why wouldn't Romandorf just confess to all his crimes? Most authorities at the time believed Romandorf was holding his information as his bargaining chip to postpone the gallows. However, he never played that card, taking what he knew to the grave.

In the end, the Whatcom County portion to the story, while sinister and shocking, played only as a sideshow to the larger scheme of things in Stevens County. How many were slain by the hand of Romandorf in Whatcom County? One, two or four, we don't know. Today, only a few landmarks survive. A former butcher shop is presently a bar. There are a few headstones of those involved. The killer's home was knocked down in 2014, but an old stone root cellar remains on the property. Meanwhile, in Maple Falls, old-timers still point toward the hill were the Romandorf ranch once stood and claim that bodies are still buried somewhere on the "The Murder Farm," as they refer to it today.

Maple Falls and Frank Romandorf

Born a logging town, Maple Falls was rapidly laid out and plotted even as the trees still dominated the landscape in 1900-01. Homesteaders, squatters and hermits were overrun by the tidal wave of civilization progressively working inland from Bellingham Bay. Within a year, the King Lumber Mill was providing the milled timbers and shakes needed to build the growing township from the forest. The dark rutted path meandering through the woods toward Silver Lake soon became the Silver Lake Road, one of the main business throughways for the community. Crossing it to the south was Maple Avenue, where high stumps still dotted the lanes. Overnight, so it seemed, hotels, saloons, mercantile stores, logging offices and a host of other business with their wooden facades sprang up like mushrooms, with their planked sidewalks, hitching rails, and outhouses in the rear.

Maple Falls was built faster than tree stumps could be removed from roads. Circa: 1901. Deming Library.

So "wild" was this frontier town to the visiting city-dweller's eye, that author Frances Bruce Todd, in her west county history, *Trail Through the Woods*,

77

recounts the first impressions of Justus Schmidel visiting from Germany one winter's eve in 1906.

Stepping off from the train depot into Maple Falls, one cold snowy night, Schmidel said it felt like "a throwback to the Wild West frontier." After checking into the "seediest" of hotels, full of fleas, he heard the proprietor holler out, "bear-fight!" Seeing the lobby entry full of sleeping men huddled around a wood stove leap to their feet and clear out, the curious Schmidel followed behind. Here it was, in the middle of January as he rounded the rear of the hotel in deep snow, that the German saw a large bonfire and a densely packed crowd. There was a sizeable cage with a wooden den attached to the rear of it. A large drunken logger was standing in snow stripping his shirt off and flexing his muscles, while another man was running around the crowd taking bets. Another man, inside the cage, took a long pole and began poking something hidden inside the den. To Schmidel's shock and amazement, a large growling bear emerged, and soon beast and logger were locked in combat. They fought hand-to-paw for the next twenty minutes. Returning to his native land, Schmidel authored this story as part of his experiences and adventures in America titled: "Die Harte Schule: Eriebnisse in America."

Maple Falls about the time Frank Romandorf arrived during the spring of 1904. Deming Library.

It was in this remote hinterland that another native German by the name Frank E. Romandorf arrived in Maple Falls during the spring of 1904. Romandorf had purchased, through a tax sale, a parcel of land with a ranch-cabin on a hill above the Nooksack River. It was said that he had come by way of Chicago some time ago, where he had left his wife Margaret, a former widow, in care of her two daughters, Bessie and Mattie. There was also a son, Edward. Romandorf had lived with them in Chicago a short time, before moving further west to establish a new family home.

Frances Bruce Todd, before she became a noted local author and Maple Falls historian, was a woman with roots running deep into that community. Living amongst homesteaders, she is one of the few reliable resources of Maple Falls' humble beginnings, and of the Romandorf family. Todd claims that Margaret and her three children were living in Missouri when Frank Romandorf came to live there. Frank courted the widow, and married her later in Pennsylvania. The children all assumed the Romandorf name at his request. But it's become questionable if the couple was ever married at all, or whether Edward, Eddie or Ed was actually Frank's own sibling or child, or was from Margaret's previous marriage. There is also the possibility that Edward was born to Frank and Margaret out of wedlock in 1889, and that Frank couldn't leave his son behind. For this reason, Frank moved them to Fremont, Nebraska.

At the end of this mysterious story, there is some evidence indicating that all of the children were Romandorf's, but who really knows? The relationship between Frank and his wife Margaret seemed more a bond of convenience than of love. Maybe she made an excellent passive partner in his schemes? She may have lacked self-esteem, and felt no self-worth doing her husband's bidding. No doubt Frank dominated her, or he held some mysterious control we don't understand. Margaret will always remain a puzzling figure of the family. The question remains, was she a simpleton, a pawn, or a cunning, intelligent woman? The family was always uprooted, as Frank bounced around the country for unknown reasons. Whenever Frank was in legal troubles, Margaret stood in defense of her husband, but never at his side.

Frank Romandorf no doubt had his brushes with the law while they were together. The first known written account was October 3, 1890, just after relocating to Nebraska. Romandorf and an accomplice, nineteen-year-old Harry Thomas, put their hand to cattle rustling. The *Omaha World Herald* headlined: "Romandorf's Dilemma, Paying Debts with Other People's Stock Not a Good Plan." The headline obviously indicated which villain was in charge. The two had stolen eighteen head of cattle belonging to Phillip Scott, who was quite perturbed. A dozen were sold to a Mrs. McCleneghan, with Romandorf and Thomas receiving fifty-dollars in cash and the balance credited on a note.

The editor of the *Omaha World Herald* added in a snarling remark, "Mr. Romandorf will have a hard time to make an explanation good enough to keep him out of the penitentiary." Apparently his explanation didn't meet the judges' approval. In February 1891, Sheriff Mallon escorted Romandorf to serve 29 months in the Nebraska State Penitentiary.

His folly didn't end there. On January 21, 1903, Isaac Cahn filed suit to foreclose a mortgage upon ten acres of land on the outskirts of Lincoln. The agreed amount was $3,000 with a payment of $25 and an agreement of $150 to be paid every six months thereafter. Also, the contract stipulated, a mill building on the property was to be relocated and put into operating condition, of which $2,000 was expended to have the work happen. Another party named Michener furnished the greater part of the materials for this work.

It appears that the ever-conniving Romandorf, holding the greater sum of Michener's investment, plus materials, now held more funds than his twenty-five dollar layout to Cahn for the property. Romandorf may have been attempting to make a dash for it. Michener was no fool, and set up a cross-petition, a mechanic's lien of $810, plus interest on the land. Romandorf would say in the future that he lost his savings in Nebraska, due to bad investments. This just may have been that investment.

Between January 1903 and the spring of 1904, there is no account of Frank Romandorf's movements, but much speculation. He moved the family to Chicago and into a house fraudulently obtained through a trade of Nebraska property, which was already mortgaged. Romandorf was also reportedly in Seattle and British Columbia before finally settling into Maple Falls. Hollis B. Fultz, a criminologist and special investigator for the Washington State Attorney General's office, took an interest in the Romandorf case during the 1940s. He interviewed then-retired Bellingham detective Thomas DeHaven, who would pass away in 1944. DeHaven's handwritten notes established Romandorf as arriving in Bellingham in the spring of 1904 and securing employment as a butcher. Later Romandorf bought the butcher shop. DeHaven remembered these details as he had, on occasion, questioned Romandorf regarding stolen cattle sold from his butcher's block. This was before his son Edward arrived in Maple Falls.

DeHaven was asked about Romandorf's physical appearance in 1904. His notes indicated, "He appeared to be about 55 years of age, Five-feet, six-inches tall, a heavy shock of grey hair, grey mustache and beard. He had squinty eyes and his nose was flattened across the bridge. An upper tooth was missing on each side of his mouth. He seemed to have plenty of money when he came to town."

Penitentiary records in 1911 state: Age: 63, 5-foot 8-inches with grey hair and brownish-blue eyes. Teeth were in bad condition. His build was entered as medium, with a sallow (pale-yellow) complexion. Distinguishing marks listed a left index finger amputated at third joint. A lengthy vertical scar located on the outer right lower leg. Toenails on each great toe are deformed. DeHaven was fairly accurate in his seven year prior description.

Soon after arriving, DeHaven continues, Romandorf purchased a "tax-title ranch abutting the property of James Logan. It was heavily forested and needed clearing. The timber was good and Romandorf could make good money off the land. Then, his son Ed Romandorf appeared." That is about the time that people disappeared.

ROMANDORF'S CABIN

American Reveille

Romandorf hired his shingle-bolt cutters and other workers from various Seattle labor agencies, not wanting locals on his property. For Romandorf, these workers were easier to abuse and mistreat, as they had little recourse. He demanded that they stay on his property and not enter town if they wished to retain their employment. They would get paid at the end of the season, or when their agreement was up. Those who managed to talk with locals living in the vicinity often complained of the poor living conditions, terrible food and not receiving their pay. Many of these men came and went without notice. It was said that Romandorf made it a practice of never paying his help and always quarreled with the men whenever they asked for their wages. To the best of anyone's knowledge, they simply left, returning to Seattle.

Where Grim Tragedies May Soon Be Unearthed

THE LOGAN HOMESTEAD

American Reveille

One such man who answered the call was Fred Helms, a German himself, who came to Maple Falls in early 1905. He owned property on Lake Washington and wanted to clear and develop his parcel, but didn't have the financial means or equipment. Working for Frank Romandorf seemed like a good prospect to Helms. Helms and Romandorf came to a mutual and beneficial agreement that satisfied both parties. Helms would cut shingle-bolts and clear land for Romandorf, with the understanding that he and Ed would take a team to clear Helms' own acreage on Lake Washington after one year's work.

Romandorf cautioned Helms against leaving the ranch and urged him to never let anybody know where he was working. For seven months Helms toiled on the Romandorf spread, never leaving it, just as asked. Finally, he couldn't take it any longer and quit because of the poor living conditions, meager board and food. He just wanted a square meal. Helms walked into Maple Falls to stay with a former friend, John Groves, a shoemaker. This was mid-summer of 1905. After several days thinking it over, he decided to go back to the ranch and finish the agreement. He had only five months left. He told Groves his intentions, so that he could get his own land cleared next spring. Groves never heard from Helms again.

Thomas DeHaven remembered: "A man by the name Fred Helms was employed by Romandorf in 1905, under some kind of work-trade agreement. He disappeared while working there in November and was never seen again. He (Helms) owned a place on Lake Washington. I understand Romandorf later showed up with a deed to it."

Helms was known to be missing, but there was no report of a crime brought against Romandorf, so DeHaven had nothing to investigate. People came and went daily, and there was nothing unusual about people buying or selling land.

Eventually, money was sent to Margaret in Chicago, which would pay the travel expenses for her and her daughters to come to Maple Falls in early 1906. Edward, who was about seventeen years old, had come earlier and helped Frank fix the ranch up for their arrival. They milled their own lumber from the property and added onto the existing structure. Edward also secured work in Maple Falls as a butcher, presumably through his father's connections, and possibly with the party to whom he sold his own business. By the winter of 1905-06, all was ready to move the rest of the family in.

Frances Bruce Todd wrote, "Bessie recalled that it was a cold, chilly day in March when they arrived on the B.B. & B.C. Railroad. There was about six inches of snow on the ground. As they departed from the train depot the town of crude buildings, sidewalks and gravel streets beheld their eyes."

Frank Romandorf's occupation at the time of their arrival was listed as "buying and selling horses and wagons, along with working the farm," according to Todd.

In Spring 1906, Jack Green showed up from Seattle. He worked in the King Lumber Mill and lodged with Lyle Heaton, proprietor of the Silver Lake Hotel. Green became well acquainted with the towns' folk and area. He liked Maple Falls and considered moving there; an agreement was struck with Frank Romandorf that in return for one year's work cutting shingle-bolts, he would receive a five-acre lot on the outskirts of Maple Falls along the Silver Lake Road.

But even with the family on the property, people continued to disappear. DeHaven recalled: "In the summer of 1906 (June or July) Jack Green, who had been working at the ranch, asked Justice of the Peace C. W. Beal for a warrant charging attempted murder against Ed Romandorf, saying young Romandorf had tried to push him against a running shingle saw in a mill where they were working." On several other occasions, Ed threw bolts from the chute aiming directly at Green's head. A solid hit would surely have killed him.

DeHaven was with Beal that day witnessing the conversation. After some second thoughts, Green worried if he pursued the warrant, Frank Romandorf might hold the money owed to him. "Green told us he was going out to Romandorf's to try to collect eight months' wages due him, and that he would tell us whether or not to serve a warrant after he returned. Justice Beal remembered the day as well:

> "I made out the warrant and he kept explaining to me how he
> hated to work under such circumstances, but that he would not
> quit because of the land. By the time I finished the warrant and
> was ready to serve it, he said he wanted me to leave it in my desk
> and that he would go back and settle up with Romandorf and pay

for the land in some other way. He was going to return and let me know how he settled, but from that day to this, I have never heard from him."

Before going to Romandorf's, Green stopped by to see his old friend Lyle Heaton at the hotel. Green had sold him a crop of potatoes he had grown on a vacant strip of land. He told Heaton, "I'm going up to the Romandorf ranch and settle up. I'll come back this afternoon and help you dig up those potatoes." Heaton thanked Green for the help, and said he would have several hoes and potato forks ready when he returned.

When Jack failed to return, both Beal and Heaton went searching. Frank Romandorf claimed that indeed had Green stopped by and received his back pay, and that Ed and Green had settled their differences. With his work completed, money in hand, Green was satisfied on all accounts and left the area. Romandorf had no idea where the man intended to go next. Beal and Heaton didn't know what to make of this, but they had their suspicions that something wasn't right. There was nothing to follow up on, other than the fact that Romandorf was and always had been an odd character.

The Romandorfs were not exactly the friendliest neighbors in Maple Falls. When in town they made no acknowledgements to folks as they passed by and never associated with the townspeople in any way. When talked to, Frank just ignored them. Hunters or trespassers were not allowed on the 160-acre property. If caught, they were escorted off. Millard Burnside's property abutted the German's property. He was inconveniently compelled to build a roundabout road to his homestead, two miles west of the Romandorf place without crossing over any portion of it. Burnside said the "grim-face malignant…was always posted on the short and private road to keep him from crossing the forbidden ground." Deputy Sheriff George McLaughlin, Justice of the Peace C. W. Beal, Game Warden D. P. Castor and residents Art Burges,

Mrs. J. H. Fitch and Millard Burnside all claimed to have been chased off the property. Sometimes with a club in hand, other times by rifle.

James Logan

James F. Logan was a Scotsman who lived alone on his thirty-three acre ranch for many years. He immigrated to the United States in 1874, coming to Renton, Washington by 1889 and then Whatcom County a year or two later. In 1891 he joined the county road commission working toward extending the wagon road into what would eventually become Maple Falls. Logan was a prospector in the Mount Baker mining district, and for a time he was joined in his quest for riches by his younger brother Hugh. With nothing gained after several years on their claim, Logan decided to concentrate on his farm, and Hugh moved on. Local tales had it that Logan had money hidden inside his cabin, possibly under his floorboards. If so, he never bettered his life with it. By 1904 he had a new neighbor, Frank E. Romandorf.

By all appearances the two neighbors lived in harmony for the first two years. But on several occasions during the summer of 1906, the townsfolk of Maple Falls heard the two men wrangling over a horse that Romandorf had sold to Logan. Then in late September, Logan's barn mysteriously burned to the ground. There was no evidence that Romandorf was involved, and certainly nothing forecasting physical violence on the horizon. By October 1906 that rapidly changed. A terrific storm of wind and rain swept through the Nooksack valley, overflowing riverbanks and uprooting trees, causing great damage.

After the storm passed, Logan wasn't seen, nor heard from for days. Curiosity led one of the neighbors to investigate the property. Logan wasn't found anywhere, and his cabin was undisturbed. There was immediate concern that Logan may have been struck by a falling tree and trapped, or even killed. Sheriff Andrew Williams was notified of the concerns for the missing man. Williams organized a search party that scoured the woods in the vicinity, but they found no trace of the missing man. The rumored "pot of gold" in the cabin was immediately ruled out as a factor in his disappearance, as Logan's rooms weren't turned out. Williams determined there was no indication of any foul play committed within the home.

Out in the pasture near the cabin, the blotted corpse of Logan's horse was found with a bullet in its head (some accounts claim "bullet-riddled"). It was soon discovered that Logan's neighbor Frank Romandorf was also missing. Margaret and the children claimed to know nothing of Frank's whereabouts since the storm. Were they now looking for two missing men? Did one involve the other in foul play? James Logan was well known, and liked, and not seen as a man likely to leave without telling someone. Sheriff Williams suggested possible murder, and the search for Logan or his body was taken up with renewed efforts.

Others thought Williams was exaggerating the situation, offering that one of the men might have been in trouble near the banks of the turbulent Nooksack River during the violent storm. While one was aiding the other, the two men could have fallen in and were swept away in the river's floodwaters. Taken as a consideration, Williams organized a second party to search along the riverbanks. All anyone knew for sure, was that Frank Romandorf and James Logan vanished that night from Maple Falls.

Discovering no bodies, no evidence of foul play or any further clues leading to the men's disappearance, the search was halted in a shroud of mystery. Then, several weeks later, Sheriff Williams received his first big break in the case. On November 15, 1906, Allen H. Strickfaden, postmaster and editor of the Maple Falls newspaper, The *Leader*, received a letter from James Logan mailed from Seattle. It was hand-written in a labored scrawl:

"Please state that I have gone to the old country. I have sold my place; Please send my mail to Hoboken, New Jersey. I will

go there on the 26th of this Month. Tell all the boys goodbye."
Signed James Logan.

The letter aroused Strickfaden's suspicion, who turned it over to Sheriff Williams at once, declaring it a forgery. The postmaster knew Logan's handwriting, and knew his friend would never have left so suddenly without seeing him first. The letter was intended, so thought Williams, as a ruse, to throw the law off the scent, and to dispel the theory that Logan was murdered. It was to provide evidence that he was alive and on his way to Scotland.

Sheriff Williams began another intensive search at both the Romandorf and Logan ranches, but the only clue of foul play was the dead horse discovered earlier. Still, the letter led Williams to suspect the German was definitely connected with Logan's disappearance. Unknown to Williams, the Whatcom County Courthouse, in Bellingham, received a deed of sale dated October 5, 1906, mailed from Chicago, signed by James F. Logan, transferring the ranch to a Frank O. Rankin. The purchase price was $5,000. James Logan's homestead now showed up on county records as a legitimate land transfer, although the buyer never materialized.

Around January 1907 Ed Romandorf found himself in trouble with Sheriff Williams for selling a mortgaged house. The matter was settled out of court, and Ed left Whatcom County for good. The rest of the family continued to stay on the property, but would later move to Seattle.

During the autumn hunting season of 1907, a hunter discovered the leg bone of a man in the wood lot directly behind the Logan place. The bone was found by Liston Bower, a Maple Falls resident who immediately turned it over to the sheriff. The bone appeared to have been washed up from the river, as it was well cleaned and smooth. With the discovery of a body part now in hand, Williams sent a dispatch of inquiry to authorities in Scotland, and to Logan's relatives. James Logan had not returned to his homeland.

Margaret and her daughters stayed on the ranch until 1909. Several years after Frank Romandorf had seemingly abandoned them, the family continued to drive off intruders seeking to trespass. Strange stories persisted and circulated about the timidity and bizarre nature of the three Romandorf women. They hid from people behind trees and buildings when someone passed by. They were seen peeking until it was safe to come out again. Seldom would they venture into town.

"When Romandorf left," said Millard Burnside, "they couldn't get the feed for their stock, and the cows and pigs began to drop dead from starvation." Burnside eventually stepped in and bought feed, as he couldn't stand to see animals die. When Margaret decided to leave the home, Burnside convinced her to lease the farm to him. She spent a week destroying papers and things around the house. "I waited for her to leave before turning my stock over to graze. That's what I wanted the place for. After they left I searched every nook and corner, but found nothing that would have given me a hint of where they came from, how they lived, or what sort of people they were. The place was cleared of every scrap of paper and writing." Besides grazing land, Burnside must have been pleased to have his old shortcut to his homestead back again.

Frank Romandorf, alias James Logan

In the late fall of 1906, a man by the name James Logan purchased the "Baslington" ranch in the vicinity of Cedonia, (Bissell) Stevens County, near the Columbia River in eastern Washington. It was once the homestead of Englishman Thomas Baslington and his wife Emma. The two had come to Washington Territory by wagon, and broke the turf on their newly acquired land sometime prior to 1885.

By the Spring of 1907, Logan had added to the acreage, establishing the fictitious "Cascade Land & Cattle Company." He hired two farm hands,

Ed Lewis and "Tennessee" Jack F. Tisth to work the estate. The ranch had substantial livestock holdings of over a dozen horses and ponies, 186 cattle and milking cows, eleven hogs, six dozen chickens, sheep, ducks, geese and a scotch collie.

During the fall of 1907, Logan struck a deal with David R. Shively, of nearby Addy, Washington, to act as an intermediary in selling Shively's 160 acres of land. It seems Shively had enough of the pioneer life, and wanted off his homestead. Logan said he would make some inquires with friends in Chicago, and would get back to him. Logan arranged the sale of the homestead and arranged that the sale would be closed in Spokane.

Hollis Fultz records the last conversation (February 1908) between Shively and his old friend, Addy druggist Alfred Weatherman. It was in regard to Logan making the sale. "Logan's getting me a good price," said Shively. "When I get my money I'm going back East and see my folks. Maybe I'll stay there." Henceforth, there was no great surprise in Addy when Shively failed to return.

Shively was said to have departed with a large trunk by train to Spokane on March 1 to meet with Logan.

Shively and Logan celebrated the transfer of Shively's land with a toast. Little did Shively notice, that Logan had laced his drink with poison. It is not known whether the poison killed the man outright, or simply incapacitated him until the deathblow was administered. After Shively was killed, he was crammed inside his own steamer trunk and shipped immediately to the Baslington ranch. Logan wired ahead instructions for his hands to retrieve the trunk at the train depot at Blue Creek and to bury it. No questions were to be asked of its contents. The men followed their boss' orders to the letter.

On March 6, a deed of transfer arrived in Colville, the county seat of Stevens, turning the property over to a George A. Herman of Chicago. That summer, the deed was again transferred to James Monaghan of Spokane for the sum of $6,000. The deed was duly witnessed, and notarized by James Allen, with Logan handling the transaction on commission.

In August 1909 James Logan decided they needed a housekeeper to do the cooking. Maybe the men grew sick of their own culinary skills. While in Spokane on a business trip, Logan struck up a conversation on the matter with friend, Fred Schuelein, a German cigar shop owner, who claimed to know the perfect woman. Introductions were made to forty-five-year-old Mrs. Agnes Janson (Agnus Vinegar), a newly arrived Bohemian widow from the old country. Fultz says she was a "buxom woman of only forty years, not pretty, but wholesome, and Logan courted her from their first meeting." This certainly gives rise to suspicions, regarding Romandorf's legal marriage to Margaret. Were they actually married? If so, was Romandorf contemplating divorce, or marrying under his newly adopted name of Logan?

By September, Agnes Janson finally agreed to go to the ranch, and departed the home of her good friend Mrs. Margaret Aherns. Before leaving she told Aherns, "If we are suited we will be married." Janson took the train to Blue Creek, where Logan retrieved her.

Three weeks later, Logan was back at Aherns claiming there would be wedding bells soon. He gathered up the last of Janson's belongings, including a cow. Before leaving, Margaret handed Logan some mail that had arrived for Janson. One letter perked Logan's interest with its foreign stamps. He tore open the envelope and took the letter to a friend who could translate the letter for him. He soon learned that fourteen thousand marks ($3,500 in 1909 dollars) had been deposited into a Berlin bank account and was being forwarded to her, as requested. The large sum aroused Logan's greedy desires like a fever.

Logan soon hatched a cunning plan and was prepared to implement it on his return home. During the horse-wagon ride back to his ranch, the German stopped fifteen miles out at the turnoff to the abandoned Hurgesheimer ranch. It was a piece of property he had considered purchasing. Logan located a concealed area in the wood and dismounted his wagon. Clearing a spot of open ground, he moved some large dead logs by horse-hitch into a pile, eventually constructing a large pyre. Finishing his scheme, he excitedly headed home. Wasting no time, he proposed to Agnes and told neighbors they would honeymoon in Germany.

Late on the evening of October 27, 1909, the couple loaded two trunks and a heavy wicker basket onto Logan's carriage and headed for the Blue Creek depot. Before leaving, Logan told Ed Lewis he would hand the team over to Johnny Cline, who would return the horses to the ranch from the depot. A light autumn rain began to fall along the way, but didn't hinder their travel. At some point on the road, Logan told his wife-to-be that he misjudged the time, and was a bit confused of their direction in the darkness. He thought it best to camp at the old Hurgesheimer place, and get an early start in the morning. Janson had traveled the route only once before, and was unfamiliar with their route. Turning off the road, they were seen by Colville merchant Al Stayt, who took no great notice as he passed.

Agnes Janson probably took no unusual notice, until Logan popped two bullets into the side of her head. The despicable act was done at the gate entering the property, as Logan never thought to cover up the blood and brain tissue, which would be discovered on the ground later. He dragged Janson's lifeless body onto the pre-built and awaiting pyre, dumped her body on the logs and ignited a raging fire.

A half-mile away, the night sky glowed orange and the crackling fire awoke thirty-four-year-old hunter Ira Gifford from his slumber. He in turn woke his brother Elmer and Uncle Charlie from their damp bedrolls. Ira wanted to see what was happening. But his brother just rolled over and fell back asleep. Morrison E. "Od" Taylor, a rancher abutting the Hurgesheimer property, saw the black smoke at six o'clock the following morning, and saddled a horse to see if the Hurgesheimer place was still standing. Coming onto the scene, a fire some six feet round burned with flames leaping as high. Judging from the amount of ash, he figured the blaze had raged all night.

Taylor discovered Logan fast asleep under his carriage. "What goes on here?" he demanded, waking the slumbering man. Logan, with a prepared story to give, told Taylor nonchalantly that he was taking his housekeeper to the depot when one of his horses suddenly got the colic. He was fortunate that a passerby took her the rest of the way, as not to miss the train. He then took the horses off the road to bleed the sick one. Taylor didn't inquire the need of such a huge fire. Satisfied, he rode back home, returning to check on the fire at noon. It still burned, and Logan was still asleep.

Later that afternoon the Giffords circled around the woods during their hunt, and came upon the site. The fire by this time was reduced to hot embers, and Logan was long gone. The men marveled at the large burned-out section of earth encasing the bonfire. Hugging in closer, the men noticed what appeared to be the ashen cinder casting of a human hand. Spooked, the trio ran to Taylor's house and told him of their discovery. Taylor knew all along something wasn't right.

Sheriff William H. Graham, in Colville, received an urgent call from Taylor, notifying him that a horrid murder had taken place nearby. Sheriff Graham arrived on the scene just before dark, with coroner Dr. A. B. Cook and Stevens County Prosecutor Hugh Kirkpatrick. They were just in time to catch sight of the macabre find in the golden glow of the setting sun. Graham attempted to gently lift the ashen hand from the pit, but it disintegrated instantly into powder.

Graham had come out from Virginia with his young family to homestead sometime before 1887. His wife had passed in 1896; she was only 36, leaving him to raise their four daughters and son. By 1906 only two daughters were at home.

That's when Graham accepted the elected position of Stevens County sheriff. Graham had recently taken a new wife, and that wasn't easy on the family. He and the kids had supported one another for over a dozen years without a mother figure. He was now 47 years old, his daughters Mollie 28 and Mattie 26. His new wife, Stella (DeGrenif) was only 25 years old, and having a tough time settling in.

When he became sheriff, Graham thought the most he'd have to worry about were cattle rustlers. He was ill prepared to deal with a homicidal maniac. This was going to be a long night. Graham sent word home to Stella that he wouldn't be home anytime soon.

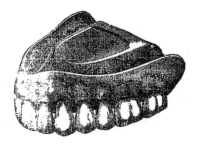

One of the few remains from the cremation of Agnes Janson, her upper bridgework.

After the pyre cooled, investigators sifted through the ash and discovered metallic articles belonging to a woman: corset stays, wire from a hat, a buckle, brooch and hat pin, bone fragments and a part of upper bridgework.

There were also spent brass cartridges found nearby belonging to a .32 S&W long, a revolver that fired rifle bullets. It was obvious that something sinister happened to Agnes Janson, if indeed the remains in the ashes were those of the housekeeper and would-be wife.

The night Logan drove into the Hurgesheimer ranch it had rained just enough to soak the ground, leaving a traceable set of carriage tracks. At sunrise, Graham backtracked the sunken carriage wheels to the road and eventually pulled into the Baslington ranch, James Logan's Cascade Land & Cattle Company. The two hands, Ed Lewis and "Tennessee" Jack Tisth, were outside working and volunteered what they knew, when Cline arrived with the horses. Cline told the sheriff that Logan boarded the train alone to Spokane. Cline also mentioned seeing a substantially large revolver in the luggage. At Blue Creek, Logan had indeed checked his luggage through, but he got off the train in Hillyard with a single trunk, just outside Spokane. There he boarded yet another train, doubling back to the small town of Davenport.

James Logan walked into the Davenport Bank to withdraw Agnes Janson's account, pretending to be her husband. He handed cashier M. W. Anderson a power-of-attorney document and showed him the deed to the Baslington ranch, establishing the title transfer from "George Hilton" to himself as a form of local identification. Anderson wouldn't buy Logan's story and refused to withdraw Janson's account. Anderson had never seen the man before, and found it odd that he would come to Davenport to empty the account rather than Colville or Spokane. Furious, Logan stomped out of the bank and headed to the saloon, where he held a room.

Meanwhile, Sheriff Graham had little difficulty tracking down Logan. It was confusing why Logan would choose Davenport, an obscure place to run. Was he hiding out? Graham called his law counterpart in Davenport, Sheriff Gardiner, and informed him that unless Logan had jumped train, he should be somewhere in his town. Gardiner's search first took him to the

Davenport bank, the only place of importance in town, and was informed by Anderson that the scrubby little foreigner was just there.

Moments later, the sheriff and his deputies apprehended Logan in his hotel room. As Graham entered the wanted man's room, Logan was found rummaging through some papers in the trunk that traveled with him. Inside, a treasure trove was discovered, described by author Fultz as "a strange assortment of instruments, documents and utensils, not such as an honest man would carry." Logan carried blank documents for land and property transactions, several pending transaction, and others in various names. There were several stamps for use on bank drafts, check cancellations, and subscribe payee. There were stamps to cancel and date train passenger tickets, several notary republic seals. Blank checks. Inks in various colors, and solvents to remove ink. The contents also showed checks allegedly written by D. R. Shively, previous owner of the ranch in Addy. There was a handwritten note stating, "All papers in box at Unity Safe Deposit Company, Chicago." Sheriff Gardiner knew he had just made a great haul, but in regard to what?

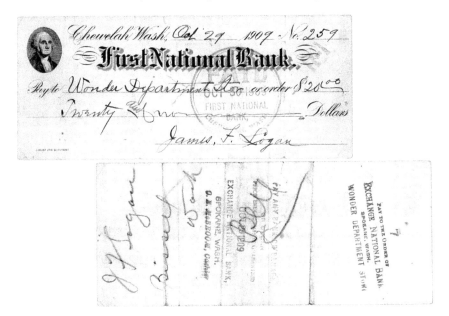

One of the fraudulent checks Romandorf cashed in John Logan's name. Romandorf had a supply of inks and stamps for all his falsified transactions. Washington State Archives, Olympia.

Sheriff Graham was no less interested, and especially in one particular document: the deeds for the Baslington ranch, transferring it from George Hilton to James Logan. The transaction occurred in a small mining town north of Colville, an out of the way location. It was signed, witnessed and executed before E. B. Bernhardt, a notary public republic of Washington state. Graham was familiar with all the legal notaries of his district, but had never heard of a Bernhardt. Neither did officials in Olympia when he inquired.

Graham returned to Colville, where the two hired hands Lewis and Tisth were being held in the city jail as material witnesses. Graham questioned the men about their employer and what they knew of him. When Graham pressed the name Hilton on the men, Lewis spoke up, saying that he was George Hilton, confusing the sheriff further.

Again, Hollis Fultz comes forward with his research notes: "I am George Hilton, that is my real name. I was born in Omaha, and my father's real name is Edward Hilton. I am a nephew of Logan, who married my mother's sister. I came to Stevens County from Missoula, Montana, in 1908. I hadn't seen Logan for many years until we met in this county." Graham held out the deed to the ranch, asking Lewis, or Hilton, why he would sell his own ranch to the man he now worked for. Lewis became flustered, not expecting the question. He claimed he was indeed the owner under the name of Hilton. "No," said Graham, "the deed and bill of sale found in Logan's trunk claims Logan owns the ranch." Lewis was adamant that he was the owner of the Baslington ranch, and not his Uncle Frank.

Sheriff William Graham found the entire affair rooted in suspicion. A cremated woman, Logan on the run, the trunk contents, the hired hands, Hilton's explanations and his slip of the tongue, "Uncle Frank." The parties involved used multiple names as aliases, and one wouldn't do that unless they were wanted or running from something. The sheriff decided the best course of action was to photograph his prisoners and send a circular to newspapers and law enforcement throughout the Northwest.

Whatcom County, 1909

Edward Lewis alias George Romandorf is shown in the small cut.

On Thursday, November 11, 1909, former Sheriff Andrew Williams was startled when he saw the photos in the newspaper. "James Logan and Ed Lewis," the caption read, "arrested in Colville, Spokane County, for the murder of Mrs. Agnes Janson." A hyped story followed that both Logan and Lewis were caught red-handed at the scene of a huge bonfire burning the evidence of a woman's body. "Janson," it said, "was lured to Logan's home with a promise of marriage, only to steal her wealth."

Except the photograph before Williams was not of James Logan, but of Frank Romandorf, who was wanted on suspicion of the possible murder of James Logan, and for the questioning of several missing persons. The shady deals Romandorf made under James Logan's name in Spokane and

Stevens County were his downfall. The chilling names of Romandorf and Logan again reawakened the community to the foul play they suspected in Maple Falls. After three years of mystery, during which time the sheriff's office searched diligently for any trace of a suspect or the victims, it appeared as if some answers would soon be forthcoming.

Whatcom County Sheriff-elect, Spencer Van Zandt, who replaced Williams two years prior, saw the circular sent to his office. Looking over the photographs, he had the same reaction as his predecessor. These were the Romandorfs, both father and son. Sheriff Williams' unsolved case of two missing county men, maybe more. It seemed to Van Zandt that Frank Romandorf had been living under the name of James Logan ever since he left Whatcom county three years earlier. The sheriff looked over the dispatch of photographs and the circular letter asking for additional information.

Van Zandt took the photographs to Maple Falls, showing them to folks who were more acquainted with both Logan and Romandorf. All identified the images as being Frank and Edward Romandorf. With his list of witnesses identifying the prisoners in his hand, Van Zandt telephoned Sheriff Graham in Colville, verifying who it was they had in custody. Van Zandt asked if their suspects gave up any information on Whatcom County. Graham at that point knew nothing of the Logan affair. Sheriff Van Zandt then indicated that he or another party would journey over the mountains to interview the prisoners. He relayed his suspicions regarding Frank Romandorf, and wanted a statement from the man leading to the spot where Logan's remains might be found. With Romandorf found, Van Zandt now assumed that Logan was indeed murdered and his corpse buried in some remote spot near or on his ranch.

It had not been known if a murder was committed in Maple Falls, but circumstantial evidence was piling up against Romandorf, and now his alleged murders in Stevens County were not helping the former Whatcom County resident. Van Zandt next paid a visit to his predecessor, Andrew

Williams. Van Zandt showed the former sheriff the photos. Williams commented on seeing them in the newspapers. Looking at Frank Romandorf again, Williams recalled that at the time the man wore a heavy beard, while the picture showed a face with only a heavy mustache. Williams stated that there was no proof that a crime had been committed. There was a violent storm that night swelling the river, and it was possible, for whatever reason, the two might have been swept away. If that were the case, the question lingered, why would Romandorf abandon his wife, children and possessions and take James Logan's name?

Williams recounted that after a search of the neighboring homesteads, he spent $250.00 of county money searching both banks of the North Fork of the Nooksack River between Maple Falls and Lynden. If Logan's and Romandorf's bodies had indeed gotten into the river, they could easily have been carried far down the swift river beyond all hope of recovery. As for the property, his search party probed for soft soil in vain, trying to locate a freshly dug grave. "No," William's responded to Van Zandt's query. "Suspicion against Frank Romandorf three years ago was not very strong."

Possibly, because it was originally his case, Andrew Williams was asked to travel with Bellingham Detective Thomas DeHaven to Stevens County. They would confront Frank Romandorf over his crimes in Whatcom. Fultz describes that encounter, from his interview notes with DeHaven. Romandorf simply laughed at Williams, when accused of murdering James Logan. "How could I murder Logan when I am Logan? I suppose when you start trailing me back and find out I was once in South Africa you will accuse me of doing things like that down there too."

The remark caused Sheriff William Graham to take a pause and think. His circular brought about a significant response from Whatcom County; what if he took it further? Graham next questioned people who interacted with Logan in the Colville area. He soon discovered Logan had indeed talked about striking it rich in South Africa, but losing it all in a bad Nebraska land deal. Inquires sent to the British South African Police Service by Graham yielded a great deal of information. The man called Logan was wanted for questioning in their own investigations over the deaths of eight men killed in a theft for diamonds during the 1890s. The heist was valued at about $15,000. Further more, it was discovered Logan's real name was William Frederick Jahns. It was determined by South African authorities that Jahns entered the United States through New Orleans. After which, he disappeared. Jahns admitted to coming through that port on the vessel *Australia.*

Trial

William Frederick Jahns, alias Frank Romandorf, alias James Logan, went on trial January 3, 1910, at Superior Court in Colville. Because he was arrested as James Logan, he was tried as James Logan, regardless of his true name. Attorneys Lewis Jesseph and Leo Grinstead represented Logan, with lead attorney Henry N. Martin sitting in on the case. County Prosecutor Hugh Kirkpatrick and attorney Merritt represented the State. Judge Daniel H. Carey, age 47, presided.

Ed Lewis, George Hilton or Edward Romandorf cowardly did everything he could on the witness stand to distance himself from Logan, but admitted he was the son of Frank Romandorf. After his run-ins with Whatcom's law officers, DeHaven and Williams, he had little choice but to admit he held the name Romandorf while living in Maple Falls. Lewis adamantly denied knowledge of any murders, and claimed not to have known this side of his father's character. Continuing with his compulsive lying, he even denied Margaret Romandorf as his mother, stating that he was the son of his father's first wife.

Lewis also claimed the Baslington ranch belonged to him, but could not explain how he came by it. Stevens County records show the property belonging to Logan, but the record was clouded, according to officials.

During the investigation of the Romandorf family history, Margaret Romandorf was soon located living at 316 (or 317) 16th Avenue in North Seattle. The King County sheriff and a Seattle reporter questioned her about her husband. She readily admitted that her husband lived near Colville and that the family had lived in Maple Falls, where they still had a home. They were married in Pennsylvania, she said, moved to Nebraska, Chicago and later on to Maple Falls. Now she and her daughters had settled in Seattle. She was shown photographs of Frank Romandorf, and a younger fellow, claiming to be George Hilton, a nephew of Romandorf. "No," said Margaret, "that's Edward Romandorf, my son." Margaret went on to state that there were no domestic difficulties between her and her husband and disclaimed any knowledge of violence or that Frank was ever previously in custody. Their relationship was such that she and daughter Bessie had spent the previous summer at her husband's ranch. "We left in August, just shortly before Mrs. Janson arrived," she said. At about this time, Bessie entered the room and intervened, ending any further questioning of her mother.

There was no mention as to whether she knew if her husband was planning to abandon her and the children in Maple Falls. Why did he leave? When did they reestablish contact, or why she was now living in Seattle and not with her husband in Colville?

Logan's defense soon fell apart as mounting evidence was introduced to the court. First the large revolver taken from Logan's custody was introduced, with matching empty cartridges found at the crime scene. Then a box was brought forth. Prosecutor Kirkpatrick made a somber approach toward the jury to display the contents. Laid out in front of them were fragments of skull, vertebrae, and bone intermixed with some ash. A gold upper-plate from the woman's mouth, two heart-shaped earrings, metal fragments from clothing and a beautifully handcrafted brooch, which somehow managed to survive the intense blaze.

"Od" Taylor took the stand and pointed toward the defendant, saying that was the man who tended the fire at the old Hurgesheimer homestead last November. Taylor said he talked with Logan, who was standing between him and the fire. He talked randomly, mumbling to himself, and stood between him and the fire throughout. August Bruckner, a forty-three-year-old German immigrant and Stevens County farmer, testified that he was one of the volunteers sifting though the ash finding remains.

It was Bruckner who found the brooch. The court was silent except for muffled tears that came from Mrs. Margaret Aherns, as she broke down on the stand while identifying jewelry belonging to her dear friend, Agnes Janson. Fultz wrote, "That brooch belonged to Agnes," said Mrs. Ahern. "She loved it so deeply she would not even allow me to touch it. It was a gift of her dearly beloved husband." After the testimony defense attorney, Henry Martin asked for an adjournment until the following day.

The defense termed the box of remains as a "mess of stuff," but a week of witnesses soon painted a vivid picture of the woman whom the "stuff" once belonged too. Logan began demonstrating signs of anxiety as he listened to the testimony. Two bank cashiers next took the stand. One from the Old National Bank in Spokane explained the currency transfer from Berlin, and how that procedure worked. Next came Anderson, from the Bank of Davenport, who refused to hand over to Logan the account of Agnes Janson.

Colville newspapers reported that "at times Logan would jabber unintelligently during the court proceedings, and at other times he shouts in anger when names of persons, supposed in years gone-by to have excited his enmity, were mentioned. Leaving the court he screamed and screamed for the first time, in what officers termed a fit." Some claimed it was a performance, to plea for insanity. Others believed Logan didn't need to act, as he was insane.

Defense attorneys Lewis Jesseph and Leo Grinstead ordered a mental evaluation on Logan. Dr. M. F. Setter of Spokane and fellow colleague Dr.

Lee B. Harvey of Colville performed the observation. Logan was a bit elusive at first, not wanting to give up all his secrets, not even in his own defense, but loved the attention he was receiving. Logan knew very well after the first day of trial, that he was in a precarious situation and the scales were tipping against him. Playing a cunning game of survival, he decided to play the insane card on the professionals. He would get out of the predicament yet.

He claimed none of this was his fault. He had a paranoiac obsession that people were out to kill him, so he was forced to do away with them first. Enemies were following him, and that was the true reason for his erratic movements all over the world. He was forced to protect himself constantly. Therefore, all his killings were obviously in self-defense. The doctors saw through this veneer and declared Logan not insane, but a cold calculated killer with a lust for murder. There was also a clear obsession, for committing murder for gain, and not protection as claimed. Therefore the physicians refused to support Logan in his defense.

And It Continues

It was a severe blow for the defense, which abandoned using their doctors' testimony. But the state was certainly interested, and subpoenaed Setter and Harvey to the stand to recount what transpired in Logan's cell that evening.

Failing to prove himself mentally incompetent to his doctors, Logan demanded the opportunity the following day to speak on his own defense. Henry Martin was dead set against Logan taking the stand. Logan insisted that he must address the court, even against the advice of his attorneys. He arose several times from his seat, breaking into the proceedings and demanding to talk. Judge Carey told Logan to sit down and to shut up or he would be escorted to his cell. Carey informed the accused that he could not be forced to testify against himself, nor was it advised in his particular situation.

Carey reminded Attorneys Lewis Jesseph and Leo Grinstead that defense was barred from pleading insanity, because the 1909 state session laws provided that the insanity plea must be made at the opening of the trial, or not at all.

In the end, Logan got his way and took the stand. It seemed the old man decided that coming clean, or to an extent anyway, might save his neck from the noose. He was still attempting to sway the jury with insanity. Again, Hollis Fultz came to the rescue with his earlier research on the case:

"My true name is William Frederick Jahns. I killed eight men in South America and stole their diamonds. I had $85,000 when I landed in New Orleans after the Boer War, but lost most of it in a business deal in Nebraska."

"I killed Agnes Janson. I prepared the log pile several days before I shot her and threw her on the fire."

"I killed James Logan at Maple Falls. Logan had it in for me and so I got the better of this old enemy. My real name is Jahns, but most of the time in America I have gone by Frank Romandorf. I ran away from Germany to avoid military service. I threw Logan's body in an old culvert not far from the house. The horse just happened to get in the way and I shot him."

"I killed Dave Shively. He met me in Spokane to close the deal for his farm. I gave him drugs in the hotel room and put his body in his own trunk. I shipped him back to the Baslington ranch. His bones are buried on a hill back of the house, if the coyotes haven't dug them up."

"I killed Fred Helms and Jack Green at Maple Falls. I killed all these people and many more whom I don't even remember. I've killed from Canada to Africa, and that is not all."

Logan rose to his feet from within the stand; his eyes were glaring; his voice rose to a scream; he looked directly at Ed Romandorf: "Other hands than mine will kill Od Taylor for what he did here to me." Then he sat back down and buried his head in his hands, sobbing, "I'm crazy. I'm crazy. I was afraid of them all."

Maple Falls, January 1910

On hearing of Romandorf's murder confession, and the disposal of the true James Logan's body, a posse heavily armed with picks and shovels, lead by Deputy Sheriff McLaughlin headed toward Maple Falls. Locals eager to search for their old friend, murdered more than three years ago, greeted the group. A lack of details in the confession compelled McLaughlin to examine the ground under three bridges for Logan's remains. One small bridge was located within 200 yards of the deserted homestead. The other two bridges were about a quarter-mile distant, and the ground beneath these would be dug up if the first failed to give up a corpse.

Romandorf Must Die!

Guilty of murder in the first degree was the verdict of the jury in Colville. The jury took two ballots, the first being ten for conviction, two for acquittal. The second ballot was unanimous for a verdict of guilty. As Jahns heard the verdict read by the clerk of court, he fell mechanically into his seat, eyeing the jurors closely. Then suddenly a smile passed over his face. It was a ghastly grin on his wrinkled face. He laughed to himself, and shook his head approvingly. Judge Daniel Carey had handed the case to the jury on Friday, January 20, 1910, with instructions from the court after closing remarks by the prosecution. Counsel for Logan did not address the jury for closing remarks.

In pronouncing sentence, Judge Carey condemned Jahns for the demented and cowardly act of killing Janson simply to gain a few dollars. "I have thought over your case a great deal and decided carefully between life imprisonment and a death sentence," said the judge, "and feel justified in sending you to the gallows. The record shows one of the most brutish crimes I have ever heard of. It does not seem possible there is a man living who could treat a woman in this cruel manner."

Through it all, Jahns grinned and smiled at Carey. He stared into the judge's eyes as he heard himself claimed the greatest monster in the history of Washington. When asked if he had anything to say, the prisoner giggled a

"No." The judge said he had decided on the death sentence after reading the crimes committed by the prisoner and his attempts to play insanity before the court. "You are not insane and never were," said Carey. "You played the part well, and if you attempted it two months earlier you might have escaped the gallows. I think this is not the first deed of this kind you are guilty of." Judge Carey didn't go further, but it seemed Maple Falls was on his mind.

Judge Carey next overruled a motion by defense for an "arrest of judgment" and for a new trial when the defense made exception to the ruling. With little hesitation, Carey carried out sentence. On Friday, the 21st day of April 1911, William Frederick Jahns, alias James Logan and Frank Romandorf would hang by the neck at the State Penitentiary at Walla Walla until dead. Carey's last order of business was to clear James Logan's name from the record, for that of William Frederick Jahns. When Jahns was told he would hang by the neck, he just nodded his head approvingly, his expression never changing. After the sentence he chatted and laughed at his attorneys.

On being taken back to his cell, Jahns giggled and skipped. He rushed ahead of his guards up the stairs for a word with his son Ed, who sat in his own cell. Entering the cell room, he ran up to his boy with a glowing smile and said, "It was murder in the first degree," as if he couldn't be more proud. As Jahns entered the steel tank that housed him, other prisoners called out: "What is it, old man?" and again he returned the answer: "Murder in the first degree!"

After the steel doors clanked shut the jailers walked around to the cell door, and asked if everything was right with him? Jahns answered cheerfully: "Don't this look it?" and the officers were amazed to see the old man do a jig in his cell. Sheriff William Graham placed a double guard over the convicted killer, not sure if the prisoner were mad and would potentially harm himself.

Continuing the Search

Meanwhile, back in Maple Falls, the search was underway for Logan. A small culvert under the town bridge, two hundred yards from the Logan cabin, was torn up at both ends, but the bones of the rancher were not found. The grounds beneath the bridge were spaded thoroughly, but there was no evidence that the ground had ever been disturbed. The other two bridges were county road bridges, and the grounds beneath these were examined, but nothing was found.

It was hardly believed possible that Romandorf (as he was still known in Maple Falls) would have risked disposing of the victim's corpse where discovery would be certain. Deputy Sheriff McLaughlin believed Romandorf to be a very clever criminal who would have either burned his victim, or disposed of the body by burying it deeply into the ground far from the cabin. He had every foot of ground within a quarter mile combed for disturbed soil. McLaughlin had no doubt that Romandorf was telling the truth when he confessed to the murder, but believed he had lied about where he hid the body.

Expecting the rancher's bones to be discovered, the Bellingham *American Reveille* newspaper dispatched a staff reporter and photographer to

Maple Falls to await developments. While they waited, photos of the abandoned Romandorf and Logan cabins were taken for the Sunday edition. With the posse failing to locate Logan, the enterprising young correspondent committed the foul act of dressing Maple Falls' blacksmith William Murray with clothing and a cap, such as Logan was known to wear. Murray was then arranged for a photograph as Logan, which appeared in the papers over the following weekend to the horror of Maple Falls residents.

Former Sheriff Andrew Williams, who investigated Logan's disappearance three years before, was interviewed by reporters regarding the confession. William's didn't believe Romandorf would have buried the body under a bridge, partially because the body would have been easily discovered:

"The bridge over the Nooksack, to which I suppose Romandorf refers," declared Williams, "is about a mile away from Logan's old home. It does not seem possible that Romandorf would take the chances of dragging the body this far out to get rid of it."

"That Logan was killed or drugged inside the house was the theory at the time of the disappearance." Williams figured a man as strong as Logan would have been drugged to be taken by surprise. There was no sign of a struggle, no blood, and the home wasn't in disarray.

"Logan's hat and coat and glasses, which he wore every day were found inside the house, indicating that the rancher could not have been far away at the time. Sometime after Logan's disappearance we found a bottle of opium (laudanum), the label on the bottle was new and part of the contents missing. The label bore the name of Bell, the druggist who does business in Everson. I went to Bell to learn who purchased the bottle of liquid opium? He didn't know, but it was not Logan. I firmly believe that this liquid was used to drug Logan and that his body was dragged about 200 feet away and thrown into the river during the height of the storm."

Frank Romandorf may very well have used the ferocious storm as a cover to do away with James Logan. Williams recalled that during the widening search for Logan, three days after his disappearance had been discovered, "We found a place where some heavy object had been dragged across a little sandbar and evidently dumped into the river. We spent several days searching the banks of the river for miles on both sides, but you'll remember there was a heavy storm just before that and the river was flooded. The body might have been caught on a snag and held so that it could not be discovered."

The search continued through several days of rain, until finally, it was suspended until further news was received from Colville. Deputy Sheriff McLaughlin gave a press interview to let the people of Whatcom know how they were progressing in the search for Logan, and hopefully in discovering the remains of both Helms and Green. He reminded reporters that a mile and a half separated the two ranches, meaning there was a lot of ground to cover. James Logan's home had been dug up to a depth of four feet in areas, revealing nothing. Logan's floor wooden floorboards were pulled up, and the ground dug underneath; even the ground under the chicken-coop wasn't spared the spade. Another crew went to the rail trestle of the Bellingham Bay & British Columbia 200 yards away and searched beneath the structure.

McLaughlin believed Logan's body was buried somewhere in Maple Falls and not pitched into the Nooksack River, as some have claimed. He remembered at the time of the murder, the slough between the Logan home and the river was so full with water that Logan's body could not have been taken to the river without a boat, and Logan had no boat. The water in the slough was so sluggish in current it acted more as a moat between land and the river. A body could not have been carried away into the river. He also discounted fires in the area at the time, as it was a very wet fall. Besides, the town residents would certainly have investigated a fire of any great magnitude that would consume a body.

From Colville to Walla Walla

After the trial, defense attorneys Henry Martin, Lewis Jesseph and Leo Grinstead took William Frederick Jahns' appeal to the Washington State Supreme Court in Olympia. They first challenged the courts findings and Judge Daniel Carey's ruling of murder in the first degree. They next claimed the murder of Janson was not premeditated. Their other petitions included jury competency, and even the qualification of one particular juror to sit on the court trial.

A Colville reporter visited William Frederick Jahns for a talk, while awaiting word from the Supreme Court. Jahns liked to talk about himself, but not about his killings. "I am going to take the whole case to Governor (Marion) Hay," Jahns told the reporter, "and ask him to have the attorney general make a thorough investigation. I am not going to go as quick as some people think. I will get out yet."

William Frederick Jahns (Romandorf's true identity) wrote this coded manuscript that he claimed to be unintelligible to all, but himself. He said, "Here is a history of the affair, but you can't read it until you have the key to it. The key, he said, would be found among his belongings if he should hang. It wasn't. Washington State Archives, Olympia.

Jahns next produced a hand-written manuscript that appeared to look like some form of hieroglyphics, a code, unintelligible to all but himself. He said, "Here is a history of the affair, but you can't read it until you have the key to it. Somebody will get the key when the time comes, and they will find out things that will astonish them." The key, he said, would be found among his belongings if he should hang.

On Tuesday, February 25, 1911, an officially sealed letter arrived from Olympia; the State Supreme Court upheld the Stevens County Superior Court judgment of guilty and Jahns' death sentence. While the prisoner had known for several days of a decision reached by the Supreme Court, he didn't know the ruling until he was ushered into the courtroom at noon.

Judge Daniel Carey broke the silence of the courtroom: "Mr. Jesseph, we are now about to proceed to carry out the mandate of the Supreme Court. Have you anything to say?"

Council Lewis Jesseph: "Not a word."

Judge Carey: "The prisoner will stand. The order and judgment heretofore made and sustained by the Supreme Court will stand and the date of execution will be fixed as April 21, 1911. That is all. The sheriff will take the prisoner."

William Frederick Jahns was re-sentenced, and even the death penalty was a surprise to him, for he had hoped that the judgment would be reduced to life. "Well," said Jahns with a smile, "they can only hang me once and it will be over." He then bowed his head in the courtroom as if meditating, upon raising it again his expression changed, and his eyes clenched looking toward the judge. He raised his voice in a confident tone and said, "This woman I am charged with killing is alive. I know it and shall at once set about bringing the fact to light."

He also claimed James Logan wasn't dead either, though he'd originally claimed him to be slain by his own hands. Jahns claimed he took Logan to Seattle, where he got him drunk on the waterfront. He hired thugs to crack him over the head and shanghaied him onto a departing ship to get Logan out of the way. "Logan," he supposed "was having a better life for himself cruising somewhere in the South Seas."

Immediately after his second sentencing, Stevens County Sheriff William Miller had prearranged Jahns' transfer from Colville to Spokane, and then onto Walla Walla by train. Miller remembered, "It was a cold day and the prisoner was protected by fur robes while conveyed in a sleigh to the station." No one was allowed to converse with the prisoner, but Jahns laughed and talked with his guards.

William Frederick Jahns entered the gates to the Washington State Penitentiary at Walla Walla, on February 26, 1911, becoming prisoner No. 5998. His convict biographical statement claimed he had schooling only to the eighth grade, as he left to become a soldier. He also claimed to have left Germany to escape compulsory military service. In the same record he said he left home at sixteen to see the country. Furthermore Jahns claimed in the same document to have served in the Brazilian army before coming to the United States.

Somewhere back in Germany, Jahns said, he had four brothers and two sisters, but mentioned no town or their names. His mother died when he was a child, and his father followed when he was 28 years old. When questioned, "to what do you attribute your present troubles, and account of the crime,"

Jahns answered simply, "Circumstances." He added, "Hired lawyer, jury trial and found guilty."

On March 31 a smoldering sawdust fire was investigated on the former property of David Shively. It was located a mile and a half north of Addy, close to the Colville River. The giant sawdust mound was the result of several years' of accumulation at the old E. S. Budrey Mill, long since ceased. As it was early spring, no one took the smoldering too seriously. If anything, it was an opportunity to burn the mound off. Eventually it was investigated, to make sure a fire hadn't spread off the mound. Since the fire started, the sawdust had burned down tens of feet. The investigators must have thought they had discovered a chest of gold when they saw a steamer trunk sticking out of the pile. Eagerly, they opened it to extract its bounty, but were instead thrown back by the stench of the cooked remains of Shively's folded body.

Addy's Deputy Walter Woodward forwarded the news to Colville. People who knew Shively, and had the stomach for it, viewed the remains for positive identification. The only recognizable feature was his head.

On April 12, Warden C. S. Reed put forward to Jahns a plea from Addy for details about the recently discovered Shively. Reed produced news clipping and photos, asking for closure. Reed wrote back to the county sheriff that Jahns "denies all knowledge...saying he is not only innocent of that crime, but of all others. If he knows anything regarding this or any other crime it is impossible to get it out of him."

At 5:30 am, on Friday, April 21, William Frederick Jahns was led from his cell to the gallows. After a few words from the prison chaplain, Jahns declared he had killed no one. In a short note to Jahns' two daughters in Seattle the chaplain wrote, "Their father's life was taken this morning at about 5:40 o'clock. Death was instantaneous...." On April 24 the daughters received a small package from the penitentiary with a few articles belonging to their father. It consisted of his spectacles, fountain pen and two pencils that he used.

The Murder Farm

After his death, Warden C. S. Reed received letters for several years asking about Jahns, alias Logan and Romandorf. Some requested his description, no doubt curious if he were someone they crossed paths with or had done them wrong. No doubt Jahns had a long list of enemies searching for him. One interesting letter came from Lordsburg, California, written five days before Jahns' hanging. The writer claimed a man by the name of James Logan; had left a child in their possession in 1893 and was never heard from again. He wished to see a photo to see if it were the same man. In closing, the writer asked not to publish his inquiry, as "I would not have the child know its father was a murderer." Is this yet another mystery involving the true James Logan?

Hollis Fultz in 1945 paid a visit to Jahns' defense attorney, Leo Grinstead in Colville. Thirty-four years later, Grinstead shared some information with the chief investigator for the state attorney general. Grinstead gave Fultz a large red leather wallet containing letters and documents belonging to Jahns. It came into his position after his client was sent to Walla Walla, and he had held on to it since. The letters traced portions of his travels from February 1901 to 1903-04. There was evidence in the wallet indicating that Jahns had murdered both Helms and Green in Maple Falls. Duplicates of the deeds to their properties were enclosed, each notarized with a fake seal found in Jahns' possession, with the handwriting identical on both deeds.

Grinstead also disclosed some of the contents of a black-covered diary Jahns kept after his arrest. The attorney recorded its contents, but didn't present these at trail. One of the items he jotted down was Jahns' Last Will and Testament. It read in part:

"All papers in Unity Safe Deposit Company Box. No property in my name. You will find in Key of Information how and system to work. Unity Safety Deposit Box, 1921 Dearborn, Street, Chicago. You will find all papers in that box.

-- House and lot in Chicago.

-- House and lot in Terre Haute, Indiana.

-- Five lots in Gary, Indiana.

-- One lot at Indiana Harbor, Indiana.

-- One thousand two hundred and eighty acres in Oregon.

-- Nine and one-half acres on Lake Washington, Seattle. (Presumably Fred Helms' property)

-- There will arrive from the Reulconto Bank of Berlin Germany, a draft to pay $1,150 in notes at the Old National Bank in Spokane."

It seems logical that William Frederick Jahns may have been responsible for numerous deaths and missing persons during his years of wandering. No one kills with such ease, comfort and disregard without years of experience. I suspect Jahns might have even left Germany after his first killing or killings. He quite possibly botched the deed and became a wanted man, forced to flee his homeland.

That's hypothetical, of course. Whatever the reasoning for his trail of destruction, Jahns did eventually adhere to a distinct modus operandi to his killings. He killed for property gain and profit. Ed Trimble, formerly deputy sheriff under Andrew Williams, now working as deputy treasurer of Bellingham in 1910, made this observation of Jahns: "I can say this much without hesitation. In his eyes murder was a light crime as compared with parting with money...I have come to the conclusion that his religion and mission in life was just this: Never spend a cent."

Jahns methodically developed a plan of attack by incapacitating his victims and then killing them outright. Afterwards, he would hide or destroy the body. He would transfer the newly-acquired property by deed of sale to a fictitious individual, and then, in good time, transfer it again through other aliases, before ultimately transferring it into his own name, or one he was conveniently using. He carried with him always a trunk full of authentic, stolen, counterfeit, or official-looking documents, bogus deeds, checks, legal instruments, letters, official seals, stamps, inks, and all the necessities to dupe the unsuspecting victim.

While his killing skills could be extremely violent and decisively quick, they were methodical, demonstrating a great level of cleverness and precision. Being a man in his early sixties when apprehended, he would have had to be cunning in defeating men much younger and stronger than he. Jahns was no amateur in his killing sprees. He would have had to perform dozens of such slayings to remain so cool and calm during their performances. His crime scenes were clean, bloodless and undisturbed. So what happened in the case of Agnes Janson?

Only the finest of killers can walk amongst us unknowingly, with their true identities hidden. If a serial killer were that proficient, we wouldn't know of their existence, as they wouldn't be known or caught. There would be no trail, no evidence, no body. They would likely prey upon victims no one would miss. Jahns blundered in his last murder by breaking all of his own rules, which made him sloppy. He was impulsive at the scent of money and thought he could make quick haste of Janson when he discovered she had come into money.

But he was too close to his victim, who was his housekeeper and potential wife. He had too many witnesses. He had a translator read her letter to him, establishing the fact that he knew she had money. They were last seen leaving together for the train depot by his hired hands, and said as much to the sheriff the following day. Johnny Cline, taking the horses back to the ranch, established that Jahns was alone at the depot. And the night Jahns cremated Janson's body only provided a beacon that drew spectators. The only conclusion is that Jahns was planning to abandon his Baslington farm and Washington State after draining Janson's account. That would surely have made him a wanted man, and open a series of investigations into his past. Basically, he screwed up.

Another possibility was that Jahns was seriously going mad, or senile. He very well may have been slipping at his age, making mistakes he otherwise would not have made in the past. Some supporting evidence may be drawn by his character and antics after arrest and while on trial.

The life of William Frederick Jahns is inundated in mystery, lies, and deceit. Even his family is not immune from such vagueness, which at times offers even greater mystery than Jahns. At least we know he was a fanatical psychopath, but what of his family? Who were they really? Were Margaret and her daughters so naïve as not to have suspected anything out of the ordinary? What about Jahns' mysterious departure from Maple Falls after killing Logan? Margaret, his own "wife," never even attempted to contact authorities that he was missing after the storm, nor even after the search for Logan started. Was she praying he was dead? Or did she know far more than authorities suspected? Jahns disappeared, and next reappeared in Colville with a sizeable ranch, but the family didn't join him, even though they knew where he was. Margaret and daughter Bessie visited in August 1910, and must have heard Jahns being addressed by their former missing neighbor's name. It begs the question, how much they really knew and how much they may have participated in Jahns' schemes?

The lack of answers to these questions continues. Here are some relevant issues and facts to ponder. The 1900 census does confirm the Romandorf family living in Lincoln, Lancaster County, Nebraska. Romandorf claims he was born in Pennsylvania, which we know is false. Margaret was born in 1865. Her daughters Bessie, Mattie, and son Ed were born in 1881, 1884 and 1889 respectively. The census states they were born in Nebraska. Yet, we are also led to believe they were born in Pennsylvania and fathered by Margaret's first husband. Her son Ed, Eddie, or Edward, and with as many aliases as Jahns, has a reputation that certainly follows that of Romandorf's. Once in his teens, Edward stayed in the shadow of the man he seemed to admire. One alias Ed Romandorf used most often was Lewis, interesting for what transpires later.

Margaret claimed they were married in Pennsylvania, but there is no record of them being either legally or emotionally bonded to one another. Margaret even knew that Agnes Janson was moving into the Jahns' Baslington ranch under the pretext of marriage. As her "husband" stood trial for murder, Margaret stayed in Seattle. When visited by authorities, she looked at photos and stated they were of her husband and son. After the verdict was announced, Margaret moved with her daughters out of the city, leaving no forwarding address with her landlord or the post office.

Penniless, Margaret moved what was left of her family into the only property she knew they legally owned, in Maple Falls. Here they lived out the rest of their lives as recluses, taking on the surname Lewis, the very same name that Edward took as his own. We may assume that Lewis was Margaret's first husband's name and the initial family name, thereby throwing the yoke of Romandorf off their shoulders forever. At the same time, the women ostracized Edward, having nothing to do with brother and son again. From the day William Frederick Jahns confessed to the Whatcom County slayings, his former Maple Falls ranch would forever be known as "The Murder Farm."

Margaret and her family were for years shunned in Maple Falls. She combated locals coming on the property looking for bodies or curiously watching them. "While game warden, I went up there," said D. P. Castor. "I told the women I was on official business and that they had to let me cross their place…but they stood out quite a while and would not let me pass…I'd like to see that ranch searched for the bodies of those two hired men, but it is such a wilderness now there is little chance of finding anything that might be there."

Millard Burnside concurred with Castor that it would be impossible to search the place now. "It's greatly changed from what it was when

Romandorf left…There are a thousand stumps and holes and thickets which would take hundreds of men to search." The only opportunity to learn any of Romandorf's secrets, thought Burnside and the locals, was to get Ed Romandorf back to Maple Falls.

Today

In 2014 I visited the site of the family home where Frank Romandorf once lived. I missed seeing the structure by weeks, as it had been torn down. Some rubble still lay on the property, and Romandorf's root cellar was still fully intact. The present owner showed me the land survey records that indicated that "A. Lewis, spinsters, sole and only heirs, formerly known by surname of Romandorf," had once owned the property.

The Romandorf home as it sat on the Silver Lake Road in 2014, before it was torn down. Whatcom County Assessors.

122

I was introduced to Romandorf's neighbors, who are now in their eighties. They still remember the stories of the old "murder farm" and the mad German who once lived there from local folklore. They would point in the direction of the hill behind town where the Romandorf house once stood, and say, "There're bodies buried all over those woods." A few folks who are old enough remember the spinster sisters well. I was told a few stories about them. Apparently they had two houses on the property. The original was by the road, and a newer, but still rustic home was located further up on the property. Bob Buckenmeyer, an abutter, told me they lived totally off the grid. No electricity, heat or running water. In the summer they walked in their long dark dresses with walking sticks to the lower house, where there was a steel, gravity-feed water tank leading into the house. The sun heated it. That's where they took showers. The sink was a small basin, and a door off its hinges served as a table. They would walk the short distance into town once a week to the grocers.

The final resting place of sisters Bessie and Marjorie Lewis. The Romandorf daughters died spinsters fearing they had murderous genes running through their blood. Photo taken by the author.

Folks claimed the sisters didn't talk about Romandorf, but one rumor perked my interest. The sisters vowed to live together as spinsters, never to marry or have children for fear that the insanity that Frank and Ed Lewis shared could run in the family blood. Was William Frederick Jahns, or Frank Romandorf their real father?

Marjorie (Mattie) passed away first, on April 26, 1968. Bellingham's Bayview Cemetery records list her as the daughter of Romandorf and Margaret (McIntyre) Lewis. Born September 15, 1888/89, Nebraska.

Bessie the eldest followed on February 28, 1970. She was listed as daughter of Francis E. and Margaret (McIntyre) Lewis. Born April 4, 1887, in Omaha, Nebraska. The dates and places are not the same as the 1910 census; big surprise. Edward was never heard from again.

The last twenty acres of the James Logan homestead washed down the Nooksack River during a big flood of 1955.

With his hanging, William Frederick Jahns carried to his grave the secrets to several Whatcom County murder mysteries that have long plagued the minds of those who sought to unravel them. While no physical evidence tied Jahns to the death of James Logan, speculation, motive, circumstantial evidence and his subsequent crimes showed that he was quite capable. But one mysterious murder has been loosely pointed toward the mad German, and if so, it excelled in brutality far beyond his other killings. While the circumstances are not so closely connected, there is a strong belief prevailing in the minds of local authorities that Romandorf is the man who killed Frederick L. Dames, the Elk Street butcher.

SOURCES

www.ancestry.com

Bellingham Directory: 1905, 1906, 1909, 1910, and 1911.

Bellingham Herald: 11/13/1906, 11/11/1909, 11/12/09, 11/15/09, 11/16/09, 1/3 1910, 1/4/10, 1/13/10, 1/20/10, 1/21/10, 1/24/10, 1/25/10, 1/26/10, 1/28/10, 2/13/10, 4/25/10, 6/11/10, 3/3/11, 2/27/1911, 3/31/11, 4/8/10, 4/13/11, 4/21/11.

California Voter Register: 1866-1898

Cemetery Records of Whatcom County: Series II, Vol. XII, Bayview Cemetery through 1985. Compiled and Published by: Whatcom Genealogical Soc. 1999.

Correspondence related to William Frederick Jahns held at the Washington State Archives.

Fultz, Hollis B., *Famous Northwest Manhunts and Murder Mysteries*. Elma, WA: Fulco Publications, 1955.

www.geneologybank.com

Gibson, Elizabeth, *Outlaw Tales of Washington*. Guilford, Conn: The Globe Pequot Press, 2002.

Heritage Quest

Nebraska State Historical Society, Prison Records 1870-1990.

New York Passenger Lists.

Northern State Hospital Admission Index, June 1929. Washington State Archives, Northwest Regional Branch.

Omaha World Herald: 11/3/1890, 2/20/1891.

Reports of Cases in the Supreme Court of Nebraska: January and September terms, 1903. Volume IV. Isaac Cahn VS. Romandorf, Filed January 21, 1903. No. 12,528. Appeal from the district court for Lancaster County, Nebraska.

State of Washington, Walla Walla State Penitentiary Convict Description, 1911.

State of Washington VS. William Frederick Jahns, for the County of Stevens.

State of Washington VS. William Frederick Jahns, Return of Execution.

Stevens County Superior Court Sheriff Custody Orders.

Todd, Frances Bruce, *Trail Through the Woods: History of Western Whatcom County, Washington.* Gateway Press. 1972.

U.S. Census. Whatcom County, Washington. 1890, 1900, 1910, 1920, 1940.

U.S. Civil War Pension Files: 1861-1934.

Washington State Penitentiary, Penitentiary Inmate Register.

Chapter 5
Who Butchered the Elk Street Butcher?

Frederick L. Dames. Puget Sound American.

Sometime between the hours of 10 pm, Tuesday, April 11, and 8:15 am, Wednesday April 12, 1905, someone brutally murdered Frederick L. Dames, proprietor of the Palace Meat Market at 1017 Elk (State) Street. Dames lived in a little shack directly behind his business in the Northern Pacific alley.

A sixteen-year-old employee Edward Leonard, who would clean the meat market each morning before opening, discovered the butcher's mutilated body. He also worked as Dames' delivery boy for the rest of the day.

What he saw that morning would haunt the youngster for the rest of his life. Dames' home was turned inside-out, everything smashed. On the floor beside the butcher's bed laid the brutally beaten body of his employer.

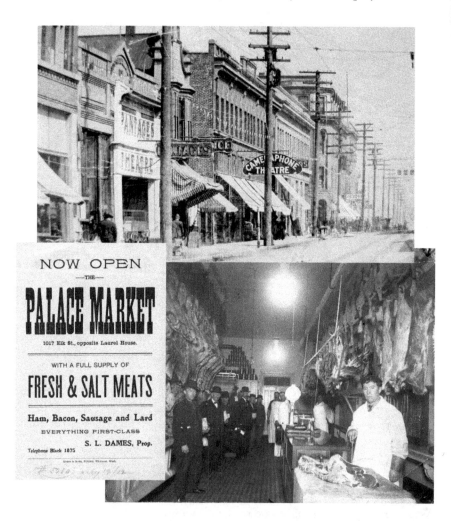

Top: Upper Elk Street toward Holly Street in the early 1900s, about the time Dames moved to the city. Laura Jacoby's Galen Biery Collection. Lower left: Opening announcement for the Palace Meat Market, 1903. Note the mistake in the initials, S. instead of F. L. Dames. Edson & Irish Collection, Whatcom Museum. Lower left: The interior of the old Palace Meat Market after it became the "Sanitation Meat Market" in 1912. This image was taken about 1915; little had changed in its appearance. By 1912, Swiss sausage maker, Hans Oberleitner, owns the market" and will add an extension to the left side of the original Dames establishment. The market will stay in the family until the 1960s. Whatcom Museum.

A violent spray of blood splattered the small room, revealing the desperate struggle for life that had occurred. The butcher's skull was crushed in from multiple blows and cleaved by a hatchet. A screwdriver wielded by the killer struck Dames numerous times in both the front and back of his head. The last blow embedded the steel length of the screwdriver through his head. Looking on, Leonard saw an enormous pool of blood surrounding the body. He stepped closer to be sure his boss was truly dead.

Dames' skin was ashen, with a ghostly appearance. The attack was so brutal that on closer inspection the boy saw that the old man's face was split and caved in. Leonard could see smashed skull fragments and brain-matter trickle from the wound. One of the butcher's eyes dangled from its socket, and his lips had turned a dark grey in color.

The Palace Meat Market (renamed Sanitary Meat Market by 1912) during the high school seniors' march. Wilber J. Sandison Collection, Whatcom Museum.

Lothaire Dames

Frederick Lothar Dames (Lothaire Dames) arrived in New York City on July 17, 1858, on the 548 ton bark *Owego*, departing from Le Havre, France.

129

Captain R. Morse was Master of the sailing vessel. The passenger manifest lists his family originating from the Principality of Luxembourg, but Dames would later claim East Prussia, which is far more likely. The sixteen-year-old came to America with his parents, Christian Friederick (45) and Anna (36), and brothers August (18), Jacob (8) and sister Friederike or Friederke (5). Little else is heard of Christian Friederick. He Americanized his name and became simply Fred. Fred and Anna almost immediately left the big city for Milwaukee, Wisconsin. There, Fred established himself as a butcher (meat dealer or pork butcher) and his wife, a housekeeper.

There is credible evidence that the Dames family had previous family members living in Prairie Du Rocher, Randolph County, Illinois. The 1860 census listed the daughter Friederike, but no Jacob. He would have been seven. Was he dead, or an extended family member who was brought to America and passed off as a son? By 1890 Anna was a widow, and supported herself as a fruit dealer.

Frederick L. Dames soon sought his own adventures. After coming to America, he took his father's given name, and changed his own, Lothaire to Lothar, which became his middle name. He took up the trade of a butcher, most likely learned from his father, and carried those skills throughout his life. Dames was a strapping figure, standing five foot nine in height. He was said to have a light complexion, steely grey eyes and dark hair. He left home at age twenty-one, a single man, but not for marriage. In June 1863 he was drafted into the Union Army, serving as a corporal in the 16th Iowa Infantry Regiment's A Company. At some point during the Civil War, he lost the middle finger on his left hand, close to the hand. His brother August enlisted, and served as a private in the 5th Wisconsin Infantry Regiment; Co. C. He, too, survived the war.

Dames next appeared in Mountain City, Elko, Nevada in 1870, prospecting for silver and living with six other miners in a dusty cabin. Four years later he's found in Eureka County where he became a naturalized citizen. By

1879, not ready to give up prospecting, Dames arrived in Bodie, California, searching for the elusive mother lode. Failing to get rich quick, he turned up in New Mexico for a short stint. Finally, Dames arrived in Long Beach, California where he opened a meat market in 1886, putting to use the trade his father had taught him.

Long Beach became one of his longest layovers, where he stayed until the 1890s before moving onto Portland, Oregon. A few years later, Dames relocated to Bellingham, Washington, where he purchased 25 feet of building frontage on Elk Street. By the spring of 1902, Martin Sinsdorfer, a mason by trade, built the building where Dames would hang his shingle, calling it the "Palace Meat Market."

What Brute Force!

Frederick Dames' young apprentice Edward Leonard entered the market at 7:00 am through the back door, as he did each and every morning. Dames always left the door unlocked for the boy to clean before he arrived to open the market. The back door had a simple latch, and Leonard once asked the butcher if he feared robbery. Dames responded that he was a very light sleeper and could detect any outside movement. When he heard the boy's arrival each morning, he knew it was time to rise. But Dames wouldn't rise that particular Wednesday. An hour passed, and the butcher failed to appear in the market for work.

It wasn't like Dames to be late, so Leonard telephoned David E. Bartruff, owner of the Washington Hotel, where Dames had a custom of breakfasting each morning. Bartuff told the boy that Dames failed to appear that morning for his breakfast ritual. Thinking his boss had overslept, he went looking out back in the Great Northern alley to rouse him out of his shack. He called out to Dames from outside his shack, but received no reply. The door was slightly ajar, an inch or so, when Leonard pushed it open the rest of the way. He was horrified to find Dames lying dead on the floor in a pool of his own blood. Leonard ran from the shack, retreating back inside the market, and telephoned Bartruff, who ran down to the Palace Meat Market to see what had transpired. Along the way, he enlisted the assistance of Dames' friend and fellow butcher, Frank Marz.

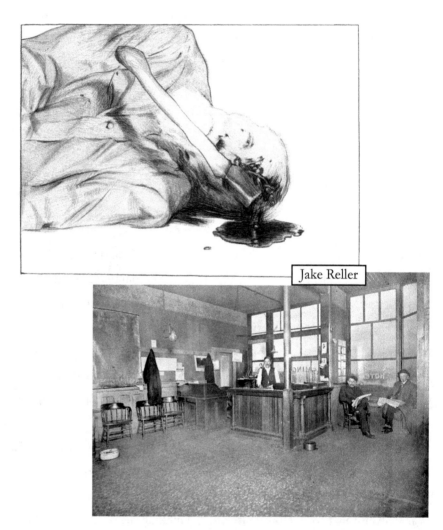

Jake Reller

David E. Bartuff at the check-in counter of the Washington Hotel at 1130 Dock Street. After a panicked Edward Leonard reported that the butcher had been murdered, Bartuff was one of the first on the scene. Whatcom Museum.

In hysterics, Leonard let the men into the shop and then led them out back to the shack. The scene before them was just as the boy had said. Dames was dead. Blood stains were everywhere, illustrating the violent struggle that ensued some hours ago. The bed sheets were wound into a bloody bundle. The interior of the shack was in total disarray. After a survey to verify Leonard's findings, the men notified the Bellingham police. Detective's Bert DeHaven and Thomas Nugent, being the first officers on the scene, were just as horrified by the ferocity of the slaying. Chief of Police Oliver P. Woody arrived for a look and to greet reporters. Police Captain Jack Parberry followed on his coattails. The body was left untouched, until coroner Henry Thompson arrived.

The sixty-three-year-old Dames must have put up a hell of a struggle thought the detectives. He was lying flat on his back upon the floor, his hair completely matted and blood-soaked, his face and head hacked and dashed in by a dozen severe blows. A deep, ghastly cut to the back of the skull and another to the front, held a foot-long screwdriver, which penetrated through the butcher's head, pinning it to the floorboards of his shack. His nightclothes were torn from his body. His fists heavily bruised and nicked by cuts from a brutal fight. Half the poor man's face was cleaved away.

DeHaven couldn't help but marvel at the screwdriver impaled through the butcher's head, and the hatchet, nearly disappeared inside the skull, with only the wood handle sticking upward. What brute force could have accomplished such a feat? All about, there were signs of a great struggle. Dames' few pieces of furniture were smashed to pieces, along with the only light bulb in the shack, which dangled from the ceiling.

DeHaven and Nugent combed the dark crime scene, but couldn't determine if robbery or revenge was the motive of the slaying. If robbery was the intention, something went terribly wrong. The detectives believed whatever money Dames had on the premises was taken, as none was to be found. He had made a bank deposit at noon the previous day, but brought twenty dollars in change back to the market. It was assumed that the money, and any amount taken in after noontime the previous day, would have still been on his person. Dames was in the habit of making daily deposits, so as to not have cash lying around.

Officers believed it was likely that the murderer or murderers waited for Dames to retire to his bed, when he was most vulnerable, before attacking him. They may have been lying in wait inside his shack, or rushed in from the outside, surprising the butcher. The best scenario suggested robbery, with two sinister culprits attacking Dames at once. They may have planned on subduing him, and then questioning him as to where he hid his money. But Dames wasn't going to allow that. He put up a fierce fight.

Very few clues were available, only a rusty hatchet and the skull-embedded screwdriver. When the light bulb was replaced to help aid detectives in their work, they discovered that the switch had been in the on position. The thorough manner in which Dames' clothing and property were ransacked pointed to a motive of robbery. Whether they were searching for money, documents, or something of more value in the butcher's possession, was unknown.

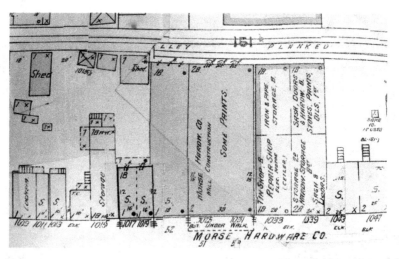

The Elk Street block, shown from a Sanborn map, circa 1910. 1017 is where the Palace Meat market was located. Note the building directly in the rear marked "shed" along the alley; that was the butcher's home, where his body was discovered. Whatcom Museum.

Even his pockets were turned inside out, according to police. Nothing of any value was known to be in the shack. Frederick Dames was not a poor man, but lived an extremely frugal lifestyle, especially absent of a wife or any courtships. He was known to have property and a banking account in the value of at least $12,000. He owned the building where the Palace Meat Market stood. Dames had confided to close associates, claimed newspapers, that people wondered what he was worth, but they would have to wait until he had passed away to find out. It was known locally that he recently sold a brickyard in Texas for a substantial sum.

Detectives concluded that the door was left unlocked, for there was no evidence of forced entry. They discounted a late caller, as Dames had few friends, and none whom he would receive so late at night. They concluded the murderer, or murderers, had entered quietly and stepped silently toward the head of the bed, and turned on the overhanging wire light bulb, striking the first blow. Perhaps the sudden illumination in the dark room threw the assailant's aim into a glancing blow of the side of the butcher's head. This gave Dames just enough time to recover and grapple with his foe. But it was no use, as his opponent swung again and again, cutting the butcher down. During the ensuing battle, the bulb was broken, prompting the assailant to swing wildly. Once all was quiet, the killer kneeled down beside his victim and struck wooden matches to see if Dames was dead.

No one in the neighborhood heard anything out of the ordinary that night. The Olswangs, a Russian family who owned a second-hand shop next door, retired to bed at 11 pm, and claimed the night was a quiet one. They had dogs in their store that were silent all night. Dames rented a space in his building to Fred G. Rauch, a German immigrant who owned a jewelry store. Rauch also reported no disturbances. Even patrolman DeFries, while walking his beat in the alley each half-hour, heard not even a cat stir. The Great Northern alley wasn't well lit, but the tracks ran down its center, with an elevated planked boardwalk running along the length on both sides of the tracks. This was for supply wagons to enter the backs of businesses, of course, but a man's foot could be quite audible to the patrolman. At 1 am, DeFries started up the alley and met the Bellingham Bay & British Columbia Railway's night watchman. After they greeted each other, the patrolman swung through the alley again. A robber would have had to know DeFries' routine, and to commit his act in no more than fifteen minutes.

Fredrick Dames was last seen alive by Robert McDonald, the cook at the Washington Hotel on the corner of Chestnut and Cornwall Streets. McDonald was engaged in conversation with Dames a few minutes after 9:00 pm, on Tuesday night. He was acquainted with Dames while in Missoula, Montana from some years back. They walked together until reaching the corner of Elk and Laurel; it was about 9:17. McDonald told investigators they were talking of old times, and discussing Dames' plan for the installation of an oven he had on order. He was quite excited with his business, and all seemed fine for the butcher. McDonald last saw Dames enter his shop, as he continued up the hill toward his home on Garden Street.

Dr. Henry Thompson held a coroner's inquest was held that Wednesday afternoon, in Sheriff Andrew Williams' office at the Whatcom Courthouse. Jurors hastily assembled included: Daniel McCush, R. B. Stuart, W. H. Gibbs, J. S. Burrows, F. J. Herberger, and S. B. Van Zandt. Witnesses were David Bartruff, and young Edward Leonard. Their findings were obvious: "Death was caused by unlawful means at the hands of person or persons unknown." When asked about the hatchet used, Leonard claimed he had never seen it before. Dames had the boy clean his living quarters periodically, but the hatchet was not Dames'. Edward said he had asked for an axe to split kindling wood, and the old man could only offer a hefty doubled-bladed axe that was difficult for him to wield. First assumptions were that the hatchet came from a boat, as it was heavily rusted and corroded, as if long exposed to seawater.

KILLED WITH A HAND-AXE

Frederick L. Dames' Head Split Wide After Fierce Struggle In His Room

Another clue included a man's overcoat found floating in the water a few feet from shore. The coat had stains indicating lard, possibly belonging to the butcher. Leonard was shown the evidence, but failed to recognize the long coat.

In the meantime, as authorities made a more thorough investigation, Thompson filed in the Superior Court an immediate application for "Special Letters of Administration," to locate relatives by tracking down what was known of the Dames' history. He also asked to file a petition before the court for immediate access to the estate of the deceased, to prevent the spoilage of perishable meat just purchased the day before, amounting to a value of $75.00. The petition was granted.

The Investigation

Bellingham Detective Thomas Nugent believed the murder was a robbery gone awry. By the afternoon of the second day, he walked a reporter through his findings:

"I believe that the crime was committed by two men. They evidently entered the place with the intention of robbing the old

137

man. After securing what money he had in his clothing they probably concluded that there was more in the bed. While they were trying to go through the bed the old man discovered them and started to make a resistance. He was struck with the little axe, which must have been in the cabin. The first blow was not sufficient to stun him and he got to his feet in a struggle for life. In the scuffle, which followed the bulb of the electric light was broken, and the place left in darkness. Unable to see his victim the murderer continued to hack him with the hatchet after he was dead. When Dames went to the floor the murderer struck matches to be sure his victim was dead. Not satisfied in the dim light he drove the screwdriver into his brain to complete his work. Whoever committed the murder wanted to be sure the man was dead and, on that account, I believe Dames recognized his assailants."

Regardless, whether or not robbery was a motive, other officers on the case were clueless to the savage brutality of the attack. The prolonged assault and violence suggested a revenge slaying, settling an old score. Or a worst case, the murder was a madman with a lust for blood. This was the working theory of Officer Ralph Jones, who, unlike his colleagues, believed that the crime was committed by a man who had brooded over some imaginary or real wrong done to him for years, and finally discovered an opportunity for revenge. That was the opinion he gave reporters.

After the local press had their guided tour of the crime scene and interviewed various police officers and detectives, they quickly wrote their own interpretations and theories in the following day's news. A reporter for The *Puget Sound American* had his own speculations on whom to look for. "...The deed was not accomplished by an American," claimed the writer. "The crime bears certain marks of revenge by a hot headed man...a resemblance to the horrible crimes committed by the Italian or the Greek. Crimes ascribed to the Vendetta, the Ku-Klux, the Chinese Tongs…"

MURDER MYSTERY
BAFFLING POLICE

F. L. Dames, an Elk Street Shop Keeper, Brutally Butchered in His own Home by an Unknown Assassin

LEAVES NO CLEW

Detectives Inclined to Believe That Old Man was Slain by Desperate Burglar···Money is Missing

A new clue materialized with the discovery of two newspapers, smeared in blood, concealed at Darum Trunkey's wood yard at the end of Elk Street. The papers were still in the shape in which they were folded for delivery. They were covered in blood, suggesting someone had used them to wipe their hands, and then concealed the papers in a stack of lumber. Detectives were encouraged that the evidence at least indicated a direction in which the killer or killers ran.

Canvassing the area, authorities questioned a laundress by the name of Mrs. Anderson, who lived in the same alley but a block west of Dames. When asked if she knew of any unusual happenings Tuesday night, Anderson reported she had heard two men run past her place at midnight, making a great deal of noise. She was able to hear them for some distance after they passed. It was hoped that a search along the alley, and from Elk Street to the water's edge, would produce further clues or evidence. Detectives figured that with a murder so gruesome as Dames', the killer would have been covered in blood, and their first instincts would be to conceal their clothes. A search was made of every conceivable hiding place in the vicinity of the crime scene, but to no avail.

Sheriff Andrew Williams offered his services canvassing the waterfront with DeHaven and Nugent. A bloody shirt was discovered in an abandoned shack between the Bellingham Bay Improvement Company Lumberyard and the old coalbunkers. Further questioning in the area indicated that two or three men occasionally slept in the shack. Two of the men were identified as William Donnelly and Charles Davis. Donnelly was a sailor native to Ireland, who had sailor jumped ship while in port, and presently worked as a longshoreman as needed at the docks. He befriended Englishman Charles Davis, who at times worked as a boilermaker when needing cash. Otherwise the two were known for petty theft and hard drinking. When found later in the day, they both denied any knowledge of the bloody shirt, claiming not to have slept in the shack for some time. It was suggested the bloody shirt might have been the result of sloppy needlework done by a heroin addict, as they were known to shoot up in the waterfront shacks. The men looked as if they had been in a brawl, but they lived on the waterfront, and drank in the worst establishments, so appearances meant little. Sheriff Williams felt uneasy about the two men, but there was no evidence suggesting that they were in the shack that night, with the exception of the laundress hearing two men running in that direction.

Williams questioned the men further, discovering some alterations to their story. One addition was that the night before the crime, Charles Weatherford stayed with them at the shack, but was tossed out. Weatherford was a well-known chronic drunk, living wherever he could flop for the night. Following up on Weatherford, Williams found that two hours before Dames' body was discovered he had told Mrs. Nettie Jones, of 305 1/2 West Holly, that the Elk Street butcher had been murdered. He was in an excitable drunken stupor, claimed Jones. (We'll get to Charles Weatherford soon.)

Additional information was received on April 26 that strengthened a theory that the "killers" may have fled by train. DeHaven and Nugent questioned a section crew working on the Northern Pacific rail-line the week the butcher was murdered. At that time the crew was working in the alley next to the butcher's shack. The workers observed a man coming out of Dames' backyard a few days before the crime, during the early morning hours. He seemed to be scouting around Dames' dwelling. The morning before the murder, two odd characters approached the same crew working in the vicinity of the old coalbunkers. Striking up a conversation, the two asked for information in regard to the routes of the several railway lines. Two of the crewmen quickly recognized one of the men as the same coming out of the butcher's yard several days before. The recognized stranger was a "very large man, strong and rawboned."

At this point detectives theorized that two assailants were involved. Did the men escape by train? That was a possibility. The detectives notified Sheriff Williams to investigate his county sources and secure witnesses on the Bellingham Bay & British Columbia Railway train that night, covering all potential departure times. It was a distinct possibility, but DeHaven and Nugent weren't buying that theory. Why would the killer or killers risk riding in a train couch where they could be easily identified? The detectives, after viewing the crime scene, knew the murderers would be covered in blood. It was impossible in darkness to cleanse themselves and their clothing of the amount of blood splattered around Dames' room. It would be impossible to hide their deed on the train, unless the madmen panicked and attempted to dash across the border at Sumas into Canada.

That led detectives to thinking the villains escaped by boat. If they indeed fled by boat, the rusty hatchet may support that theory. Plus, there was the lard-stained coat that was found in the water. If Edward Leonard was wrong about the coat, then it may have been used to cover the killer's bloody clothes. The men would have undoubtedly panicked for fear of being caught, after the ruckus in the shack. They would have bolted from the hovel after their prolonged struggle, killing Dames, their only witness.

141

Detectives surmised they could have run south along the Northern Pacific alley toward the old coalbunker to an awaiting boat. In doing so, they alerted Mrs. Anderson, the laundress, by making too much clamor in the alley during their hasty escape. The culprits would also have had to keep a sharp eye for patrolman DeFries making his thirty-minute rounds.

At some point, emerging at the end of Elk Street, the men stopped long enough to wipe their hands with some newspapers, then wedged them into one of Darum Trunkey's woodpiles. They would have moved on to the abandoned shack near the coalbunkers next. The killers would have taken refuge for a few moments to gather themselves, checked to see if they were followed, and looked to see if the rest of the escape route was clear to the waterline.

One of the murderers may have been the larger, stronger, and more fearless of the two. He undoubtedly would have been more aggressive,

locked in mortal combat with Dames, and the recipient of most of the victim's blood splatter. He would have acquired the long coat from Dames for concealment on the way out. Once hidden in the shack, his companion may have scouted ahead, while he stripped off the coat and bloody shirt, then placed the coat back on. After the last leg of the escape to the boat, the coat was stripped off and tossed into the water. Washing away the evidence, the two would have slithered off before daybreak.

Aftermath

Frederick L. Dames was laid to rest the afternoon of Friday, April 14. As a show of respect, the butchers of the city closed their shops to attend the services. He was buried at Bayview cemetery, paid for by the Butchers Union & Steadman Post GAR.

The tombstone of Frederick L. Dames. The murdered butcher was buried at Bayview Cemetery, paid for by the Butchers Union and the Steadman Post GAR. Out of respect, all the butchers and meat markets in the city closed and employees attended the funeral. Photo taken by the author.

Frederick Dames previously owned a meat shop in Portland, Oregon, before coming to Bellingham in 1903. C. L. Parrish, a deputy clerk to the

State of Oregon's land board of Portland, was well acquainted and a good friend of Dames, providing Bellingham police with the butcher's background. Parrish's relationship with Dames dated back to 1879, when they prospected together. Dames also had a meat market in Bodie, California, during that time. Parrish followed Dames to New Mexico in 1881-82, and also kept his books in Portland from 1900-02. Parrish told the *Weekly Oregon Statesman* he was mystified to any motive of vengeance:

> "Mr. Dames was a butcher by trade and a large robust, clean man, of pleasing appearance and fine business tact, and at age 60 was capable of doing a day's work equal to any man of 30. He had no bad habits, retired and arose early and was always attentive to business. He had a reputation of running his business in a straight forward manner."

In Bellingham, Dames had a reputation as being peculiarly reserved regarding his business and private affairs, but had a good number of friends. To several, he confided that he had made bitter enemies over the years, but always maintained silence when asked the nature of the trouble to which he referred.

REWARD OFFERED
BY THE CITY AND COUNTY FOR THE
MURDERER
OF FREDERICK L. DAMES
$500!

With no new clues to follow, and all leads dead-ended, a plea went out for a posted reward. On April 26, Olympia Governor Albert Mead agreed, and proclaimed a $500 reward for the conviction of the killer or killers of Frederick L. Dames. Whatcom County matched the reward. The City of Bellingham offered a similar bounty of its own.

A major crack in the mysterious case came on June 23, not in solving the slaying, but a breakthrough in Dames' personal history. On that date, a petition arrived from Milwaukee to be filed in Probate by Anna Dames, for her son's estate. Fred Dames had long since passed, according to the document. Anna swore on oath that she was the "last sole and only heir at law of said Frederick L. Dames." No mention was made as to whatever happened to Frederick's brothers, August and Jacob, and his sister, who had all made the voyage together to New York City in 1858 aboard the *Owego*.

But there was soon in issue over the petition, confusing Judge Jeremiah Neterer as to its authenticity. He ordered an investigation into the matter for full disclosure. It was soon discovered that attorneys Dorr & Hadley, representing their client, "filed through the mistake and misunderstanding of counsel growing out of the fact that the said Anna Dames speaks German only and does not understand or speak English...an erroneous impression had been given...that Anna Dames was the mother of the deceased."

This confusion was cleared up and a new petition was refiled into Probate on December 19, 1905. The woman in question was none other than Dames' sister Friederike, now Anna Friedericka Wellhausen. From her petition we learn a little more about her brother. Anna explains that Frederick's true mother passed away when he was a child in Prussia, and that "subsequent to the death of said mother and about three years thereafter... Christian Frederick Dames married Anna Disgen." Anna was the daughter of Frederick's father and a half-sister by blood of the deceased, and his sole surviving heir.

Judge Neterer was satisfied, but would not finalize the estate, nor distribute it or discharge Henry Thompson as administrator yet. Neterer further directed newspapers to publish his order looking for further heirs for four consecutive weeks. Administrator Thompson was to carry on his circular mailing to any and all locations where Dames once lived.

Meanwhile, detectives conducted further inquiries with the few acquaintances who knew Dames in Bellingham. It just seemed strange to authorities that Dames would start so many businesses, only to desert them and move on again. Was he running from someone who may have caught up with the butcher that fateful night? But his past was a closed book to detectives. He disliked talking about his past. He never talked about family. He had a quick temper, and word was that it was easy to engage him in a quarrel. He often remarked about enemies attacking him. It was widely believed his assertions were made in jest, or as boasts.

On May 20, Sheriff Williams arrested William Donnelly and Charles Davis for enticing one Michael Connelly to bed with them for the night in their waterfront shack, the same hovel where Williams had discovered the bloody shirt weeks earlier. The two men assaulted Connelly, beat him senseless, stole twenty dollars, and tossed him out. He was so sure of their complicity in the slaying of Lothaire Dames that Williams asked Judge Jeremiah Neterer on August 18 for the maximum sentence, in hopes that he could successfully prove their involvement while incarcerated. He feared that if given a chance, the men would leave town and melt into the underworld of some other city.

146

William Donnelly and Charles Davis. Washington State Archives, Olympia.

Donnelly would change his story later in his application for parole claiming that:

"Davis took some money from a logger and he (Davis) met me about two blocks from where the money was gotten and Davis invited me to take a drink with him, which I did, and for that reason and no other, I was arrested and detained in jail for over three months. Then Davis (who was an ex-convict) persuaded

147

me to plead guilty in order that he might get a lighter sentence, which I did."

Judge Neterer agreed with Williams, and hoped that the sheriff could connect the two felons to the Dames case. On August 24, 1905, both men were sentenced to hard labor at Walla Walla for grand larceny. Neterer threw the book at them, with Davis serving until August 1, 1908 and Davis, until August 17. Three year sentences for $20.00 was a high price to pay. In the end, Sheriff Williams believed the two men were guilty of slaying Frederick Dames, but could never prove it.

The Dames case remained unsolved, becoming dormant for nearly five years, that is, until Frank Romandorf was arrested in Stevens County. With the brutality of Romandorf's murders coming to light, his admission to the demise of Logan, Helm and Green, it was all that was needed to condemn the killer for the murder of the Elk Street butcher. As far as the *Bellingham Herald* and the *Bellingham Reveille* were concerned, the case was unraveled. On Sunday, February 13, 1910, Bellingham awoke to the banner headlines: "Dames Murder Mystery solved, Romandorf Killed Elk Street Butcher." A double column header in the *Herald* stated: "One More Name Is Added To List Of Fiend's Victims."

Suddenly, an entirely new story surfaced of a relationship between Dames and Romandorf, where five years before, the name Romandorf never appeared during the butcher's investigation. In the Colville jail, Romandorf, with a list of aliases, was awaiting transport to the Washington State Penitentiary at Walla Walla, where he was to swing by the neck. Never once did he mention the name Frederick Dames from his cell. But the *Herald* printed that Dames met his death at the hands of Frank Romandorf, "the arch murderer."

Dames and Romandorf, it was claimed, were warm personal friends. They both came from the same locality in Germany, although we are clueless as to where Romandorf was born in Germany. The papers continued that they had known each other for several years in Bellingham. Then came a vicious quarrel between the two men. An altercation was said to have occurred in the Palace Meat Market, where Dames allegedly threw Romandorf from his shop and into the street. Furthermore, "individuals" (who would appear if needed) had seen the killer in the city on the very night the horrible murder was committed, and now all clues indicated that Romandorf murdered Dames. Yes, if called upon by the authorities, witnesses would go on the record and sign an affidavit to that effect of what they had seen.

Another anonymous witness claimed to have been present when the two men quarreled in the market and saw Dames throw a heavy steel meat cleaver at Romandorf, driving him into the street. The incident was said to be over an order of spoiled meat sent to Maple Falls on the Bellingham Bay & British Columbia Railway. Romandorf entered the butcher shop accusing Dames of shipping him spoiled meat, saying he refused to pay for it. An argument ensued, involving the hurled clever, and "Romandorf dodging it in the nick of time. He vowed an oath to return and get even," according to the witness.

Romandorf was said to have left the city in a rage for Maple Falls. He wasn't seen in Bellingham again, until witnesses saw him standing on Elk Street just a few hours prior to when the ghastly deed was committed. Authorities were certain that the murderer left the city immediately, and Romandorf did live outside the city. "Everything indicates," claimed the *Herald*, "that after he had satisfied his lust for the life of his former friend he left the city as quickly as possible…"

It's understandable that Bellingham and Whatcom County needed a conclusion to the heinous murders that took place in its environs. With the capture and exposure of Frank Romandorf, the last of the puzzle pieces fit nicely, ending a terrible mystery. Did William Frederick Jahns actually murder the Elk Street butcher? Had they been friends?

After the Colville verdict, authorities in Whatcom County made no comment on a connection between Jahns and Dames. The trial and conviction of Jahns, for the murder of Dames was only made in the local newspapers. The February 13, 1910, *Bellingham Herald* even stated, "…it is now clear that the slayer of Dames was Romandorf, it is not necessary to look for a motive…Killing seems to have been his business in life." The newspapers printed lots of ink indicating they had evidence and witnesses "ready to come forward" if asked. Oddly, it seems that even after Jahns was dead, and the threat of any reprisal lifted, no one came forward and no names appeared.

No proof or evidence ever came forward that the two men shared anything in common, other than possibly their heritage. Even the quarrel over spoiled meat, which was supposed to have led to Dames' demise, was never substantiated, coming only after Jahns's trial. The "spoiled meat" story alone conjures various questions. Why would Jahns, a frugal man, pay to have meat shipped in from Bellingham when he owned a ranch? First, both Jahns and his son Edward were butchers, who were capable of butchering their own cattle. Second, Maple Falls had several meat markets in operation at the time.

S. N. Prosser owned a meat market, with George E. Prosser as his butcher. A. W. Bell, who advertised fresh meats, fish and sausage, fresh mincemeat in bulk, owned another at the time. S. H. Birdwell had a meat market in operation, as L.A. Skelton purchased half interest in it in June 1906. Leonard Spaulding was a butcher in 1905, opening a meat market in 1906. Martin Fleming butchered and sold meat under a canopy for several years before George King built a butcher shop on the site in September 1906.

Another observation in the Dames murder is that of motive. William Frederick Jahns wasn't just a killer, but a meticulous predator in search of profit and gain. He collected property and substantial money from his victims. Not all his crimes were murder. He was involved in many swindles that involved making fictitious deals, and knowing when to run. He neither put down roots, nor made friends with people who could betray him. Even the relationship with his family is murky.

Jahns was cunning in the way he made people disappear, and in obtaining their property. He made it a profession. That is why it seems improbable that he would confront Dames in combat, in a populated area, and under conditions out of his control. Jahns debilitated his victims with poison, and then killed them off; this was not the case with Dames. Jahns took precautions, making his victims disappear and giving the appearance that they had moved on, leaving as few questions behind as possible. The murderer of Dames took great chances and made a shoddy job of the assault. Aside from his overly ambitious murder of Agnes Janson, Jahns was clean in execution and disposal. That is why most of his victims were never found.

Most convincing is that Jahns did not kill for revenge, but for profit and gain. The Bellingham newspapers played on the fact that Jahns killed Dames out of revenge for humiliating him in his shop. Jahns was a coward, and would not kill to protect his ego. There was no evidence that Jahns intended to murder the butcher and then deed his meat market over to himself.

That being said, were William Donnelly and Charles Davis the true murderers committing an awfully botched robbery? Was there another side to William Frederick Jahns that we know nothing about, regarding his history with Dames? Did some devious past catch up to Frederick L. Dames, who mysteriously moved every few years, and never married? Or did an unknown drifter get away with the murder?

Superior Court, September 4, 1906

It had been nearly seventeen months since the slaying of the Elk Street butcher, and it was time, so decided Judge Jeremiah Neterer, for distribution of the estate. Whatcom County Coroner Henry Thompson handed over to the court his final report on the assets, accounts and payments made on the Dames estate. Virgil Peringer, his own attorney, accompanied Thompson for legal advice. Anna Fredericka Wellhausen, claiming to be sole heir, appeared with Dorr & Hadley, her attorneys. Judge Neterer went over the final accounts in the courtroom, with all satisfied with the administration of Dames' estate. Neterer so ordered, verbally recorded into the record that on:

"Tuesday, the 4th day of September, 1906, at the hour of 9:30 o'clock A.M. and directing that all persons interested in said estate appearing…It is furthered ordered and decreed, that all remaining funds ($1553.96) and all property remaining…is hereby distributed…to Anna Fredericka Wellhausen. And of all other property belonging to said deceased at the time of his death wherever situated and which has been or may hereafter be discovered. (Which was believed to be a lot.) As hereby ordered, that said administrator be discharged and his bondsmen released. Done in open court today."

The Redlight Bar is the present occupant of the Palace Meat Market in 2014. Little has changed with the structure itself. Frederick Dames would be proud. Photo taken by the author.

The alley in back has totally changed since 1905. The Great Northern doesn't rumble down the tracks any longer. The rails and elevated platforms are gone. All the shacks, sheds, and living quarters are long since past. Photo taken by the author.

SOURCES

www.ancestry.com

American Reveille: 4/13/1905, 4/14/05, 4/19/05, 4/15/05, 4/16/05, 11/13/1906, 11/14/06, 11/15/06, 1/25/1910, 1/15/10, 1/16/10, 1/22/10, 1/23/10, 1/26/10, 1/27/10, 1/28/10, 1/29/10.

Bellingham Directory: 1904, 1905, and 1906.

Bellingham Herald: 4/12/1905, 4/13/05, 4/14/05, 4/15/05, 4/17/05, 4/26/05, 6/21/05, 11/12/1909, 2/13/1910.

Bellingham Police Records, Washington State Regional Archives.

Cemetery Records of Whatcom County: Series II, Vol. XII, Bayview Cemetery through 1985. Compiled and published by Whatcom Genealogical Soc. 1999.

www.geneologybank.com

Heritage Quest

Puget Sound American: 4/12/1905, 4/19/05, 4/20/05.

Washington Superior Court for Whatcom County, Probate No. 1224, 1905.

Whatcom County Coroner Inquest, page 86.

U.S. Census. Whatcom County, Washington, California, Illinois, Nevada: 1880 1890, 1900.

Part II

Chapter 6
Who is Charles Weatherford?

January 1908. Cartoon by unknown artist. *Bellingham Reveille.*

On January 18, 1908, another strange specter rose from the ashes of the Frederick L. Dames murder. On a hand-written note, Judge John Kneumann, Justice of the Peace, Sumas Precinct, took the confession of W. T. Hatton of Clearbrook, Whatcom County, who said under oath that Charles Weatherford killed butcher Dames with a hatchet. Kneumann's note said:

"Chas. Weatherford, who was present, admitted to the court that he killed the butcher. W. T. Hatton said there were two witnesses. Chas. Spalding and Emil Spangmore were sent for. Both witnesses said they heard Weatherford say that he killed the butcher with a hatchet." Continuing the judge added, "Under the circumstance the court believes it will commit said Chas, Weatherford, as he appeared to be of unsound mind. Committed to Superior Court this 18th day of January 1908."

The headline of the *Bellingham Herald* acknowledged: "Suspect In Dames Murder Case Arrested." It was the first breakthrough in nearly four years. Charles Weatherford was quickly ushered into the county jail. Not released to the public in 1905 was the fact that Weatherford was one of the first suspected in the Dames murder. He was placed under arrest and "sweated" thoroughly, but maintained his innocence, Sheriff Andrew Williams released to the papers. No evidence connected him to the murder, and authorities could extract nothing incriminating. All they had was his drunken reference to Mrs. Nettie Jones, that the butcher had been murdered, before it was reported.

Jones told police that she had met Weatherford at Eureka Station on the trolley line to Lake Whatcom. She remembered their meeting occurred about six o'clock in the morning on the day of the murder. Weatherford told her of the murdered butcher, giving details and the manner in which the body was found. This was two hours before Edward Leonard discovered his employer.

Williams was acquainted with another story at the time, that a tramp had entered the shop through the back door a few days before the murder, asking for money. Dames was infuriated by the rear door intrusion and refused to give any money. Then the tramp became insulting toward the butcher, and Dames struck the man, knocking him to the floor. He then kicked him continually out the door. Williams believed the tramp was Weatherford.

Although forced to let Weatherford go, Sheriff Williams had his suspicions, and kept the suspect under surveillance. Williams said later that after leaving the jail, Weatherford, whom Williams referred to as the "hobo," was followed through various parts of the county, where he spent considerable time between Sumas, Everson and Maple Falls before returning to Bellingham. Williams noted Weatherford worked a few pickup jobs along the way and was well known by the Bellingham Bay & British Columbia Railway line, for having to toss him off the train often.

Drinking heavily one evening, Weatherford struck up a conversation with Hatton, Spalding and Spangmore. He soon told them a strange story of how he had helped murder Dames, and gave robbery and revenge as the motive for the killing. It is not known if Weatherford was a drunk in 1905, but by 1908 he was a raving alcoholic. It was quite possible he was just bragging that he did something big. It's also possible he was guiltily living with the ghosts of that night, became an alcoholic, and that he was telling the truth. He had told Hatton he kept himself literally soaked in whisky, as he lived in terror that someone was after him since that night.

After his arrest, Weatherford refused to talk any further, and when questioned by Deputy Sheriff Ed Trimble at the county jail, he declined to make any statements. He just sat in a chair, rocking back and forth. Two other men were also suspected to have acted in some capacity in the dastardly crime, Charles Davis and William Donnelly, but as their crimes couldn't be proven, they were eventually held on larceny charges. Williams had hopes that when their terms expired he could meet them at the release gate with a new warrant, charging each one with the murder of Dames.

Charles Weatherford appeared a wild man before his jailers. From the moment he was arrested, he held a fixed grin so large that all that was left of his teeth were exposed. It revoltingly matched his facial expression of bulging bloodshot eyes, embedded grime, wild hair and a matted beard encrusted in filth. A caricature of his crazed manifestation appeared in the *American Reveille*. The stench of the man and his clothing was so repulsive that Williams ordered the prisoner be washed and new clothing found for him.

On January 19, prosecuting attorney Virgil Peringer took Weatherford to Dames' shack to reenact the crime. Weatherford declared that he did not commit the murder, but was a witness. He told in detail how the butcher was killed and where the body was found. He claimed to have come in as two men were finishing their deed. Williams and Trimble were surprised that while at the murder scene, Weatherford talked with a great degree of intelligence. His "terribly disgusting grin was forgotten." But when returned to his cell he "again resumed the role of the imbecile." Peringer later said he was in a quandary as what to do with Weatherford. He was of the opinion that Weatherford was crazy, and only imagined he committed the crime. The *Bellingham Herald* went so far as to report: "Murder's Mind Is Gone, with his Brain Badly Bent Self Confessed Criminal is Held in Jail Pending Determination of Procedure."

Sheriff Williams believed the man was either in on the murder or knew who was. He had a suspicion that when the crime was committed Weatherford was implicated in it somehow, but had no evidence as proof. He was aware that Weatherford was a hobo and a drunkard, living in abandoned shacks along the waterfront. He also knew Weatherford was acquainted with Davis and Donnelly, who Williams was sure had committed the murder.

Not important at the time was that the two had tossed Weatherford out of their shack the day before Dames was murdered. And then there was Weatherford's statement to Mrs. Nettie Jones, claiming Dames was murdered two hours before young Edward Leonard discovered the body. What stunned Williams now was Weatherford's mental deterioration and heavy drinking in the time since the murder. Something was clearly eating the man to death.

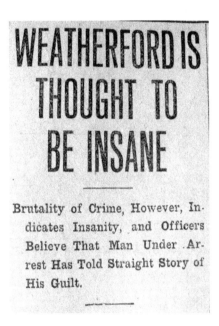

WEATHERFORD IS THOUGHT TO BE INSANE

Brutality of Crime, However, Indicates Insanity, and Officers Believe That Man Under Arrest Has Told Straight Story of His Guilt.

Charles Weatherford was now suffering from severe alcohol withdrawals. He sat in his cell, "silent and moody," refusing to talk, and repudiating the confession he had made to W. T. Hatton and others. So severe was his physical condition that by February 10 authorities reported Weatherford was "suffering greatly from drying out." It was hoped that a long rest would get the alcohol out of his system, and possibly restore his memory to some level of a normal condition.

His jailers were perplexed. Opinions differed as to whether Weatherford committed the crime, and had to talk as a result of it preying upon his mind, or whether he was demented, thinking he had been involved. During his withdrawals, and at lucid moments, he still clung to his first story after arrested, that he knew who killed Frederick Dames, but that he was not implicated. Then he would deny these statements, crediting himself with the deed.

"At times he talks coherently and at other times he doesn't," Williams said. "If he would only lie completely or stick to the truth, then he would know what to do. At times (Weatherford) tells a very circumstantial story in connection with the murder, and relates details in a comprehensive manner, but the next minute he will make the most absurd statements."

Sheriff Williams believed the man knew something, but it was nearly impossible to figure out what. He was determined to hold him, stating the man's brain was somewhat clearer, and believed in another month or so he would tell just how much he knew about the murder. Regardless, if Weatherford should snap out of his delirium, and provide details yet unknown in the case, the damage might already be done. Having Weatherford as a witness in a court of law, he would be deemed a lunatic and any jury would find him insane.

While the prisoner recovered, Williams may have discovered something. During a lucid conversation, Weatherford made claim that between the hours of 6 and 7 o'clock on the morning of the Dames murder, before the body was found, he was standing on Elk Street. A youth on a bicycle came up to him asking the whereabouts of the butcher shop, to which Weatherford claimed to warn the youth off by replying, "Don't go near Dames's butcher shop."

Sheriff Williams inserted an advertisement in the *Bellingham Herald* seeking knowledge of this youth who might remember the conversation with Charles Weatherford on the morning of the murder. Williams was making all efforts to prove some his prisoner's allegations.

"Spooks"

In response to his query for the boys' whereabouts, the Dames case took yet another twisted turn. A mysterious letter was received from a woman who signed her name as "Spirits," a spook who could not be communicated with. The letter claimed knowledge of the Dames case. The story broke in the *Bellingham Herald*, to the embarrassment of Williams, along with the fact that he had received half a dozen letters written by the woman over the past few months.

The sheriff admitted the woman "sets forth many interesting details in her (last) letter as to how the murder was committed and implicates certain persons." She also referred to the talk between Weatherford and the boy on the bicycle the morning of the murder. Ordinarily, no attention would be paid to such "missives," assured the sheriff, but the woman told such a compelling circumstantial story and seemed to know so much about it that Williams intended to follow through. The *Herald* mocked Williams, proclaiming the sheriff was inclined to follow the "French theory in all crimes, 'Cherchez la femme,' which generally leads to the solution of the mystery."

In one of the Spirit's letters, she said that she was controlled by "supernatural powers" and that the sheriff cannot see her. To which Williams replied that he was willing to take a chance at being able to catch a glimpse of a spook, and declared that he did not care what time she chose to visit him, just so the Spirit appeared and cleared up the problem that was worrying him.

Obsessive, Sheriff Williams left Bellingham on several trips hoping to follow up on clues as to the identity of "Spirits." On April 28 Williams made another effort, leaving for Burlington and Mount Vernon, in neighboring Skagit County, hoping to meet the spook. He left telling reporters he thought he was now on the trail of the mysterious woman. On his return, Williams claimed he was successful in finding "a woman" who he believed had some information he was seeking to solve the mystery. Unfortunately, he said, she wasn't the woman who signed herself Spirit.

By September, Weatherford was proving a great disappointment to Sheriff Williams, the county prosecutor, and local authorities. The myth of their prisoner's gruesome participation in the Dames murder was waning. It was becoming apparent that Weatherford was merely a simpleton, who most likely had nothing to do with the killing, "his story being the mere delusion of a weak mind." If he had knowledge of the crime, it was believed to have been long lost in a brain eaten away by alcohol poisoning. He became a docile trustee, gaining privileges working outside and cleaning the jail cells, creating a happy home. For possibly the first time, he had a roof, a clean cell, clothes, food and a warm bed.

Sheriff Andrew Williams lost his reelection to Spencer Van Zandt in November, 1908. In reference to the new sheriff's inheritance of Charles Weatherford, he was dubbed the proprietor of "The Happy Home, Hotel Van Zandt," much to the lawman's scorn. Van Zandt leaned on the county prosecuting attorney to file an affidavit in Superior Court to dismiss his prisoner, as he was "not of the right mind...and has told several conflicting stories." There was no sufficient evidence to hold the prisoner, who considered the county jail his home. When informed that he would be released, Weatherford became much aggrieved, telling the new sheriff-elect, "There may be a law forcing you to put a man in jail, but I never heard of a law forcing you to make him leave." Van Zandt eventually got his way and Charles Weatherford was released. Whatever Charles Weatherford knew, it was long lost in his own mind.

A last memory lingered in a poem penned by cellmate J. A. Sills, an Alaskan miner held for forgery. ("Frank" in the fifth stanza is the jailer, and "Stanley" the cook.)

They bid me leave my happy home,
    they bid me hit the trail.
To wander from the comforts of the
    dear old county jail;
From the strong steel tank that shelters me
    from the winds that blow.
They bid me hike, but you bet your
    your life, I ain't going to go.

I said I was a murderer when first I
    came to stay;
Yet after this they heartlessly now
    bid me go away.

I'll say I killed another man-two
    -men-ten men-a score.
And if that does not satisfy, I'll say
    a dozen more.

The woman's ward is occupied, but I
    can sleep within:
To ask me now to seek for work
    would be a deadly sin;
The thought of going fills my eyes
    with bitter blinding tears;
Oh, leave me yet a little while-say
    ten or twenty years.

Oh, ask me, woo me not to leave my
    dear old county jail.
Who, then would sweep the corridor
    or dump the garbage pail?
I get my grub; I get my rags, tobacco,
    too I get;
Thou sweetest snap I ever struck, I
    cannot leave you yet.

I love the dear old county jail, so safe
    and snug within:
I even love the dear old spoon with
    which my spuds I skin.
I love the soup, I love the mush,
    the stew and all the rest:
And not one wave of trouble rolls
    o'er my peaceful breast.

I love the sheriff. Frank, I love; and
    Stanley I love too;
I even love my work because I have
    not much to do;
I love to sing my sad, sweet song, as
    o'er life's sea I sail;
Be it ever so humble, there's no
    place like jail.

SOURCES

American Reveille: 1/28/1908.

Bellingham Herald: 4/12/1905, 1/13/1908, 1/14/08, 1/15/08, 2/13/08, 2/10/08 2/15/08, 3/2/08, 3/19/08, 4/28/08, 4/29/08, 5/7/08, 9/25/08, 12/6/08.

Proceedings 792, Jan 18, 1908, with notes by Judge John Kneumann, Justice of the Peace, Sumas Precinct.

Whatcom Criminal Index: No. 792 1/18/08 Book 3.

Chapter 7
Tunnel No. 21

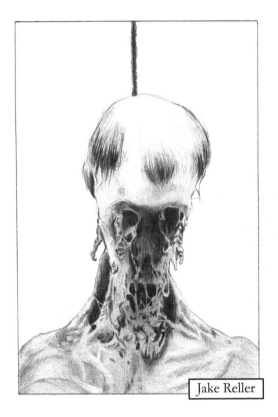

Jake Reller

Some mysteries go unsolved, never to be answered. They become puzzles that stir our imagination until our minds run amuck, attempting to solve the unsolvable. Imagine walking down a street and stumbling across a violent crime scene. You'd naturally try to put the pieces together and figure out the series of events that led to your unpleasant discovery. There is an underlying tendency for the human mind to want to solve mysteries or puzzles.

The dusty bowels of many police departments throughout the world are stuffed full of such "Cold Case Files." Most will never be solved. A number of these unsolved cases carry a curse for the fanatical and obsessed detective. This is the case that follows them into their retirements, becoming personal fixations. This is the case that got away.

The short story below is one such cold case from South Bellingham. It was never unraveled. Authorities, baffled and finding no evidence, were determined foul play existed, but was it suicide?

Tunnel 21. Galen Biery Collection, Whatcom Museum.

A Stroll Down the Tracks

On Monday, September 11, 1911, Arnold, owner of Arnold & Shaver Reality Co. on Elk Street and dealing in land and farm loans, was walking south on the railroad tracks from South Bellingham. Why Arnold was walking the tracks that day isn't known. There certainly wasn't much in the way of realty or farms on his route. Yet, on a warm, sunny day the course Arnold traveled was along the beautifully scenic edge of Bellingham Bay. Eventually, Arnold approached the first of the Great Northern rail tunnels. He may have paused awhile, not wanting to risk being caught inside if a train should pass through.

Whatever transpired next is speculation. Perhaps Arnold paused looking over the bay, lighting a cigarette before his long walk back to his office. Maybe there was a distinctive stench of death in the air, and Arnold was investigating its whereabouts. Arnold may have heard the distinctive "caw, caw, caw" of a murder of crows hovering overhead and looked up. He didn't tell us how he made his discovery, but Arnold must have stumbled backwards, shaken to find the decomposed remains of a man suspended from the limb of an alder tree overhead.

The sight high above must have been dreadful. A corpse dangled above the tunnel entrance just out of eyesight of a train engineer when passing beneath. Astounded, Arnold noticed the hanging corpse had no clothing on its body accept its underwear and boots. It must have been hanging for quite some time, as the tissues were brownish, covered by a waxy substance and slowly dissolving. This may have been partially due to the dampness, so near the saltwater. The organs and cavities had long since ruptured, and the body's nails had long since fallen off. Most disturbing to Arnold was that the face was unrecognizable. The fellow's neck was blackened, stretched and twisted by the strangling rope. The crows had removed the eyes, nose and lips, exposing gaping holes on the corpse's face. The teeth were broad and wide, making a freakish grin. Regaining his composure, the realtor headed back to town to report his ghoulish find to the police.

Arnold notified police of his discovery by mid-afternoon, but authorities were unsuccessful in locating coroner N. Whitney Wear. Eventually he was reached by telephone about 6 o'clock, but for some reason he made no investigation of the case until early Tuesday morning. From Arnold's description, authorities may have decided an extra day wouldn't hurt. An officer was dispatched for what must have been the unpleasant duty of standing watch over the hanging corpse overnight, preventing the body from being disturbed by onlookers or kids throwing stones at the corpse.

BODY HANGS IN BREEZE FOR TWO MONTHS

Decomposed Remains of Unknown Man Who Had Evidently Been Dead for Weeks Is Found Suspended From Limb of Alder Tree Just Outside North End of Great Northern Tunnel In South Bellingham—Discovery Is Made by C. E. Arnold Who Notifies Coroner—Investigation Is Made Today.

BODY IS CLOTHED ONLY IN UNDERWEAR

Body Is Clothed Only In Underwear

After the body had been swinging in the channel breezes for a period estimated by Coroner Wear to be that of two months, the coroner and the police conducted an on-the-spot investigation, searching for clues. Wear noted the body was obviously badly decomposed and there was no clue as to the man's identity. The only item found was an empty, leather money pouch. Wear figured the body to be that of a man, 30 to 35 years old. The body was curiously clothed only in underwear, shoes and socks. Though a thorough search of the brush in the vicinity of the hanging tree was conducted, no trace of the man's outer garments were found. After viewing the remains, the coroner ordered the corpse to be cut down and brought to the undertaking establishment of Stokes & Wickman, where it would await identification.

A few days later police released a statement claiming that they had not the slightest clue as to the identity of the man, and expressed the opinion that the case could have been one of murder rather than suicide. "Unless the man was mentally unbalanced and threw his clothing into the bay before suspending himself by the neck from a tree, the police recognize a possibility that foul play was responsible for the outcome." One theory posited was that someone who was fleeing the area for some unknown reason encountered the John Doe on the tracks. That person may have seized the poor victim and killed him for his clothing, with shoes not fitting. The leather purse was emptied of money and identification and tossed aside. The secluded location made the crime possible, and it could be made to look like a suicide, but police couldn't explain the origin of the rope.

Autopsies, or postmortem examinations, have been around for thousands of years, yet they were still rather crude at the turn of the twentieth century. In cases when the corpse was unknown, it often made for an interesting study for dissection. Galen Biery Collection, Whatcom Museum

The only description police could offer newspapers was that the remains were terribly decomposed, "but so far as it is possible to judge, the body is that of a man of 30 to 35 years of age, of medium height and weight." The well-worn, empty leather purse found near the body was retained as a possible clue to the identity of the man, along with one of the shoes in case someone eventually came forward. The body found a resting spot in Potters field.

It was another cold case for Bellingham.

SOURCES

Bellingham Herald: 9/11/1911.

Chapter 8
The Cobbler

Love triangles seldom end well. One only need watch a performance of Ruggero Leoncavallo's tragic opera, *Pagliacci* to see the mother of all love triangles come to its deadly conclusion.

"Play your part, while you're in torment! You won't know what you're doing, or what you're saying. It must be done! Force yourself! Well, are you not a man? No, just a clown!"

Ruggero Leoncavallo, *Pagliacci*, Act one Canio:

The story of Edward and Clara Gaultier, and J. Horton Thurston, is a prime example of one such love triangle, ending with disastrous results. It has all the elements of a classic tragedy: a jilted husband, who is too passive, forgiving, tormented, and willing to sacrifice his own dignity for his true love; a wife with strong sexual desires, who could not care less how much she humiliates her husband; and a rival, who is cool, calculating and manipulative, with no concern for the damage he inflicts on others. Sooner or later, the situation was bound to come to a catastrophic conclusion.

This was the situation near Blaine, Washington, on the night of September 26, 1918. The populace of this fishing community on the Canadian border had expected to awake any morning to read in newspapers the impending news that the Great War in France was over, and that the "boys were coming home." That, in fact would be the case in about six weeks time. Instead, on this particular morning, they woke to the banner headline: "Double Murder At Blaine."

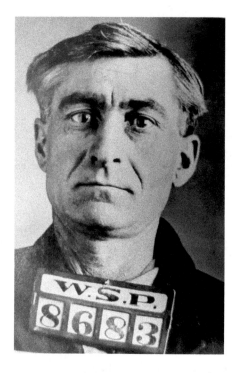

Edward S. Gaultier, the cobbler. Was he the fool everyone thought? Inmate No. 8683. Washington State Archives, Olympia.

Gaultier

Edward Stephen Gaultier was born in the tiny community of Charles City, Iowa on September 26, 1875. A child of protestant, French-Canadian parentage, his mother died when he was just six years old. His father, overcome by depression and grief from this loss, never remarried, nor fully recovered. His sister Clara, who was not much older than Edward, cared for her little brother. There was another brother in the mix, Andrew, but there is little known of him from this period.

His father, who was eventually committed to an insane asylum, placed Edward in a boarding school where he was educated and raised. At twenty years of age, and standing five foot six, he left school to head west, finding work as a cowpuncher. In 1899, Gaultier, by reason of an accidental gunshot wound, lost a portion of his foot. Due to the injury, he was partially crippled, suffered great physical pain for years, and became very sensitive about his disfigurement. The record doesn't tell us when Gaultier lost his leg below the knee, which resulted in having a wooden leg fitted in its place and walking like a "gimp" for the rest of his life.

Two years later, in 1901, and despite his disfigured foot, he found the love of his life in a young girl named Clara Newell. She was sixteen years old, to his twenty-six. Edward remembered her as petite, with smooth dark skin, and a full head of long flowing black hair. They courted a year before Edward asked for her hand in marriage.

They lived on the plains for four years, during which time Edward farmed, hunted, and trapped. Clara bore him two children: a son, "Young" Eddie, and a daughter, "Little" Clara May. They claimed to be very happy. It was also reported that during this time Edward saved Clara from nearly drowning in a river.

Sometime in 1905, Clara decided that life on the plains no longer suited her, and she desired to leave their farm. It was decided they would head further west, where Gaultier's sister Clara Lindsey and her family had settled in Deming, Washington. There, Edward engaged in business as a shoemaker.

Sister Clara had met and married William M. Lindsey in Vancouver, British Columbia, and moved to Whatcom County shortly afterward. The Gaultiers would live in Deming four years, again claiming to be very happy and much in love with one another. Edward saved his money and made a claim upon a homestead and quickly improved upon it. Life was going so well, Edward took Clara (his wife) to the 1909 Alaska-Yukon-Pacific Expedition, staying in Seattle for a whole month.

Then Edward Gaultier's life seemed to take a turn. Clara's behavior began to change radically. Gaultier, who may have been in denial, or simply naive and embarrassed by her explicit needs, did not notice the change, but others had. Edward's sister and her family told him that his wife was seen "paying unbecoming" attention to other men in town and that she was not hiding these affections in the least, being very public with her intentions. Sister Clara said she and others had witnessed her sitting in another man's lap.

Gaultier firmly denied any truth to the rumors regarding his lovely wife, becoming angry with his sister and her family. He abruptly packed up his family and moved to Sumas, near the Canadian border. They lived there for a short time, but he couldn't ignore the rumors. In 1910, he relocated the family to the small community of Elma, in Grays Harbor County. There, he continued his cobbler trade and opened a new shop. Once again, life seemed good. They had another child, Charlie, their second son.

One day Clara came home wearing a dazzling new suit. Edward asked where she got the money for such an expensive outfit. She claimed to have purchased it herself with money she had saved aside. A week later, resulting in a direct jab to Gaultier's manhood, he received a bill for the suit from a local attorney. Confused, Gaultier asked Clara about the bill. She broke down and told her husband the truth, that another man had bought her the suit. The lawyer, the other man, sent the bill to the cobbler, quite possibly to embarrass Gaultier with the fact that his wife was having relations with him behind his back. Gaultier paid the bill, but burned the new suit. He then confronted the man, telling him to leave his wife alone.

That same week, the couple stepped out for the afternoon to attend an estate auction. A large crowd was in attendance, and Edward was having a fine time at the sale, when someone noticed the cobbler and his lovely wife. Alluding to the earlier suit incident, a loud voice bellowed forth, "Hold up a woman's suit and here's a man who will bid on it." Gaultier was greatly disturbed and embarrassed. Angry, he took his wife's hand and left.

Possibly out of fear of losing her, Edward claimed later, he would never "scold or abuse or otherwise attempt to punish his wife" for her indiscretions. Observers could not understand his choice not to punish her. Over and over, family and friends told Gaultier to make a stand or leave his wife, but he wouldn't have it. Somehow, in Gaultier's imagination, he believed the more he accepted the situation of his wife's infidelities, the more he was proving his love to her.

Gaultier worked in his cobbler shop daily, growing a larger cliental. Many loggers came in with their expensive caulked boots, wanting to have him work on them, so as to extend the life of their boots a little longer before having to purchase new ones. The Gaultier's decided to expand their business by looking for new and profitable markets. Edward would watch over the children at the shop, while Clara traveled the surrounding townships, selling the shoes her husband made. Her boundless attractiveness, even after bearing three children, was obviously an asset in her sales to stores. Ordinarily, it wasn't uncommon for a sales trip to take two or three days. During one such trip, Clara did not return or call in. After four days of hearing nothing, and fearing something had happened, Gaultier hired a sitter, closed the shop and went looking.

A few towns over, Gaultier inquired in a shoe store as to whether Clara had been in selling his shoes. He gave a description of his wife, but the shopkeeper stopped him from going any further. She's here, the keeper told him, but you won't like who she's with.

The shopkeeper directed him to a hotel at the end of a street where she frequently stayed when making her sales. Dejected, Gaultier limped on his gimp leg to the hotel address given him. He asked the front desk clerk for the number of his wife's room. Wide-eyed at seeing Gaultier in the lobby, the clerk provided the room key. Crestfallen, the cobbler knocked on the door, but no answer came. Hearing his wife's giggles through the door, Gaultier turned the key in the lock and walked into the room to find Clara naked in bed with another man. Confident that he was in no mortal danger from an enraged husband, the man in the bed just laughed as Edward gathered up his wife's clothes and escorted her back home.

Clara shamefully admitted to adultery with the man. Well… she admitted to adultery several times with the man during the night, and morning, but promised she would "never fall again." Edward, in turn, maintained his love for her. Clara said she would "always thereafter be a good true wife." He forgave her and took her back.

For whatever reason, the cobbler's business began to fail. Becoming very "blue and melancholy" Gaultier moved his family yet again. They left Elma and after several stays in various Whatcom County townships, settled in Maple Falls. In September of 1913, Edward started his shoe shop in the Lindsey Building (owned by his brother-in-law) on Lake Street, in block one. He expanded his trade to include harness and glove manufacturing

In short order, Edward's sister again approached her brother, claiming Clara was shacking up with the same fellow as the last time they lived in the area. Once again, Edward became angry with his sister and family, refusing to ever speak or have further communication with them. Still, Gaultier couldn't stay in Maple Falls any longer, so in 1914, they moved to Hamilton, a small logging town on the Skagit River.

On the surface, once again, all appeared well for the couple in Hamilton. Edward took a logging job, as there was no need for a cobbler. In 1916, Clara gave birth to another boy they named Allen. Oddly, the naive Gaultier gave no notice of the fact that both Clara and he had dark complexions and dark hair; that their other three children had dark skin and hair, and in features, all resembled their father. The new baby, however, was of very light complexion with blond curly hair, and did not in the least look like his father. Gaultier simply overlooked the obvious.

Needing more money and with more mouths to feed, Edward decided to relocate his family once again. This time to Blaine, where he believed he could work during the seasonal salmon run, and establish another cobbler shop the rest of the year. With four children underfoot, one of them a two-year-old to chase after, Edward figured Clara would be too weighed down to gallivant anymore. However, even after Clara had borne him four children, she had lost little of her youthful appearance and petite figure.

Blaine

Edward Gaultier quickly reestablished himself in the new community, opening a shop on Washington Avenue. He was well liked by the merchants and citizens. Working in the fisheries now, he understood that workers needed their shoes maintained and repaired to protect themselves against the cold and wet environment in which they functioned. They didn't always have the money to pay for the work on their shoes, but Edward trusted they would pay when they could. Many respected him for that understanding. He didn't gamble, drink, swear, or womanize. He wasn't a rich man, but he was said to be wealthy with friends and thereby deemed a respectable citizen.

City of Blaine, circa 1900. Courtesy of Bill Becht, Horseshoe Cones & Antiques, Blaine, WA.

Each night he would close up the shop, limp upstairs, and hand over his daily earnings to Clara to feed the children and pay the bills. Whether out of boredom, spite to break up the harmony, or simply guilt, Clara one day decided to tell Edward that he was not the father of baby Allen. She admitted the father was a man back in Hamilton. She expressed her "sorrow for her infidelity and sin and promised she would not fall again." Gaultier was greatly disturbed by his wife's infidelity, but believed that if she confided in him, she must truly love him. He took her into his arms, cried, and forgave her.

During their first Blaine summer, Clara would help look after the business, while Edward took a job on a fish-trap for Alaska Packers' Association at Point Roberts. He had his wages forwarded to her.

One day, Clara visited her husband at the trap and told him that she had been talking to a sixty-two-year-old rancher named John Horton Thurston (who always went by J. Horton). She reported that J. Horton wanted to go in on a gas-powered boat with Edward and start a fishing venture in the off season. Furthermore, this Thurston fellow had a seventy-acre ranch just south of Blaine and a fifteen-year-old son named Glen. Thurston had lost his wife, May, a few years before, and it seemed he was lonely. Clara said Thurston had suggested they could save money by moving onto the ranch, and Clara would keep house for their board. It wasn't much of a working ranch, with only two horses and six cows, but it would be good for the kids. She told Edward she wanted to do this.

The cobbler was shocked to see his wife visit him at work. "Well, okay," said Edward. He knew of Thurston and had talked to him from time to time, but he knew nothing of his background or reputation. Clara gave him a kiss and ran off back to town. On August 7, Edward came in from the trap to the new home on Thurston's ranch. There he met J. Horton Thurston and his son Glen. Edward's own three sons, fifteen, ten, and two years old, and his thirteen-year-old daughter, were all settled in.

Gaultier looked around the house, and seemed satisfied, but was soon disturbed to find that Clara's underclothes and stockings were under Thurston's bed, in his room. Upset, he asked his wife about this observation, only to be told that she had taken a bath in that room earlier and had not yet removed her clothes from the room. The mood darkened as Gaultier suspected the worst. He started asking her questions. Later in the day, Clara suggested that he obtain a divorce from her. "I don't want a divorce," said an astonished Gaultier. In return, Clara said that she didn't love him well enough to be his wife anymore. Edward didn't want to hear this talk any longer, and told her so. Thurston, shadowing the couple at a distance, said nothing of the confrontation, and stayed away from their conversations.

The following day, Clara repeated her desire for a divorce. Gaultier asked if there was another man, to which she replied in the negative. The mood in the household was heavy and silent. Later in the day, Thurston's son Glen approached Edward, claiming his father and Mrs. Gaultier had several times locked the children out of the house for long periods of time. Edward gave the boy a long stare of disbelief, and then reached out, squeezing Glen's shoulder, and thanked him. Edward asked his own children if this were true. They confirmed it was.

Soon, the subject of "divorce" became an open conversation in the household. Gaultier spoke loudly of his love and devotion, and tried everything to dissuade his wife from wanting a divorce. Horton, as Clara now referred to Thurston, attempted to interfere by telling Edward of the benefits of a divorce, intervening in the confrontations between the couple and always siding with Clara. Edward blamed Thurston for the disharmony in his marriage, and warned him to stay away from his wife. Horton would stay at Clara's side, and together they would walk away to avoid Gaultier when the conversation intensified.

The following week, Edward Gaultier fell into a deep depression. He slept very little, if at all. He didn't eat, and lost a great deal of weight. He worked in his cobbler shop and would return to the ranch at night to have a presence and be a barrier between Thurston and Clara. On September 17, he went to Thurston's house at ten o'clock at night and stayed outside, looking in the window, watching and waiting, until two o'clock in the morning.

He wanted to catch the two in the act of embrace, or he hoped to confront Thurston alone. When the moment arrived, he asked Thurston why his wife wanted a divorce. Thurston looked at Edward as if he were fool, and advised him to let her go.

At ten o'clock the following night, Gaultier returned to the house to discover the front door locked. A portion of the house was shrouded in darkness. He rattled the doorknob until his daughter "Little Clara" opened the door. He stepped into the dark room. She told her father that mama was in the other room kissing Mr. Thurston. Gaultier went straight into the living room. As he entered, Clara and Thurston leaped from the sofa, her dress pulled up and with no stockings. Gaultier demanded to know what was going on. He said he had been told that they were kissing one another. Horton just stood there and straightened his clothing, as if nothing had happened. Then he turned to walk toward his bedroom.

Greatly excited, and distressed, Edward told his wife that this house was no place for her and the children, and begged her to leave there for the children's sake. Thurston entered his room and left the door ajar enough to hear the conversation. Clara retired to her own room where she shared a bed with her daughter. Her husband silently followed, and sat at the edge of the bed begging her to leave and crying until 4 am. Finally, Clara said, "Now you can get a divorce if you want it; you have grounds now." He again said he didn't want one, and that he could forgive her for what he had seen. Edward "begged her in all ways not to ruin their home and to try to save her reputation." He did not sleep that night, and the next morning ate nothing.

Edward spent all day of Friday, September 20 begging her to leave. He told her, "Thurston was not a fit man to be in a house with a woman like her." At three o'clock in the afternoon the two took a walk in the woods where they could be alone. Edward went over the story of their lives together and tried to convince her how many times she had fallen, and how often he had forgiven her. Clara again tried to explain that she had lost her love for him, and simply no longer wanted to be with him.

Over the following week Gaultier visited his children each day. They cried to him that they wanted to leave and that they had seen their mother kissing and touching Mr. Thurston. But he wouldn't take them from their mother.

On the twenty-second, Gaultier went from Blaine to the ranch to see his wife. The previous day he was in Bellingham, where people told him that his wife and Thurston were seen walking in town hand-in-hand, kissing on the street. Several men told him that Thurston was a man of bad reputation. When a woman told Edward of this, he expressed surprise, to which the woman exclaimed, "Is that anything new to you?" Edward hung his head in shame and limped away. Arriving at Thurston's house, he was let in.

Gaultier was a shell of a man by now, hunched over with bloodshot, sunken eyes. He lost weight from lack of appetite. When he confronted Clara again, she just stood there in the kitchen denying nothing. "I told you I had no feelings for you." Gaultier turned to Thurston and told him he was taking his wife away, but Horton put his foot down, stating if she wanted to stay Edward could not take her. "She is happy here with me." Edward spent the night at the ranch, but did not undress or sleep, nor did he eat in the morning.

On the twenty-third, Clara went into Bellingham to see if she could obtain a divorce without her husband's consent. That night Edward decided to stay on the boat with Eddie, his eldest son, for company. He wrote a letter to his wife stating he would kill himself. He would have Eddie deliver it in the morning. Edward went to the edge of the boat for a long time contemplating his troubles, then made up his mind to try reconciliation again. He tore up the letter, and then wrote a second letter about how he had suffered for her. At four o'clock he woke his son to carry the letter to his mother. Edward told him to tell his mother to sell everything, furniture, tools, etc. as they would start over. He told his son to watch over the children until he arrived later.

During the forenoon of the twenty-fourth, he again went to see his wife to talk her out of a divorce, and that evening had a "friendly" talk with both Clara and Thurston. His mind-set seemed to be changing, but no one could put a finger on his thoughts. He stayed the night at the ranch and although his body was tired, his mind raced and would not rest. He could not sleep. At midnight he got up, dressed and sat on the edge of the bed, smoking. In the morning he decided to pay a visit to Thurston's stepson, Noble McClurg, who lived in Bellingham.

Noble, 28 years old, was a sawyer by trade. Edward asked the fellow what sort of man Thurston was. He told him of the relationship his stepfather was having with his wife. The stepson said, "This didn't surprise him at all," following that "the man would stoop to a new low to do anything." Noble sat Edward down on his porch and shared all the history of Thurston, as he knew it.

J. Horton Thurston was married twice in Michigan. His first wife, Minnie, married Thurston in 1881 and bore him five children. In Almont, on May 22, 1900, Minnie filed for divorce on grounds of "extreme cruelty and non-support." The divorce was not contested and promptly given on July 30.

Thurston didn't remain inactive long, moving into the household of the widowed May McClurg, as a boarder. Exactly when is not known, but Thurston did appear on the 1900 census taken on June 8. Noble was just 9 years old at the time, living in the home with his uncle and sister. His father had been dead awhile and he knew his mother was lonely. Noble surmised that Horton and his mother had been an item before his divorce. May soon after married Horton, moving the family to Whatcom County. May passed away on July 2, 1917, at the young age of 45.

Noble told Edward that within a month of his mother's death, Thurston had proposed marriage to another woman who was his housekeeper. When that didn't work out, Thurston got a girl of about sixteen years old for a housekeeper and offered to give her a piano if she would sleep with him for a month. He also told Edward that his stepfather had once stolen a farmer's wife from her husband, and then threw her out when the fun was over. All this transpired in just a year before Clara came along. He reported that Thurston was an evil man of the worst reputation!

Gaultier went back to his wife and told her of his recent discoveries, and that he felt sick and worn out from her ill treatment of him. He declared he felt "out of his mind, feeling like that of a drunken man." Edward threatened to have Thurston arrested. Clara told her husband, "Ed, are you going bugs going down there and listening to everything people tell you…" That afternoon Gaultier told Thurston he knew all about him and the revolting details of having stolen another man's wife. Thurston had been sick all day, complaining of stomach pains. He remained indoors, moving from bed to sofa and back, trying to stay comfortable. Thurston ignored the jilted husband, and rolled over with a smirk running across his face.

That evening, Gaultier attempted to eat a bit of food, only to become nauseated. Sitting at the kitchen table, he told the two elder boys that neighbors had reported seeing a coon in the area of the reservoir. Apparently it was getting into mischief and becoming an annoyance. "Was anyone up for a hunt?" he asked. Clara told her husband he looked too sick to be out on such a cold September night, and he should just retire for the night. Edward answered that he could not sleep, but wanted to tire himself out so he might be able to. "Young" Eddie was game to go out with his father, and Glen also wanted in on the midnight hunt.

Thurston took to his bed early, claiming sickness. Clara tucked in "Little" Clara and snuggled up beside her and fell asleep. Edward lay next to her wide-eyed. As it became late, Edward got the boys moving and they were off on the hunt.

After an hour or so walking in darkness, the trio managed to tree their prey by the reservoir, but they were unable to get a clear shot because of their dull lights. Gaultier told the boys to stay put while he ran back to fetch an axe at the ranch to chop the tree down. He built the boys a fire by the trunk to keep the coon treed, and the boys warm. Then he searched about the ground for his tobacco pipe, lost in the drama of the chase. His gimp leg was sore that evening, due to running on uneven ground in the dark. On his return, he fell hard and had a difficult time using his wooden leg to get back on his feet. He was aided by his rifle, which he used as a cane.

Returning to the house, Edward attempted to reenter by the door he had left unlocked nearly two hours before. Forcing the door open, he limped through the kitchen toward the living room. From the kitchen threshold he could see a sliver of light shining in from Thurston's side room. Stealthily entering the living room, he heard heavy moans and movement. Circling around the sofa, Edward saw his wife and Thurston lying side by side. She had her arm around his neck and he had her bed skirts pulled up, his hand in an "unmentionable position between her legs." Neither noticed, nor changed position as Edward stood there.

Gaultier watched the couple on the sofa for a short time. He had caught Clara with another man before, but this time it was different. She and her lover had run him down for weeks, humiliating him in front of his children and the town. He was exhausted from agonizing over her, and now, watching her on the sofa, he suddenly realized what she had been telling him for some time. She didn't care. She truly didn't love him anymore.

Edward snapped out of his trance, and may have even been surprised when the startled adulteress and her consort noticed Gaultier's figure in the shadows. Thurston leapt to his feet.

"Did you get a coon?" asked a startled Thurston.

"No," replied Gaultier with complete lack of expression or emotion, "I didn't get a coon, but this is the second time I have found you two like this, and you both may as well get ready to die."

With the barrel of Gaultier's .30-.30 caliber lever-action rifle thrust toward him, Thurston became understandably nervous. The usually cowardly

Gaultier had wildness in his eyes not seen by Clara and Horton before. Thurston knew immediately from Gaultier's cold voice that he was in a dilemma. "Now Ed, lower that rifle and let's talk some sense," a panicked Thurston stammered out. Gaultier said nothing. Then Thurston offered Gaultier a thousand dollars, along with his half interest in the fishing boat, which was jointly owned between the two men, if he would just go away and leave them alone.

Again, Gaultier said in a monotone voice, "Thurston, get ready to die."

Clara leaped up off the sofa, lowered her skirts, and walked toward her husband, laughing in his face. "He won't shoot," she taunted Edward in front of her lover. By this time, Thurston was readjusting himself, tucking in his shirt. "Calm down and let's talk," said Horton, regaining a more relaxed and manipulative composure.

"He won't shoot," declared Clara again. "He wouldn't dare shoot" and giggled, knowing that after all she had put her husband through, he had never taken any form of action against her or any reprisal against her lovers.

Thurston must have thought differently after Clara's mocking. Staring into Gaultier's tired and bloodshot eyes, for the first time he saw calmness in them, as if the jilted husband knew what he had to do. J. Horton Thurston saw what was coming and attempted to escape, but Edward Gaultier was faster. He fired his rifle; the bullet ripped through the rancher's abdomen and knocked him over a chair, which flipped over on its back. Thurston's body skidded to a halt on the floor, already dead.

Edward ejected the shell cartridge, reloaded the chamber with another round, and turned his rifle onto a horrified Clara. He shot her as well. The slug penetrated his wife's left breast and exited her back near the spine. She dropped onto the living room floor in a heap. Death at such close range was instantaneous.

Jake Reller

Calmly, as if a great weight had been lifted from his shoulders, yet still terrified, Gaultier collected his children from their warm beds and took them across the road to the home of Alfred H. Wilson. Wilson was co-owner of Wilson & Brown Grocery in Blaine, not far from Gaultier's own cobbler shop along Washington Avenue. Alfred lived with his wife Elizabeth on the property of real estate broker I. M. Scott.

With his children in tears, Edward banged on Wilson's door until it opened. A very distressed Gaultier informed Wilson what he had done. "Please douse your lights," he told Wilson in a gruff tone. "I don't want eyes laid upon me." Then Edward asked Wilson if he would please call Byron Kingsley, constable of Blaine, stating he was ready to face the consequences for his act.

Once notified, Constable Kingsley informed Sheriff William D. Wallace of Bellingham of the murders near Blaine. At eight o'clock that morning, Deputy Sheriff Alfred Medhurst, Sheriff Wallace, and coroner Dr. Whitney Wear left for Blaine to take Gaultier into custody. Kingsley found Gaultier awaiting him in a dark corner of the grocer's home. Coroner Wear, a Bellingham physician and surgeon, after investigating the circumstances, announced that there would be no need of an inquest.

The Trial

On the morning of September 28, prosecuting attorney Loomis Baldrey filed a complaint in the Whatcom Superior Court. He charged Edward Gaultier with murder in the first degree of his wife, Clara Gaultier. Baldrey had not decided what action he would take with respect to Gaultier's killing of J. Horton Thurston. The case was so convoluted that it would take time to unravel all the twists and turns. He believed he could build a stronger case centering on Gaultier killing his wife, and avoiding the love-triangle. Baldrey did not want a sympathetic jury siding with a heart-broken murderer. Five days later, on Thursday, October 3, Gaultier appeared for arraignment before Judge William H. Pemberton. Upon motion of his defense counsel, Walter B. Whitcomb, they waived the reading and asked for time for a doctor's consult. The court fixed the date of pleading for the following Monday morning at 10 o'clock.

Monday, October 7, Edward Gaultier limped into the Whatcom County Courthouse. He pleaded, in a soft voice, "not guilty" before Judge William Pemberton. Whitcomb followed up his client's plea, adding, "Not guilty by insanity, Your Honor." Gaultier added in a written plea that he was insane at the time he killed his wife. Gaultier accused Thurston of breaking up the harmony of his home and declared that he was justified in committing the deed. Whitcomb added that his client's mentally irresponsible condition did not exist and that Gaultier has been sane since the act was committed.

Whitcomb said that Gaultier killed not out of rage, jealousy, or passion, but was driven into madness after weeks of torment by the two dead protagonists, until he was broken by their deeds. In all efforts to save family and reputation, Edward Gaultier undeniably bore an excessive weight on his mind and shoulders, which would have otherwise crushed the average man. Whitcomb, attempted to utilize the "unwritten law of in defense of one's home."

Whitcomb in part also agreed with the state that it would be better for his client to leave Horton Thurston's murder at arms length. He was unsure as to whether this could help or hurt in Gaultier's defense. By agreeing with Baldrey's assertion to avoid the love-triangle in his own case against Gaultier, Whitcomb could avoid contending with a double-murder. In the end, both attorneys decided the key to saving or putting Edward Gaultier away lay with the relationship between husband and wife. While in theory, the two were in agreement, both the defense and the prosecution were clueless as to how to conduct their cases without alluding to Thurston.

The *Bellingham Herald* claimed the trial, set for December, was expected to be one of the most interesting events in recent history. A jury would have to determine whether or not Gaultier was insane at the time the murder or murders were committed, and whether or not he would be a safe person to be at large. The *Herald* ran a column sub-headed: "Shot To Death His Wife And Her Paramour, When He Found Them In What He Says Was A Compromising Position." After the act was committed, Gaultier said that he felt justified in its commission, considering the circumstances. Loomis Baldrey was quick to add that the alleged killer "has shown a cheerful and unconcerned attitude ever since his incarceration, once his foul deed was done," insinuating that Gaultier didn't seem in much distress for a man being accused of murder.

A jury was secured with little trouble. There were only four peremptory challenges, one by Loomis Baldrey, and three by Walter Whitcomb. One juror, a Mr. Rickenbacher who was a Swiss dairy farmer, was excused because he said he harbored prejudice against insanity as a plea of defense. A jury comprised of eight men and four women was finally selected, with two alternates in case any were "struck with the influenza." The jurors were C. M. Sherman, Emmet Farley, Helena Wolter, A. Prentiss, F. J. Hinkey, A. N. Stansell, Mary A. Hanlon, J. T. Westman, Irma E. Robertson, James Cain, Martin Oines, and Bernard Reilly. The alternates were Mrs. Botta, (number 13) and T. F. Moore (number 14).

Day One: Tuesday, December 10, 1918

With insanity as the plea of defense, the trial opened on the frosty morning of December 10, 1918, at 9:30. The case had not attracted nearly as many observers as had been predicted, with the courtroom not more than half full. Newspapers thought the court's ruling prohibiting the presence of minors (due to the graphic sexual nature of the trial) was a factor in limiting curiosity seekers. But it's more probable that attendance was greatly affected by fear of the influenza. For almost a year, the Spanish flu pandemic had been spreading death across the land. Present estimates claim that between January 1918 and December 1920, as many as 500 million people perished, five percent of the world's population. Many communities hung signs prohibiting large gatherings, for fear of spreading the modern plague. Theaters, sporting events, churches, restaurants, and other places where people congregated closed their doors until the specter of death passed.

The state would produce about a dozen witnesses and the defense approximately the same, many being the same witnesses. The state's included neighbors Alfred and Elizabeth Wilson, Constable Byron Kingsley, Coroner Dr. Whitney Wear, Sheriff William Wallace, Deputy Sheriff Alfred Medhurst,

Chris Paterson, "Young" Eddie Gaultier, "Little" Clara Gaultier, Charlie Gaultier, Dr. Eber McKinnis of Blaine, Blaine undertaker Henry B. Potter, and Glen Thurston, son of Horton Thurston.

In his opening statement, prosecutor Baldrey recited briefly the history of the case, stating that Gaultier had lived in other sections of the county and state before moving to Blaine, never permanently settling his family down. He indicated that the Gaultiers had been married about sixteen years and that Edward had gone fishing during the season, and hunted and trapped in the fall, seemingly always abandoning his wife and children. He claimed Gaultier purposely left the family at the Thurston home, where Mrs. Gaultier acted as housekeeper to pay for herself and children's board. "One reason the defendant agreed to this arrangement," said Baldrey "was his desire to have his children taken care of, but then declared to be disturbed prior to the killing by the knowledge that his wife was seeking a divorce."

Few exhibits connected with the crime were introduced in court. Those displayed were the rifle, with which it was alleged the murder was committed, seven shells said to have been in the gun, and the prosecutor's hand-drawn map of the Thurston home interior where the murder had occurred. The map was used during the examination of state witnesses as to where the bodies were found in relationship to where Gaultier was standing. The only theatrics came from the state, when Baldrey held the rifle high above his head, displaying the weapon to the jury. He then curtly made a snide remark, how it was such a large caliber rifle with which to just hunt coons.

During the first day, the prosecution called its first witness, Alfred Wilson, who lived across the road from the Thurston home and to whom Gaultier had surrendered. Wilson was asked to give detail, the circumstances as to Gaultier's arrival at his home after killing his wife. The questions were cursory and intended to inform the jury of the events in question.

The next witness called to the stand was Constable Byron Kingsley, whom Wilson telephoned and who would eventually take Gaultier into custody. Baldrey asked Kingsley to recite the phone conversation with Wilson that night. Then, Baldrey asked of the events leading to collecting of the sheriff, doctor and coroner.

Kingsley's testimony indicated that Edward Gaultier was awaiting his arrival, and remained cooperative with Wilson and authorities. Before he transported the prisoner to Bellingham, Gaultier wrote out a confession for the constable, including details leading up to the night's events, after which he signed his statement, witnessed by the prosecutor. An astonished Walter Whitcomb leaped to his feet, declaring that this was the first he had heard of this and demanded to know why he wasn't privy to such knowledge.

The third witness was undertaker Henry Potter, who took charge of the bodies. He described the position, wounds, dress and related matters, and at the request of Mr. Baldrey, took in hand an umbrella rod and used it to point to essential spots on the map of the room drawn up by the prosecution. Testimony regarding Thurston was allowed to demonstrate the distance of separation between the bodies in the room.

But the focus of the courtroom's attention centered on the testimony of the three Gaultier children, Clara, Eddie and Charlie. All were considered "bright and quick to answering questions on direct and on cross-examination clearly and openly." The attorneys permitted wide leeway in the process of examining the young witnesses. Clara, it was noted by some, made a much better witness than the average adult, showing no signs of nervousness and making her answers "without hesitation or quibbling." The two boys were also clear in their memory of the tragedy in the early hours of the morning at the farmhouse.

"From the testimony given by the children," declared the *Herald*, "they are as near eyewitnesses to the shooting, as there are alive, save Gaultier himself." The shooting followed a period of depression; grief and doubt on the part of Gaultier. All the children, even Glen Thurston, told Gaultier that his wife and Horton Thurston frequently had shown affection for each other, kissing and manifesting their love in other ways. A few days before the tragedy, claimed the older children, Gaultier had announced that whoever is responsible for breaking up his home should suffer, and that he would get even. Thurston was present during these statements, but according to the witnesses, he made no comment on Gaultier's threat. The children testified that their father had frequently broken down and cried prior to the shooting. Mrs. Gaultier had talked to the children about her obtaining a divorce, and this subject, it appears, had been discussed more or less freely about the Thurston home. All the testimony bore out the fact that Gaultier always treated his family well, still turning over all his earnings to his wife, that the mother was kindly disposed to the children and that there had not been harsh words between the father and mother in front of the children. It developed in the children's testimony that a strong feeling existed between the cheating couple, which they took little pains to conceal, and the effect it had upon Gaultier.

The children were then asked to testify to the events, which occurred centering around the coon hunt. Earlier during the night of the tragedy, the children said, they had been in Blaine. Glen Thurston had been sent to bring them home. Reaching home about 8 pm, the conversation turned to a coon hunt at the suggestion of Gaultier. He asked the two oldest boys to go with him to get a coon that had been seen near the reservoir. It was not established fully whether Thurston was invited on the hunt. At any rate, the family went to bed about 9 pm, and at around midnight Gaultier roused the boys and left the house by the back door, leaving that door unlocked. Besides Clara and Horton, the three youngest Gaultier children were left at the house.

"Little" Clara Gaultier testified that she was awakened some time later when her mother left the bed in which she, Clara and the baby were sleeping. The mother spoke to the girl, who did not answer. She lay awake, however, until she saw her mother pass out of the bedroom into the kitchen. Then she fell asleep. Next a pounding at the back door awakened her, but being only partially awake, she again drifted off to sleep. Then a gunshot roused her. Clara did not know how long the time was between the pounding on the door and the shot. Moments later, she was thoroughly awakened by a second shot. This time she remained awake but didn't get up. In a few minutes her father came to the room carrying a lamp and said, "Sister, I have killed mama and Mr. Thurston." Accompanied by the children, he went to the home of Alfred Wilson across the road.

The hunting party, according to the boys' testimony, proceeded without incident. The coon was flushed and took to a tree from which it was impossible to dislodge. Gaultier built a fire and told the boys to stay and watch the tree while he returned for an axe. He appeared, according to the testimony, in no particular hurry, spending some time looking for his lost pipe. Not finding it, he took time to mark the place with some leaves and went back home, reminding the boys that he would be back soon. On his failure to return, the boys went home to discover the bodies of one's father and the other's mother. At this point in the trial, the state emphasized the established facts that Gaultier returned home for an axe, when a neighbor's house where an axe might have been obtained was nearer. Also, that he failed to ask Thurston to accompany him on the hunt for the coon, and that the boys were left in the woods alone.

Eddie Gaultier, a shy lad, whose mumbled answers could barely be heard, described how he and Glen Thurston returned to the house, where as his father confessed, he found his mother and Mr. Thurston in a compromising position. Eddie then offered further information about the relationship between Thurston and his mother, but was cut short by the defense that Gaultier wasn't on trial for Mr. Thurston's murder. When Baldrey asked when he had first heard of any discussion concerning divorce, Eddie said his mother and Mr. Thurston discussed it regularly. He said, "Father said, he would take mother away, but Mr. Thurston said if she didn't want to leave, father couldn't make her. He was angry, and claimed "he would get even with whomever was breaking up his family."

Baldrey looked back at Whitcomb, then the two asked for a sidebar. Pemberton instead called a recess. The attorneys admitted that one transgression overlapped the other and that it would be difficult, if not impossible, to separate the two murders throughout the trial. Whitcomb also reiterated that he wanted to see the written confession held by the prosecution.

Baldrey's questioning of Gaultier's children was designed to show that the cobbler had threatened Thurston before the rancher was slain. Whitcomb asserted that the prosecutor could not connect Thurston with the case because the defendant was not charged with Thurston's murder and if the state was going to try to prove premeditation, it should confine itself to threats against Mrs. Gaultier. Baldrey retorted that the whole affair was one transaction even though he was loath to draw Thurston into play for fear of turning the murder into a crime of passion, thus bolstering Whitcomb's theory of defense.

During the recess Gaultier smoked a cigar and visited with his children in the corridor. He hadn't seen them since his arrest and was pleased to be together again. The children asked when they could all go home. Reporters noted that there seemed no resentment among the children, who now lacked a mother to nurture them. Baldrey, walking out of the courtroom, stood watching the family for a moment. He noticed another man holding Gaultier's two-year-old. The man gave Gaultier a pouch of pipe tobacco. Baldrey had noticed the unknown man attending the trial from the back of the room. Curious as to the stranger's interest, the prosecutor asked an associate to check into him.

Back in the courtroom, Gaultier sat inside the railing just behind his attorney and appeared content with the proceedings. The only sign that he was nervous was his rolling of a lead pencil between his fingers a good part of the time.

Pemberton made two rulings. The first was in regard to Whitcomb's motion that the prosecution be required to turn over to the defense for perusal the confession written and signed by Gaultier on September 26, a few hours after the killing, in which the defendant admitted to the double murder. Judge Pemberton ruled that Baldrey need not turn over Gaultier's written and sworn confession to Whitcomb, as Baldrey had informed the court that he did not intend to introduce it as evidence.

Regarding a decision to allow evidence concerning premeditated threats against J. Horton Thurston, Pemberton had no interest in adding to his workload, and no one had yet come forth to file further charges to the affair. Even Thurston's stepchildren seemed to lay low on Horton's murder. The state surely didn't want to prosecute Gaultier for the murder, and although evidence could benefit the defense, Whitcomb feared going down that rabbit-hole would put him in the position of defending his client against two murders. It was agreed by all parties to allow testimony about Thurston's participation in the murder of Clara Gaultier, so long as the murder itself wasn't put on trial. Judge Pemberton would have to lay down instructions to the jury disregarding Edward Gaultier's alleged participation in the murder of one J. Horton Thurston.

Day Two: Wednesday, December 11, 1918

Attendance on the second day of trial was much larger. Almost every seat in the courtroom was taken. It seemed that the interest created by the morning newspaper's reporting outweighed fear of the influenza, tempting people to attend the trial. Witnesses to be examined by the defense on December 10 included: Blaine's recent ex-mayor George S. Shaw, Clifford H. Barlow, manager of a Bellingham harness shop, Elizabeth Wilson, Eddie and Charlie Gaultier, and the defendant Edward Gaultier.

George Shaw, former mayor of Blaine, was brought in as a character witness. He claimed to have known Edward Gaultier for some time, and held him in the highest esteem. He vouched that the cobbler was an outstanding member of his community. Clifford Barlow, another character witness, from whom Gaultier purchased his shoe leather, claimed him to be a rare breed of man who would not cuss, drink or gamble, but more importantly, he paid his bills. Both men claimed Gaultier was a hard worker. If he was away from home, it wasn't a case of desertion, but to earn enough money to feed his family. "If you didn't see the cobbler in his shop making or repairing shoes," they claimed, "he was found on a fish-trap working twelve days stretches. If the season was over, he was catching trash fish in the bay, or maybe hunting and trapping. If neither, he was back in his shop. Edward Gaultier would not desert his family."

The most interesting testimony of the day came from Elizabeth Wilson, who took the stand in the late morning. It was to her home that Gaultier took his children after the murders. Elizabeth and Alfred were upstairs sound asleep when barking dogs suddenly awakened her and the sound of a gunshot, which sounded to have come from the woods on the night of the murder. She testified that later she heard two muffled shots nearer her home. Her first thought was that Thurston had been out bear hunting. Fifteen minutes later she heard her Scotch Collie barking and children crying. Then a knock came at the front door. Upon opening the second floor window, she and her husband learned that it was Gaultier's knock. "What's going on, Ed?" called down Alfred. The cobbler told the couple what he had done and asked for shelter for himself and the children. He also asked that Constable Byron Kingsley be called.

Elizabeth Wilson objected to her husband opening the door to a man with a gun when she heard him admit to the crime of murder, testifying that Gaultier must have been insane when he shot his wife and that she did not want a crazy man in her house. Finally, Alfred went downstairs and admitted

Gaultier and his children. He lit a lamp on the table and immediately Gaultier asked that it be extinguished, explaining that he preferred the darkness, not wanting eyes on his face. He also started for Wilson's woodshed, but Alfred told him that if he was to be under his guard he must stay in the main house. However, he did extinguish the light, and Edward returned to his children, sitting on the kitchen floor.

Elizabeth, exhibiting no fear, followed her husband downstairs and confronted Gaultier herself, asking him why he killed his wife, adding that he could have had recourse to the law. "Why did you commit this awful sin and crime?" she questioned the man sitting on her floor. She testified that Gaultier answered: "Mrs. Wilson, I lost control of myself." Mrs. Wilson stated on the stand that she will never forget to her dying day the look of horror on Gaultier's face as it was seen when Constable Kingsley turned his flashlight on him. She testified that she was greatly impressed by the weeping children and father. Nothing, she asserted, had ever impressed her as being more pathetic.

Gaultier sat on the floor below the telephone with his children and out of range of the windows. Evidently he feared that the glass might be shattered by a shot and he expressed to the Wilsons his fear of vengeance from Glen Thurston, who was armed with a gun, having been with Gaultier and Eddie on the coon hunt that night. When Kingsley later covered him with his flashlight, he cowered in horror and begged him to turn it off.

Elizabeth Wilson testified that she had never heard a father give his children better advice than Gaultier gave his offspring as he sat weeping in the darkness trying to console them. He expressed sorrow over the commission of the crime. The father urged them to be good children and grow up to be loyal citizens. Especially did he urge "Little" Clara, his daughter, to "be a good and true woman."

When court reconvened in the afternoon, the state called Deputy Sheriff Alfred L. Medhurst to the stand, who told of his measuring the house and rooms. From those measurements, a plat of the inside of the house was drawn and introduced as evidence by the state. Walter Whitcomb quickly raised his objection that the plat was not accurate and was not sufficiently identified, leaving the matter open for acceptance. Medhurst did not have his memoranda of measurements with him and verified the distances from memory.

Medhurst was then questioned as to the positioning of the bodies, the location of the bullet holes in the bodies and the single hole found embedded in the wall of the room made by the bullet that killed Clara Gaultier. He also testified that he had tried opening the back door and said it could not be forced without breaking it down, owing to the security of the lock. Medhurst testified that the door had not been broken down. The defense discovered upon cross-examination that the witness had tested the door only when the night lock was on, there being only an ordinary key lock and a night latch Yale lock. The door, it was shown, was of light material and easily sprung.

Medhurst also told of the location of various articles of furniture in the house, including two couches, upon one of which the defense contended that Gaultier came upon Thurston and his wife in a compromising position. The prosecution, for what was deemed dramatics, had a battered dining room table, a tattered lounge and a well-worn stuffed chair, all from the Thurston home, arranged in the front of the courtroom facing the jury. Medhurst said one couch was weaker than the other and volunteered the information that he knew this because when he sat down on it, the legs gave way and the couch collapsed.

It appeared from the line of testimony that the manner of the location of the bodies, the couches and other articles of furniture would have a direct bearing on the case; at least considerable time was taken while Medhurst was on the stand rearranging the furniture. No one could figure out where Baldrey was going with the examination, as no immediate conclusion was made, except that Thurston had bad taste in furniture. The deputy sheriff continued on about how he found the scene of the crime. Thurston's body was found near the dining room behind the overturned stuffed chair, and Clara's was found in the living room. The deputy sheriff pointed out that the rooms were small, and that the bodies were but a few feet apart. Medhurst said he believed the shot that killed Mrs. Gaultier entered her body at the front and came out in the middle of her back. The bullet that killed Thurston did not pierce through his body.

Day Three: Thursday, December 12, 1918

The third day of trial opened with a few additional character witnesses for the defense. Florence E. Middleton and Theodore. F. Beaudet, immigration inspector at Blaine for several years, were called first.

On the stand, Mrs. Middleton claimed that the day before the murder, she saw Gaultier walking down the street and that he had a look of a crazed man on his face. "If I had been alone when I met him I would have run away," she testified. It wasn't just that he held the glare of death, but looked like death himself. Poor Edward Gaultier had lost a considerable amount of weight, his face was gaunt, his check bones were extended and his eyes were dark, empty sockets. With the distinctive limp to his walk, he looked worse for wear.

Theo Beaudet testified that Gaultier bore a good reputation, and he knew nothing against his character. He was surprised to see him look so ragged in appearance. "Someone must have put him through a hard time," he said, alluding to the man's wife.

Letters written by Mrs. Gaultier to some of her relatives were also admitted as evidence. In these were references of her intention to seek a divorce.

Lastly, the defendant Edward Gaultier limped on his gimp leg to the witness stand. "A murderer's love of the darkness, his fear of the light and contrition over his crime, and a father's love and concern for his children immediately after he had slain their mother" figured in the testimony offered at the trial, so said the *Bellingham Herald* later.

In his testimony, Whitcomb asked Gaultier to give his background history. He asked about his boyhood days, where he attended school and where he had worked during his life. Edward shared the story of his mother's early death and how his father had never recovered, eventually going insane. For the first time he shared that his aunt, his father's sister, had also been committed to an asylum for mental illness.

Whitcomb then jumped ahead, inquiring about his livelihood in Blaine. Gaultier said he owned a cobbler's shop and also fished for a living, eventually leaving his wife and children at the Thurston home with the understanding that his wife would serve the rancher as housekeeper. He recounted instances of his wife's loss of affection for him and it was while his attorney was questioning him concerning his comings and goings and related circumstances during the days immediately prior to the crime, that his feelings overcame him. For the most part, Gaultier talked with little hesitation.

As his emotions took over, Gaultier's strained voice recited the unfaithfulness of his wife and the effect of her relationship with J. Horton Thurston on his children. He claimed the situation to be heartbreaking. In his retelling, Gaultier was overcome, and on two or three occasions tears welled to his eyes and he halted in his testimony while he applied a handkerchief.

SLAYER IS OVERCOME AS HE RECITES STORY OF WIFE'S ALLEGED INFIDELITY

GAULTIER IS PLACED ON STAND BY THE DEFENSE

Blaine Slayer Tells Life Story— Dramatic Play of Emotions Figures In Trial Today.

ALL WOOD SHIP CONTRACTS EXCEPT WHERE $200,000 IS SPENT WILL BE CANCELLED

WASHINGTON, D. C., Dec. 11.—Cancellation of all outstanding contracts for construction of wooden ships where builders have not spent more than $200,000 on a ship has been determined upon by the shipping board.

This applies to yards on the Atlantic, Gulf and Pacific coasts. Contracts for 160 ships of this type were suspended recently, and many of these are affected by the decision, though officials of the board would not attempt today to estimate the number.

The contract cost of wooden vessels averages about $700,000 and it is understood the board's experts decided that

(Continued on Page Three.)

COUNTY IS LIBERAL IN CHARLES TAWES, WELL

Under cross-examination, the state questioned him very closely. There were a few sharp exchanges between Baldrey and Whitcomb, but nothing theatrical. The most intense part of Gaultier's testimony during the afternoon was the answers to the prosecutor's questions, tending to show that he had premeditated the murder of Thurston. In this most direct line of questioning regarding the murder, Baldrey was attempting to establish whether Clara's murder was premeditated as well, or a spontaneous act.

Gaultier told Baldrey that he made a distinction between "murdering" and "killing," whereupon the prosecutor thereafter used the word "kill." Answering Baldrey's question, "When did you first determine to 'kill' Thurston?" Gaultier replied that he had told the man to get ready to die, when he found him and his wife in a compromising position, and after he (Thurston) had offered him $1,000 and his interest in the jointly owned boat, if he would go away and leave him and Clara alone. The cobbler testified that his wife said: "Ed, take the money and go away." Gaultier asserted that he did not tell Thurston to get ready to defend himself, "but," testified Gaultier, "if anybody told me to get ready to die, I would know enough to get a gun. There were lots of guns in that house, and Thurston could have gotten a gun."

"Just before I fired the fatal shot," he testified, "I saw above my wife's head a vision of the children, who were smiling and apparently prompting me to kill her."

"You're telling the court, Mr. Gaultier, that an apparition appeared before you, and it told you to kill your wife?" asked the prosecutor, with a pleasing smirk. "Yes, indeed," claimed Gaultier. Loomis Baldrey repeated to the jury in a booming voice, "With a vision of his children smiling their approval of the contemplated crime above their mother's head, he fired the shot that killed his wife."

"Is there anything else we should know?" asked Baldrey, to which the defense objected, as leading the witness. Pemberton asked the prosecution if he had a question in mind. Baldrey asked the cobbler what he did after he shot his wife. Gaultier, tearing up, said he removed his wife's shoes after the killing.

SLAYER SAYS HE HAD VISION OF CHILDREN SMILING THEIR APPROVAL AS HE SHOT WIFE

Gaultier Makes Remarkable Statement In Murder Case—Alienist and Physician Testify That He Was Insane When He Committed Crime—Slayer Makes Distinction Between Murder and Killing.

Baldrey had stressed earlier the positioning of furniture within the room. He was exceedingly careful to get the exact positions of the sofas, the stuffed chair and dining room table, as near as possible. And he strove to exhibit the exact locations where Thurston and Mrs. Gaultier were when and after Gaultier entered the house. He carefully measured the distance between the sofa and the table and on several occasions had the defendant point out on the map the positions of the furnishings and his way of travel that night within the room.

Once the crime scene setup was complete, Loomis Baldrey posited to the court a new plausible scenario, one that could prove premeditated cold-blooded murder. With the boys out of the way on the coon hunt, and the youngest children fast asleep, Edward Gaultier saw an opportunity for revenge. He knew Thurston was sick and possibly in the living room, with, no doubt, his beautiful wife watching over her lover. Gaultier crept back into the house and quietly entered the living room, finding the couple together as he suspected. Baldrey's theory to the court is that nothing happened as the defendant had claimed, that the couple was never caught in a compromising position. A new hypothesis suggested that the rancher was sitting in his battered stuffed chair when Gaultier made his presence known. He shot Thurston in the abdomen, who then flew back over in the chair onto the floor. Then he killed his wife, who was witness to the whole affair. Baldrey contended that Thurston never attempted to escape the room. Furthermore, that neither one had a chance.

To this, an astounded Whitcomb leaped from his chair objecting in the harshest tone, bellowing once again, that the defendant was not on trial for the murder of J. Horton Thurston. Whitcomb claimed the state was poisoning the jury, and a mistrial should be declared at once. In response Baldrey claimed he was not charging Gaultier for Thurston's murder, but using the unfortunate rancher's demise as a plausible excuse to kill his own wife. Even Judge Pemberton thought the prosecution was over-stretching the facts. Pemberton allowed the hypothesis, but reminded the jury that Gaultier was not on trial for Thurston's murder and that the prosecution's theory was just that. The judge called a recess.

As the trial resumed, Gaultier was called back to the stand, where Baldrey changed tactics toward discrediting the defendant. He asked the accused about the man he had witnessed in the corridor the previous day. Who was this mysterious man, who had been sitting in on the case? Gaultier shrugged, claiming not to understand the question. Baldrey then sprang on the court the introduction of evidence intending to show that said man lived in Hamilton. His name was being withheld in the evidence, but he was the true father of Allen, Gaultier's two-year old son. Baldrey asked Gaultier if some tobacco had not been handed to him yesterday, indicating that it had come from the alleged father of his son. After the court overruled an objection to this testimony, the defendant answered that he had.

The cobbler testified that he already knew of the relation between this man and his wife. Gaultier, with respect to the reported fact that his youngest child was the offspring of his wife and the Hamilton man, said that Clara had told him such was the case, but that "she had lied to me in other matters." He admitted on the stand that he had received $140 from the Hamilton man, in support for raising his son, but that he received not a penny for himself.

Furthermore, Gaultier could not see where the prosecution was going with this line of questioning, as he has lived a life of embarrassment and his little one was no embarrassment to him. He said he loved him as his own.

During the rest of the afternoon's session, Baldrey finished his rebuttal, calling Sheriff William Wallace and Deputy Sheriff Alfred Medhurst to the stand. The two testified that the night of the crime was foggy. Gaultier had testified that it was clear. Byron Kingsley, the constable who arrested Gaultier, and Medhurst contradicted Gaultier's testimony that the lock on the back door was broken, the defendant stating that he had broken it upon entering the house after returning from the unfinished coon hunt to find, as he said, his wife and Thurston in a compromising position.

Day Four: Friday, December 13, 1918

Day four of the trial opened with short testimony from several doctors who had been following the trial from the courtroom. Dr. Edward W. Stimpson gave expert opinion that Gaultier was not insane when he committed the murder. Dr. Stimpson, Dr. William W. Ballaine and Dr. Orville E. Beebe, declared that in their opinion, no man could reason and remember as Gaultier did and be insane.

In rebuttal, the sworn opinion of Dr. William C. Keyes, a Bellingham physician, and Mrs. J. J. Mustard, an alienist, who traveled to Bellingham from Olympia to study the trial, concurred that Gaultier was indeed insane when he murdered his wife. None but the opposing attorneys knew Mrs. Mustard was an alienist.

In his closing argument, prosecutor Baldrey referred to the fact that Gaultier had married his wife when she was only 16 years-old, and he 26, before her "character had been formed and fully developed." That he had afterward taken her from place to place, had sent her out as a traveling saleswoman, and had left her alone in his store while he went hunting, trapping and fishing. All this was evidently intended to show that he had not looked after her welfare as he should have done. Continuing, the prosecutor stated Gaultier had permitted her to receive gifts from other men and that he only complained after he had received a bill for a suit that some other man had given her. Baldrey contended that the defendant's anger was not caused by the gift, but that it arose from the fact that he had to pay for the suit. He introduced the anonymous man from Hamilton who was the father of Edward's youngest child. Baldrey told of Gaultier receiving money and tobacco from this man and held that all along the defendant knew that his wife had shown a weakness for other men, and he tried to show by these transactions that Gaultier looked on her doings with an eye toward financial or material advantage.

At this stage, after Baldrey had talked for about twenty minutes, Mr. Whitcomb objected that the prosecution was not confining itself strictly to the evidence and asked that the court reporter be called in to take the argument. The court so ordered. Baldrey then asked jurors whether they would not have removed their wives from temptation. The defendant, he held, knew that there was something wrong from the statements of his own children and from his own personal knowledge, his wife bringing it to his attention in part by her expressed intentions of getting a divorce.

Baldrey acknowledged that he did not blame Gaultier for being depressed, "but," he asked the jurors, "in that case would you have gone coon hunting and left your wife alone in a house with another man, and then return…unless you had intended to kill? Why did Gaultier not send the boys who were with him for an axe?" Answering his own question, Baldrey claimed that it was because he did not want Glen Thurston at the house.

Then Baldrey brought out that Gaultier had experienced "a burst of acute insanity" when he saw Thurston and his wife together on that fateful night, but he had sense enough to think of his children sleeping on the other side of the partition and of his wife, for he had ordered Thurston to "get ready to die." He also became sane when he shot his wife, Baldrey stated in an attempt to show premeditation.

Mr. Baldrey suggested that Thurston and Mrs. Gaultier were not up that night for adulterous purpose, but that Thurston had been unwell. He had gotten up from bed on that account, and that possibly, Mrs. Gaultier heard him and had risen to help him. Baldrey proposed that the two victims might not have even been on the sofa at all. Thurston may have been in the toppled chair when shot, and to dramatically illustrate the point the prosecutor sat in the very chair himself and pointed out to the jury the fact that the rancher had been shot in abdomen. He and the chair would have fallen over on impact, he demonstrated. Baldrey stood up and continued, "Gaultier intended to shoot Thurston regardless, and may have had to chase his wife to finish her too."

The defense's closing remarks came in part from a 10,000 word hypothetical question regarding the defendant's sanity, posed to the doctors in the court earlier, and this time condensed for the jury to assess:

"Assuming Edward loved his wife, Clara; and that he has no recollection of some of the events that transpired at the time of the shooting…and assuming that he immediately gave himself up and told his neighbor to send for the sheriff; that immediately after the shooting he was pale and excited and looked wild eyed. Assuming also that always prior to this time he had been a peaceable law abiding man and assuming that during the two weeks preceding the shooting he had cried many times, and assuming that he dearly loved his little daughter and that she a few days before the shooting had told him that she had seen her mother kissing Thurston, and that on several occasions at night her mother had arisen from bed and gone in her night gown to Thurston's room and stayed there for some length of time and

that he believed these things and that his little daughter understood their significance and finally assuming that his father's sister
had been insane and was insane when she died, and that his father
was insane and died in an insane asylum."

"Assuming all these things to be the facts, would the man under
investigation, in your opinion, be sane or insane at the time of
the shooting? Was the defendant in your opinion at the time of
the shooting in such mental condition that he couldn't distinguish
between right and wrong? Was the defendant able to choose between right and wrong with reference to the shooting or was he
by reason of mental disease unable to exercise his will with reference to such act?"

The court began reading instructions to the jury about 10:30 am and
finished by 11:00. In these were defined legal meanings of first and second-
degree murder, manslaughter or insanity at the time of the murder. The jury
was reminded that if Gaultier was not guilty, but insane at the time of the
crime's commission, but that he is not insane now and became sane and mentally responsible between the date of the crime and the date of the trial, they
must make that determination. The court directed the jury to take into consideration the evidence showing that Gaultier had borne a good reputation.

After being out for twenty hours, the jury at 11:15 the following morning returned a verdict of guilty in second-degree in the murder of his wife,
Clara Gaultier. Because premeditation could not be shown, the verdict stood,
and the case was not appealed.

Edward Gaultier took the verdict calmly according to some witnesses
and nervously according to others. He was willing to take a life sentence,
considering that he was 43 years of age, the judgment imposed closely ap-
proximated a life term so far as he was concerned. "I've done wrong and

am willing to take my medicine." The penalty, an indeterminate sentence between fourteen to twenty years, was imposed upon the cobbler.

Epilogue

Edward S. Gaultier was received at the state penitentiary in Walla Walla on January 6, 1919, becoming inmate 8683.

Edward S. Gaultier was received at the state penitentiary in Walla Walla on January 6, 1919, becoming inmate No. 8683. Washington State Archives, Olympia.

On January 13, a written statement was made after the trial by the prosecuting attorney's office, and placed by Loomis Baldrey into the file of Gaultier. Inside he disclosed the state's theory on the murder case, not pursued for lack of evidence:

> "The prosecution believed Gaultier knew of his wife's unfaithfulness and that he connived it so long as he benefited by it, and that he expected to benefit from Thurston, who was supposed to be well situated financially, and that when his wife finally revolted at this manner of living and decided to get a divorce, he decided to make way with her. A number of incidents support this view.

Among them, letters of Mrs. Gaultier and statements made by her."

While we'll never know if Baldrey was on to something, it is curious that the prosecution failed to dig further and uncover other tidbits concerning Gaultier's earlier incriminating history. According to the state penitentiary inmate register, Edward Gaultier had been incarcerated twice prior to coming to Washington State. The first was at age 25, in Kent, Wisconsin, in 1900, the crime unrecorded, but he returned again in 1902 for embezzlement.

Gaultier and his attorney Walter Whitcomb applied for and were denied parole in December 1922, December 1924, March 1926, 1927 and in 1928.

In 1922, Loomis Baldrey wrote, "I believe Judge Pemberton's attitude is the same as mine...I have always felt that he premeditated the act, but the jury felt otherwise. As to whether or not he has repented and would never do a similar act, those who have had close watch of him for several years, are in a better position to judge than I am."

Walter Whitcomb remembered Gaultier as an "excitable little Frenchman-like the French-Canadian of Minnesota and Wisconsin," when in 1926 he wrote a plea of clemency to Governor Louis F. Hart. He had been in the penitentiary eight years. "The chief turnkey at the jail told me that he has been a good model prisoner... he has not been locked up night and day for four years, and he is now the Guard on the Gate at the penitentiary. He is a shoemaker in charge of an attempt to establish a tannery there."

Edward Gaultier eventually won his release on December 5, 1929, which was finally approved by Governor Ronald Hartley.

As for the Gaultier children, Loomis Baldrey claimed Edward allowed his wife's brothers to adopt Clara May, and another relative to adopt Allen. Eddie and Charlie were enrolled in a Catholic school. Walter Whitcomb, however, claims that the Gaultier children were parceled out after the trial to new homes; the boys, Eddie and Charlie were put up for adoption, while

Clara May and Allen were passed onto a Catholic school to be raised. In 1924, Whitcomb wrote in a letter to the governor that the girl had made an unfortunate marriage.

Here's what is known: Eddie died in Seattle on April 6, 1924. At 21, Eddie was riding on a motorcycle when an automobile hit him. Thrown from his cycle, he collided into a telephone pole, fracturing his skull. From his obituary we learn a little more. Aunt Clara Lindsey, who helped raise her brother in Iowa, now lives at 406 Holly Street in Bellingham. Clara Lindsey, who kept a sharp eye on her sister-in-law's activities in Deming and Maple Falls, had filed suit against her own husband William on grounds of "cruel and inhuman [sic] treatment, and non-support." She won separation in December 1923, along with custody of her ten-year-old son.

Sister Clara May married a McChesney who lived in Auburn. Was it an unfortunate marriage? By the 1950s she was Clara May Woods. Allen indeed was adopted by one of his mother's brothers, becoming Allen S. Newell, and dying on July 23, 1950, leaving behind a wife, a son, and three daughters. From this we learn that the other brother, Charlie, ran a paint dealership in Seattle.

What eventually happened to Edward Gaultier isn't known. In a bizarre turn of events, in December 1929, just out of prison, he remarried a woman named Lona Gay McGill. McGill was recently divorced, just 15 months before. Edward was 54 years old to Lona's 31. In 1931, the couple was residing in Everson, where he once again established a cobbler shop. Gaultier's bad luck with women continued. On July 13, 1934 she sued him for divorce. The charges were "cruel and inhuman [sic] treatment." She was soon remarried again. The last we know of Gaultier, he took a trip to Alaska.

Glen Thurston, through the efforts of his stepbrother Noble McClurg, made sure that young Glen, now sixteen and a minor, would retain his father's property. Noble got his five brothers and sisters to sign off on any claims, giving Glen some advantage from his unfortunate life.

Nothing remains of the old Thurston home today. On the Sweet Road between Harvey Road and Dahl Lane there is about an eighth-mile of road frontage where his home may have been at one time. The plat is wooded and gives way to a ravine. Somewhere around the Dahl reservoir, just northeast of the farm, is where Gaultier left Eddie and Glen to stand guard over the treed raccoon while he fetched an axe.

The curtain now drops on the stage of this love triangle.

J. Horton Thurston buried next to his second wife, May Thurston 1871-1917. Blaine Cemetery. Photo taken by the author.

"…laugh Pagliacci through the pain that poisons your heart."

SOURCES

www.ancestry.com

Arbuckle, Barnes-Hinds, Post and Reichhardt, "A Symbol of Our Heritage,…The Old Fir Tree" Blaine Centennial History 1884-1984. Profile Publications Inc., Lynden, Washington. 1984.

Bellingham Herald: 9/26/1918, 9/27/18, 9/28/18, 10/3/18, 10/7/18, 10/16/18, 12/9/18, 12/10/18, 12/11/18, 12/12/18, 12/13/18, 12/14/18, 1/16/1919.

www.geneologybank.com

Heritage Quest

"Hypothetical Question" (No. 2298) Closing remarks of Counsel.

Whatcom County Assessor & Treasurer – Property Details.

U.S. Census. Whatcom County, Washington, California, Illinois, Nevada: 1880, 1900, 1910, 1940.

Whatcom County Index: No. 2298 9/28/19 Book 7.

Whatcom County Sheriff Records, Washington State Regional Archives, 1918.

Washington State Archives Inmate No. 5683, 1919 Inmate File Box 377.

State of Washington, VS. Edward S. Gaultier, Information for Murder in the First-Degree Case Files.

State of Washington, VS. Edward S. Gaultier, Statement of Prosecuting Attorney.

Washington State Penitentiary Clemency No. 4718.

Washington State Penitentiary, Penitentiary Inmate Register.

Whatcom County Auditor Grantor Indirect and Grantee Direct Records, 1918-1919.

Chapter 9
Sam Thompson

Samuel Thompson, or simply "Sam," as he was known by the folks of Maple Falls, was "just a happy-go-lucky Negro, always with a smile on his face and absolutely harmless," according to the local newspapers. He resided in Maple Falls for several years, spending most of his time in the saloons and card houses, earning his "bed and meals by his cheerfulness and his singing and dancing." When Bellingham train excursions passed through, Sam was always at the station and favored visitors with "old Southern melodies and danced jigs on the platform," where he received coins for his entertainment.

The Maple Falls train platform where Sam would dance for the tourist coin. Circa: 1900s. Laura Jacoby's Galen Biery Collection.

Little is known about Sam Thompson's life. The 1910 census claims Sam to be 56 years old, although his death certificate would later indicate 65.

He stated that he was born in Virginia, and his parents as well. His generally mysterious age placed him in the realm of probability of being a southern slave for eleven to twenty years. He was married fifteen years, but we know nothing of his wife. It appears she was not living in Maple Falls. When not performing for a living, Sam worked a few hours after saloon closings as a janitor. At other times Sam worked at the Gerdrum saw mill nearby.

Tuesday, December 20, 1910, wasn't one of Marion (Merry) McKinney's busier evenings. As proprietor of the Maple Bar Hotel & Saloon in Maple Falls, he strove to keep a clean and respectable establishment. Merry certainly had his challenges from the area's logging crews, prospectors, miners, trappers and hunters, but mid-week was a tad slower. Of course, McKinney still had his share of arguments, fights, drunkards, and the occasional busted furniture with which to contend. But on that particular wintery Tuesday evening, all hell would break loose.

The Wilds of Maple Falls

In 1907, McKinney had leased Lot 21-9 of the Chase addition to Maple Falls, and there he operated his establishment, first under the name of the Maple Bar Saloon, and later the Wahaloon Saloon. The Chase addition was a newer section of town, developed when the Bellingham Bay & British Columbia Railway was built. Of course the saloon was really run by Mrs. McKinney, who opened the saloon daily while Merry worked in the woods. After a hard day's labor, he would return home to operate the saloon during evening hours. Mrs. McKinney would stay on and prepare the meals.

The township of Maple Falls was growing fast as the timber industry expanded. The 1911 County Directory claimed a population of five hundred, but the following year claimed only 250. Still, a considerable amount of new businesses being built indicated that the timber industry was on the rise. The philosophy of the day was that the big trees would last forever and that an infrastructure was necessary to support continuation of their harvest. In just a few years several butcher shops, numerous saloons, hotels and an even an opera house were built. The railway had a depot, which brought further investors. The Modern Woodsmen of America constructed a meeting hall for all the logging organizations to use. Looking down Maple Avenue and Lake Street, one could see the hanging door signs for Wheeler's bakery, Nittenburg's Cigar store, Phillips grocery store, Fitch's General store, A. L. Confectionery, Allen H. Strickfaden's Maple Falls *Leader* newspaper, and Leslie Haggard's general merchandise. Toward the woods behind the hustle and bustle of the business section, two houses of ill fame were tucked away for the workingman.

Early Maple Falls, as the town was on the rise. Circa: 1903-05. Laura Jacoby's Galen Biery Collection.

Maple Falls was an unincorporated township situated on a crossroads. The east to west road ran from Glacier, at the base of Mount Baker, to Bellingham on the bay. On the north/south interior axis, it lay between Sumas, on the Canadian border, and Sedro-Woolley in Skagit County to the south. The small town had a "wild west" edge about it, with roughnecks, loggers and homesteaders cultivating the surrounding land. Centrally located on a rail-line, and becoming a communication hub, it was situated in the perfect location for many of the logging companies' offices. For those illicit individuals wanting to be stealthy in their movements, traveling through the wooded interior was the preferred conduit for various forms of illegal trafficking. Old-timers and early law enforcement notoriously knew the north-south corridor as "Smugglers Pass." It was the perfect route to bring illegal immigrants, primarily Chinese, across the border for cheap labor.

One infamous smuggler of that pass was "Terrible" Jake Terry, a former inmate of San Quentin Penitentiary. Terry smuggled hundreds of Chinese from Canada through Sumas toward Sedro-Woolley, extorting large sums of money from poor immigrants looking for work and a better life in America. Cocky and defiant of law enforcement, Terry was known to give the sheriff his route and time and day of crossing and then defy the sheriff to catch him. One night, the sheriff did!

Frances Bruce Todd, in her history of Whatcom County, *Trail Through the Woods*, recounts one such story:

> "As early as 1890s word was received by those patrolling the border of a band of Chinese that were heading south by way of Acme and Wickersham. They were lead by five, well-armed smugglers. The law officers came upon them during the night as they were nearing Sedro-Woolley. The patrol laid low until daylight. They captured the Chinese at the break of dawn, but with the loss of two of their men."

Todd wrote that at one time U.S. entry points from Canada were closed to immigrants. The four entry points were Sumas, Washington; Portal, North Dakota; Malone, New York; and Richmond, Vermont. With only these stations for foreigners to legally cross into the U.S., there was a great deal of immigrant smuggling taking place around these points. There was certainly not enough manpower to patrol the long border stretching from Blaine to beyond Sumas, under the cover of dark forests where no roads existed.

Smuggler's Pass, descending through the Maple Falls region, had many secret routes. From 1890-1924, only a handful of border patrol agents were assigned to the area, covering hundreds of square miles. These officers had no office or housing, and were given little with which to work. Those assigned to the region of Blaine to Sumas, south through the Columbia Valley toward Maple Falls, Acme, and Sedro-Woolley, considered themselves in exile.

During winter months, Maple Falls experienced fewer visitors. Saloons were filled mostly with locals and the area's working class. Most customers were known regulars, including some of the more colorful residents of the community, such as Millard Burnside, a trapper and hunter who lived somewhere in the hills above town. Burnside owned a fully-grown pet bear, but he wasn't allowed to bring him into town unless it was leashed with a chain. Even so, saloon owners fought with Burnside constantly over bringing the bear inside their establishments. Burnside complained bitterly that it was inhumane to keep the beast outside in the cold.

Grizzled prospectors, coming down off their Mount Baker claims, liked wintering in the small town, shunning the overcrowded expense of the big city of Bellingham. Most arrived wearing the same clothing they had on their backs when they left for the mountain in the spring. They were content staying close to their own kind. Besides, the money they earned from months of prospecting lasted longer in Maple Falls, with its cheaper drink and women. For them, the return to civilization known as "Maples Falls" was an annual reunion with old friends and fellow prospectors.

James Hill

Many townships are notorious for their legendary bullies, who torment the populace for sport. Maple Falls was no different. For a brief time, that holy terror was Jim Hill. Those who knew him considered Hill a mean-spirited, horrible, despicable and unpredictable beast of a man. Folks stayed out of his path, thinking Hill to be undoubtedly insane, as he was frequently called. He displayed no remorse for his actions or the pain he inflicted on others. Today he would be considered psychotic. Feared, hated, and despised, Jim Hill was avoided at all costs.

Suspiciously, Hill was noted to always have money, and he flaunted it. No one knew where it came from, as he was never known to work a day in his life, aside from an occasional few weeks at a time in the logging camps. Rumor had it that he smuggled Chinese from Canada, working the "Smuggler's Pass." It would come as no surprise, as Hill was always out in the countryside for days at a time. Others claimed he rode with a gang that had robbed banks and saloons in the region. The Janisch Saloon had been recently robbed in the town of Concrete, on the Upper Skagit River. Coincidentally, Hill wasn't in Maple Falls at the time of that holdup, but when he returned, he was flush with cash. Considering his reputation, town folk were suspicious.

Hill was infamous in the Skagit Valley as well. While a six-year resident in Concrete, he was alleged to have committed various strong-arm crimes, and was suspected of many other crimes from Sedro-Woolley to Rockport and Marblemont. Concrete authorities were always watching Hill. Each time they thought they had him, he was "always ready with a pretty fair alibi," said the Skagit sheriff.

We know more about Jim Hill's disposition than his physical features. The most detailed description came from a "special" sent to the *Bellingham Herald* from Concrete, dated January 6, 1911, about three weeks after the Janisch Saloon holdup. Concrete authorities knew their description fit Hill's profile, but out of fear, the barkeep may not have wanted to finger Hill by name. He reported the robber was wearing a blue flannel shirt, slouched hat, black overcoat and black pants, and light colored shoes. Hill didn't have much of a selection of wardrobe, and the description the barkeep gave matched clothes much like Hill's, said authorities.

Jim Hill was said to be fairly large, muscular and square-shouldered. He stood six feet in height and weighed two hundred pounds. He had a fair complexion, light hair and a growth of beard. As for his age, it was figured he was between 30 and 40 years old. Quite frankly, no one was close enough to Hill to dare ask about his background, but it was well known he was originally from Tennessee and carried a distinctive accent backing that claim.

Authorities searched the Upper Skagit, but Jim Hill had not been seen in Concrete since the morning of the holdup. Regardless, Concrete authorities concluded Hill was their man, and called him out by name.

The Act

Tuesday, December 20, 1910, was a cold winter day in Maple Falls. Jim Hill first strolled into the Maple Falls Hotel, owned and operated by William Milton Copes and his wife Anna Mae. Anna Mae detested Hill, as he was a despicable drunk, and was prone to cussing and spitting tobacco juice on her floor. Hill often threatened customers and drove them out. She didn't like the fact that he was always well armed with his rifle and six-shooter. She feared he would get drunk one day and kill someone. She also dreaded the day when her husband would be called upon to stand up to Hill to defend their business, or their lives. Before he became too inebriated, she would usually toss Hill out so he could become the problem of some other saloon.

As usual that afternoon, Hill had his six-shooter belted around his waist and his rifle in hand. He laid the rifle across a table and had a few drinks. He may have eaten some dinner, as Mrs. Copes was known as a swell cook. Upon seeing he was well armed and knowing his character, most customers gave him wide berth. Several hardy timber-men in the saloon, knowing Hill, happily exchanged words. Before long, Hill would wear out what little welcome he had and move along to the next establishment. Eventually, he arrived at Marion (Merry) McKinney's Maple Bar Hotel Saloon.

The Maple Bar Hotel had a small number of guests that night. In the saloon, a few sat having a late night supper cooked by Mrs. Emma McKinney. On the other side of the room a band of local boys were playing a game of cards. With them was Leslie McAllister. Merry was tending bar and pouring a few drinks. Jerome (Slim) Simmons, a shingle mill employee and sawyer staying overnight at the hotel, had a drink already in hand. A husky woodsman at 31, Slim had been working the area's mills for nearly a decade. He was conversing with Alfred Casey, a filer from a local mill. Also in the saloon that night was Sam Thompson, singing the southern tunes for which he was noted and dancing up a storm when asked, for a few coins of course.

The door soon flung open, blowing in a stream of cold air along with a staggering Jim Hill. Hill walked in like he owned the place, tossing his rifle down on a table as he always did. First thing, Hill eyed the card table and tried getting into a game, but was shunned. Grumbling, he staggered over to Merry McKinney for a drink.

Looking over at Sam, he told the "n___ to shut up, as he didn't want to hear any of his noise." Furthermore, Hill said he left the South to get away from Sam's kind. Sam stopped singing, but Simmons, who knew Hill, told him to lay off poor old Sam, that he was the best entertainment in town. Hill grunted, ignoring Simmons. Hill was drunk from his previous stops that night, and he wanted to play cards. No one would play with him, so he thought a little bribery might help.

As Jerome Simmons told it, Hill invited the boys to have a drink with him, on his dollar if they would let him into a game, but he told the card players, he "would not buy a drink for Thompson, the n___."

The boys relented and took Hill up on the offer, kicking back a chair for him to join in the game. The hotel guests encouraged Sam to sing some more. He complied. All seemed to be fine in the hotel after that. Hill was happy for the company, the guests and locals were drinking and throwing coins at Sam to sing and perform a jig for them. As the evening progressed, Simmons retired to his room upstairs.

While Simmons was preparing his bed, Jim Hill was playing a card game downstairs. Sam Thompson had been persuaded to sing another song from the old South. Drunk, attempting to concentrate, and possibly losing, Hill yelled at Thompson to "shut his God-dammed mouth or he would shut it for him."

When Sam failed to comply with Hill's warning, the two hundred pound bully leapt out of his chair, throwing it backward to the floor. Before anyone realized what was happening, including Sam himself, Hill grabbed his rifle in a ferocious display of violence and slammed its butt squarely down on Sam's jaw using all his brute force.

Upstairs Simmons heard Thompson scream, "For God's sake don't hit me any more!"

No reason is ascribed for the assault upon Thompson. Witnesses of the affray declared that the attack was absolutely without provocation. After striking Thompson and knocking him down, Hill leveled his rifle at a number of guests of the hotel, in front of whom the assault occurred. He threatened them until most were "driven upstairs under threat of instant death should any not obey."

Samuel Thompson screamed out in pain, bleeding profusely from his mouth, as Hill started kicking him, calling him all sorts of vile names. The hotel guests scrambled back to their rooms, but many of the locals tried rushing Hill in an attempt to save Sam.

With a crazed glare, Hill held them off with his rifle. Merry Copes was trying to protect his guests and hold back his screaming wife. At some point in the struggle, Hill dragged the dazed Thompson out of the hotel and into the frozen street, shouting more obscenities. In his rage, Hill clocked Sam again with his rifle on the back of his head.

Jerome Simmons said later that he "rushed out into the street with several other men following behind. Thompson was there with Hill lying on the ground. When the men rushed to the scene, Hill held them at bay with his rifle, daring them to come on."

Simmons slowly worked his way around to the backside of the desperado, who was slowly walking backward toward him. Marion McKinney kept Hill's attention, telling him not to do anything rash, that killing Sam wasn't worth doing prison time for. Simmons gradually drew near the enraged man, watching for a clear opportunity to rush him.

As Hill came within reach, Simmons said he threw his arms around Hill, hurling him to the ground. McKinney leapt upon him, and wrested the rifle away. The other men then jumped in and Hill was captured, placed under citizen's arrest and taken to the small local jail cell. On the way, Simmons said Hill made the following remark in a mocking tone: "It was a shame to hit old Sam that way." Simmons said that Hill seemed to take the whole matter as a joke. Simmons expressed the opinion that Hill was crazy.

The street in front of the hotel where Sam Thompson was badly beaten by the deranged Jim Hill. Laura Jacoby's Galen Biery Collection.

Sam Thompson was carried back into the hotel, and a doctor was fetched for him. Poor Sam was beaten and bruised, but he took the worst of it from Hill's rifle hit to his jaw, which hung limp, and wouldn't close. It was no doubt shattered. The doctor's priority was just to stop Sam's bleeding. There was nothing more he could do for the jaw. He would need to be rushed to Bellingham for better medical attention. All they could do was wait for the train to Bellingham.

The Following Day

Sam Thompson, in an immense amount of pain, was taken to Bellingham the following day by train, where he was admitted into St. Luke's Hospital. The Maple Falls doctor was right when he presumed that Sam's jaw was shattered.

Saint Luke's Hospital in Bellingham. After two weeks of tremendous suffering and torment from his injuries, Sam Thompson succumbed in his hospital bed on the morning of Tuesday, January 3, 1911. Laura Jacoby's Galen Biery Collection.

Deputy Sheriff Wallace Coleman left that same morning for Maple Falls, armed with a warrant sworn out by prosecuting attorney Livesey, charging Hill with assault in the second degree. Colman, not taking any chances, loaded his rifle to retrieve the burly troublemaker.

MAPLE FALLS MAN INJURED IN ROUGH HOUSE

Sam Thompson Is Brought to City for Medical Treatment—Jaw Is Smashed In Row—Warrant Is Issued for One Jim Hill Who Is Charged With Playing Role of Bad Man.

On his arrival he discovered his prisoner had escaped the Maple Falls jail the night before, soon after he was locked up. Whether he broke out himself or was released by friends in Maple Falls, Coleman was unable to ascertain, but he suspected he had help. Acting on this belief, Coleman arrested two of Hill's associates, but was later forced to release them, having little proof and no charges upon which to hold them.

On December 22, Sheriff Spencer B. Van Zandt formed and led a very large posse into the woods with hopes of capturing Jim Hill. The posse was armed with rifles and revolvers and their job was to scour the forested region between the Columbia Valley, Sumas and Maple Falls. Deputy Sheriff Wallace Coleman was already in the hills surrounding Maple Falls, following up on reports from residents who were acquainted with Hill, declaring they had seen the fugitive in the vicinity over the past few days.

The *Bellingham Herald* claimed the "country in that part of the county was heavily against the pursuers," as the vicinity of Columbia Station and Maple Falls was "wild and there is only one chance in many that Hill will be found, if he is hiding in the woods."

SHERIFF HEADS POSSE IN SEARCH OF HILL

Large Force of Men Armed With Rifles and Revolvers Is Today Searching Woods for Jim Hill, Who Is Wanted on Charge of Death of Sam Johnson, Colored, Who Is Thought to Have Died From Effect of Injury Inflicted by Hill—Search Also Made at Maple Falls.

Those who knew Hill declared that he always carried a small arsenal. When he worked in the logging camps he always carried a revolver in his belt, along with the rifle with which he cracked Sam Thompson in the jaw. "Jim Hill," according to Maple Falls residents talking with *Herald* reporters, "tried to give the impression that he was a bad man," and in that he was successful. "His first act, upon reaching Maple Falls," they stated, "was to become intoxicated." Once fully intoxicated, he would go on his rampages.

Death

After two weeks of tremendous suffering and torment from his injuries, Sam Thompson succumbed in his hospital bed on the morning of Tuesday, January 3. His jaw was so badly smashed that he was unable to eat, except what he could manage through a glass tube. His face was grossly enlarged and discolored. One of poor Sam's eyes bulged from his head, a bloody mass. Red-yellow mucus drained from his ear. There was little the doctors could do to relieve his pain, other than try to make him comfortable with laudanum and opiates. Even those powerful painkillers only dulled his pain. Headlines read: "Murder Charge Hangs Over Maple Falls." Underscored with, "Negro Dies From Blow Struck By Hill."

On February 27, 1911, a coroner's inquest was performed and reported in the Proceedings of County Commissioners of Whatcom County. Coroner N. Whitney Wear presided over the inquest, reviewing the findings of Sam's death. Several witnesses were called upon to hear testimony: Jerome Simmons, Alfred Casey, William and Emma Copes, Leslie McAllister and Marion McKinney. Others included Dr. I. W. Powell, Sam's physician and surgeon, and Dr. J. Reid Morrison, who performed the autopsy. The six men hearing evidence as jurors at the proceedings included S. E. Mullin, H. H. Griggs, Joseph Romaine, Charles LaFray, A. H. Pratt and Frank P. McQuirk. Attorney Howard Thompson was also in attendance.

Doctors Morrison and Powell were the first witnesses to give testimony. Both testified that death was caused by the injury to the jaw. Death, they said, was due to one or both of the following two causes found in an autopsy conducted the previous day: infection of the jawbone and infection at the base of the brain, both caused by the injury to the jaw. It was noted that gangrene had set in, and that when cut, the wounds oozed with a thick milky pus. Both physicians agreed Sam suffered a very painful death.

Two witnesses testified that Jim Hill had the "appearance of mania and both expressed the belief that he was crazy." Evidence was also brought forth to show that Hill was a native of Tennessee and harbored a distinct dislike for negroes. As the inquest drew its final verdict, Attorney Thompson warned the jury not to consider the evidence touching on Jim Hill's mental condition, as he required observation to make that determination.

As the probe into Jim Hill's crimes was just getting under way that December and early January of 1911, Whatcom County was hit by another tragedy that pushed the Sam Thompson case to the side and for a short time spotlighted Jim Hill again. News arrived from the county hamlet of Acme, Washington, that Justice of the Peace Audrey A. Galbraith and Key City logging manager W. B. Stevens had been gunned down in a firefight with two desperados. But that's another story!

In the first twenty-four hours of the manhunt for the Acme killers, the theory was that Jim Hill participated in the killings. It was believed Hill had finally snapped after striking down Thompson. Now a fugitive, he was desperate and had nothing to lose. It was rightly pointed out that it was no coincidence that the killers had attempted to secure work in the most out-of-the-way logging camp in the county, far up the South Fork of the Nooksack River, where Hill might hide out. "No better hiding place could be found than an isolated logging camp," said the *Bellingham Herald*.

However, as the facts unfolded and the killers of Galbraith and Stevens were apprehended, it became evident that Jim Hill had no involvement. Nothing was ever heard from Jim Hill again, and he soon faded into obscurity.

What happed to Jim Hill? Where did he go? Hill slipped away into the night on December 21 and disappeared from history. It is probable that he knew his time was up in Whatcom County, and the Upper Skagit region. He may have decided it was time to leave. If Hill had worked the Smuggler's Pass, moving human contraband, he surely had solid connections across the border. It seems plausible that the smuggler may have smuggled himself into Canada, joining his counterparts there, where he may have carried on in human trafficking. Of course, that is all speculative.

Poor Sam Thompson, with no family to care for his remains, found himself buried in the Potters Field of the Bellingham Bayview Cemetery. He has no marker or headstone.

SOURCES

Bellingham Herald: 12/20/1910, 1/4/1911, 1/5/11, 1/6/11.

Cemetery Records of Whatcom County: Series II, Vol. XII, Bayview Cemetery through 1985. Compiled and Published by: Whatcom Genealogical Soc. 1999.

Coroner's inquest reported in the Proceedings of County Commissioners of Whatcom County. February 27, 1911.

U.S. Census. Whatcom County, Washington. 1910.

Chapter 10
The Barber of Bellingham

The mother-son relationship between Elsie and Ben Worstell was one of zealous religious fanaticism. They were motivated to keep the evils of the world from entering their household. The only problem was that the son's simple mind was too weak to shield him against the local temptations that Bellingham had to offer. As if the serpent in the Garden of Eden were offering him a sweet, delicious apple, poor Ben just wanted to have a taste of the fun to be had with wine and women. He wanted to smoke, dance and meet girls. Ben defied his mother, regardless of how much she was "beat[ing] the fear of God into her son," and that wasn't a good idea.

If I were asked to whip up a movie close to this story, what would that recipe's ingredients look like? Hmm! Maybe a splash of Piper Laurie, who played the fanatic mother Margaret White in Stephen King's *Carrie*. Locking poor Ben into a prayer closet to pray for forgiveness. Then I'd add a dash of father and son, Dad and Fenton Meiks, played brilliantly by Bill Paxton and Matthew McConaughey in *Frailty*, the two having delusions of having a divine mission.

Ben

Rain was falling hard enough during the morning hours of Monday, March 6, 1933, that work was postponed for plasterer Hans W. Hansell. The home he was working in was cold and damp, as it had been raining most of the week. His boss decided to hold off on Hansell continuing the work until the mudded walls could dry. Normally, he would welcome a three-day weekend, but at the height of the Great Depression every penny counted to put food on the table.

Ben Worstell at the Washington State Penitentiary in Walla Walla on March 28, 1933. Washington State Archives, Olympia.

He shared a first floor apartment at 1323 Forest Street in Bellingham with his wife Margaret and daughters Inez, 20, and Alice, 22. Times were tough, so his daughters remained living at home, as work was difficult to obtain. Besides, the Hansells were happy to have their girls with them. Hansell had dressed and was preparing breakfast while reading the newspaper, when he heard a loud commotion from the apartment above. A few minutes later he heard a woman's shrieking scream followed by a series of continuous heavy slams against the floor. Yelling and stomping about wasn't unusual, but the Hansells had noticed a steady increase in violent behavior from the male tenant upstairs lately.

The tenant above, Mrs. Elsie Worstell, aged sixty, was actually the owner of the house. She lived with her twenty-seven year old son Benjamin D. Worstell, who went by the name of Ben. They had moved in about three weeks prior, from a previous home on High Street. The room directly above Hansell's kitchen was also Elsie's kitchen, and that was where the loud scream and sounds of a scuffle came from.

Margaret Hansell ran into the kitchen after she had heard the scream, which was followed by a crash. As she entered, a rapid slamming was rattling the ceiling. An excited Hans Hansell was heading for the apartment door, but was warned off by his wife. Mrs. Worstell had told her that Ben was a difficult boy at times, and had been a former mental patient of the Northern State hospital. She made it clear to expect some loud noises and arguing, but that Ben would never be violent toward her. She warned that an intervention could provoke problems.

Mr. Hansell agreed to hold back on investigating the disturbance, but pondered running out to call police, as he didn't own a telephone himself. Again his wife discouraged him, as Ben might have sought reprisal. Ben Worstell had frightened the couple and their two daughters on several occasions. He was a large, broad shouldered man, with a medium-stout build, standing at five foot ten and 164 pounds. He was obviously fairly strong. He appeared to have a childlike mind and was always yelling religious verses. Ben's head from chin to forehead resembled the expanding upper portion of a light bulb, all the more pronounced by an exceptionally high forehead with a deep receding hairline. His ears were small and low on his head, and he had a set of sad, droopy St. Bernard eyes and small lips.

The previous Saturday, there was so much yelling and stomping that Mrs. Hansell thought the son would kill his mother if something were not done. Both were always screaming at one another, and Ben's angry, heavy footsteps were striking the floor above so hard, she feared her plaster ceiling would crack. She called police that one time and asked that her name be withheld, fearing Ben finding out she complained. The police were not unaware of the situation, but he had done nothing wrong or illegal as of yet.

Ben Worstell was well known in Bellingham where he practiced as a barber, to the unease of authorities. He had a small business called the "Home Market Barbershop" located in the Home Market at the corner of Magnolia and Commercial Streets in the downtown business district. Detective Elmer LaPlant had arrested Ben on June 6, 1929, when he had his first emotional breakdown. Ben had to be forcefully subdued by Bellingham police inside St. Luke's Hospital for disturbing the patients, declaring he was "chosen by the Lord to deliver Satan from mankind." He was sent to the hospital, he claimed, "to pray for the sick." Worstell struck LaPlant a severe blow to the face, before being subdued by officers and taken to the city jail. He was so irrational that officers had to restrain their prisoner and could not question him for several hours. He told LaPlant later in an "excitable talk, that the Lord helps him in all sickness."

Upon testimony from four doctors and several witnesses, including Ben's own mother, Superior Court Judge Edwin Gruber committed Ben to the Northern State Hospital in Sedro-Woolley. He was diagnosed with manic depression and acute religious mania. He was described thus: "rambling voluble speech, and responded to questions quick and hesitating." His physical condition was listed as fair, but he slept very little. Ben was paroled as recovered in August 1929, after two months of hospitalization, but suffered a relapse, returning to Northern State in September 1931. He was released soon after, but again was forced to return in March 1932.

Not All is What it Seems

Elsie Marjorie Dale married Dr. Gaylord Worstell (before he became a physician) on August 26, 1893, in Iowa Falls, Iowa. They would eventually have four children, Richard, Grace, and a set of twins named Fern and Ben. The twins came on March 24, 1905. Ben's mental status was uncertain. Stories indicate that he was born premature before his sister, or that he may have lacked oxygen at birth, others said he grew up a simpleton, and retarded. A family history written by Ann Jean Worstell Cloona claimed that "the family believed Ben was retarded." But friends claimed that wasn't the case, that Ben was simply crazy. He seemed to have been a well liked and a good boy, but struggled in school, only passing three years of high school, never finishing. Whether he received special attention or was shunned isn't known. But he was especially close to his twin, Fern, who nurtured him.

Dr. Gaylord Worstell received his medical training from George Washington University, in Washington D. C. He liked the adventure of moving around the country, seeing new places and accumulating property. He settled in Big Sandy, Montana, where he built a practice that suited him, and that's where he planned to stay. Because of its small size, it was an opportunity for him to stand out and make something special of himself, unlike the competition of a large city.

As the years progressed, Elsie and Gaylord grew further apart, finding less in common with one another. Cloona claimed Elsie was too "artistic and spiritual," while Gaylord was "scientific and logical." Later in life, Elsie discovered an affinity for religion and spiritualism. She became fanatical, eventually becoming more righteous and domineering in her religious beliefs than the church itself. This, of course, annoyed Gaylord. The division in their lives eventually grew into hostility, anger, and for Gaylord, a potential hatred of having her around. One could speculate that Gaylord felt he was becoming a respectable member of Big Sandy, and Elsie was a growing embarrassment.

At some point during the early twenties, Gaylord and Elsie separated. Elsie moved to California, leaving Ben with his father. Eventually in 1923 she relocated to Bellingham, Washington where Fern was pursing a teaching degree at the Normal School (Western Washington University). By this time Ben had joined his twin sister in Bellingham. Elsie owned several homes, farms and other properties in three states.

Moving onto High Street near Fern's school may not have been her idea of the perfect home for the three of them. But with two of her children together with her again, away from Big Sandy and her husband, it must have made for a good opportunity to start over. By the summer of 1926, Fern graduated and was off to California to teach at her first job, leaving her brother in the hands of her mother and her fanatical influence.

Autos and motor stages lined up on Forest Street in preparation for departure to Bloedel Donovan's 5th annual employees' picnic, July 25, 1924. Note the two identical houses on the hill. The house to the left is 1323 Forest, the future home of Ben Worstell and his mother Elsie. Whatcom Museum.

1323 Forest Street today. The Worstell home has long been torn down. The brown house in this photo did not exist in 1933, but today fills, in part, the gap of the former house. The blue house on the corner is an exact duplicate of the house that Elsie Worstell was murdered in. Photo taken by the author.

Murder!

Moments after the screaming and pounding, all was quiet above at the Hansell residence. The noises ceased, and all was silent in the house once again. The family below stood staring up at the ceiling, as if afraid to move or make a sound. Hans Hansell heard the upstairs door slam shut and heavy footfalls of the son descending the stairway from the apartment. Once it appeared safe, Hansell hurried across his lawn to the home of Charles McCauley, his neighbor at 1325 Forest. Charlie was a house painter, and like Hans, was housebound due to the rain. Hans told McCauley about the latest happenings at the Worstell residence, thinking Ben really did something this time. Both decided to investigate. Nellie McCauley, Charlie's wife, was worried about the danger of her husband going up there, especially if Ben should return and discover them in his apartment. Charlie told her it would be all right, that he would return with news shortly.

Creeping up the stairs, they knocked on Elsie's door, but heard no movement inside. Hansell assured his neighbor that there were two people in the apartment and that only one had left. McCauley knocked on the door several times more and called out to the woman inside. Receiving no answer, he pushed the door ajar. What greeted his eyes led Charlie to run back down the stairs and down the block to telephone the police. At 10:32 an out-of-breath Charlie McCauley called from the telephone at the Model Truck & Storage Company, located at 1328 State Street, to report... a murder.

The body of Mrs. Elsie Worstell was found on the floor, near the kitchen stove. She was lying on her back staring up at the ceiling with eyes glazed over. She was wearing her winter coat, and her little hat was only a few feet away from her body. She was evidently attempting to light her gas stove when attacked; an unlighted match was still clutched in her right hand. Perhaps she was preparing a cup of tea when struck down. Her neck and throat were badly bruised, slowly turning purple. Blood had trickled from her nose, down her cheek and mouth, dripping onto the linoleum floor. Almost every appearance showed strangulation.

While a panicked McCauley ran for help, Hans returned to his family below and informed them of their discovery. He told his wife to lock the door, as he watched from the window for either the police or the return of his neighbor. To his great surprise, within minutes he saw Ben returning to the scene of the crime, climbing into his little coupe in preparation for a getaway. But Worstell gave no sign of being in any sort of hurry, if attempting escape at all. If anything, he took his time and casually drove off toward downtown. Some ten minutes later police arrived.

The investigation of the murder was assigned to Inspector LeVerne A. McMurtrie (Bureau of Identification). Bellingham Detective Sidney Van Sinderen seconded him in the investigation. County coroner Charles S. Hood arrived and pronounced death, possibly caused by a broken neck from strangulation, but reserved his findings until after a more detailed examination.

An hysterical Mrs. Hansell told detectives she had heard Worstell come home and walk about the house at 3 o'clock, Monday morning. She reported she could hear him singing and shouting religious passages. Then all was silent, as Ben must have gone to bed. She did not hear any other noises until several hours later when the mother screamed. She said the mother and son had moved into 1323 Forest Street about three weeks prior, from 708 High Street. Since that time, she said they lived in "ill fear" of Ben Worstell, because he had been in and out of the insane asylum.

When questioned by police, McCauley stated that on Sunday morning when he was on his way to a nearby store to make a purchase, Worstell ran out of his house and grabbed him by the coat, asking where he was going. He wanted to go with him. McCauley knew the man was not rational, but allowed him to accompany him to the store, and when they returned, Ben wanted a coffee. McCauley admitted to police that he was perplexed as to what to do, as he sensed an ill feeling of fear within himself.

Bellingham Prosecuting Attorney Lawrence Keplinger, upon hearing the tragic news that morning, rushed by car to the crime scene. Many of the officers securing the premises were surprised by the prosecutors' sudden appearance. Keplinger was led by a uniformed officer to the upstairs apartment, where he looked over the body of Elsie Worstell. Coroner Hood was present and pointed out some of the particulars to him. This was madness, thought Keplinger, obviously way beyond a parole violation with the Northern State Hospital in Sedro-Woolley. "Mr. Worstell will have to stand trial," said Keplinger to detectives. He will be "charged with murder and may be sent to the hospital for the insane", meaning the criminally insane ward of the state penitentiary at Walla Walla.

Lawrence Keplinger knew a little more about the case than he let on to the detectives. He knew, for instance, that Mrs. Worstell was in fact at the offices of Dr. Solon R. Boynton above the Bellingham National Bank Building at 9:20 that very morning, no more than an hour before her demise. She was confiding to her doctor that her son "has gone violently insane." She reported that Ben had been rebelling against her for weeks, and she felt her control over him slipping away. She told Boynton that the more she pounded scripture into him, the more he resisted her. The situation was such, that her attempts to save him from the devil and eternal sin were spiraling out of control. Ben had decided he wanted to stay out late at night with friends and have fun. He wanted to see girls, dance and drink beer, and even suggested that there was one girl in particular that he wanted to marry. Talk of marriage was where Elsie drew the line. She said she didn't want him to be with a woman, and refused to be the "grandmother to dummies!" Mother was losing her boy.

Elsie asked her doctor what she should do. Dr. Boynton had been the family physician for several years and told her to immediately call the prosecutor's office, offering the use of his office telephone to her. Boynton was well aware of Elsie Worstell's fiery religious fanaticism. It was the very foundation of her existence. He reasoned that Ben was too weak and simple to fend her off, and Elsie played off that disadvantage. Boynton opined that most of Ben's dysfunctions were the result of his being brutally dominated by his mother since childhood, and this was probably why Ben was in and out of the state institution. Boynton recognized that Ben was in conflict. He was making some friends and was exposed to other influences, many of which were considered normal. But these influences clashed with his mother's religious views. Weak as he was, Boynton was sympathetic with poor Ben. He reckoned that Ben was a ticking time bomb, and it was not entirely his own fault. Dr. Boynton may have even felt that reinstating Ben to the state hospital was an unfortunate solution, when Ben really only needed proper guidance, counseling and loving support, none of which he was getting at home. And certainly this kind of support was not available in 1933.

The Northern State Hospital in Sedro-Woolley. Ben's part-time home. Courtesy of Steve Pickens.

According to Dr. Boynton and Prosecutor Keplinger, Elsie had made the call to the prosecutor's office as advised. She reiterated to Keplinger her concerns regarding her son's condition. Keplinger advised her to visit his office at once, to start the process necessary to care for her son. "It may be advisable to have Ben recommitted again," he stated. It would be a simple matter at this point to have a judge sign a readmittance to Sedro-Woolley due to Ben's prior history. He would begin drafting the paperwork. Keplinger warned her for her own safety to come straight on over. Elsie left Dr. Boynton's office at 9:35. Instead of racing straight to the prosecutor's office as instructed, for whatever reason, Elsie went home. She would be dead less than an hour later.

As authorities were combing the crime scene and questioning witnesses, police were on the lookout for Ben Worstell. After the killing, they learned that Worstell drove downtown and entered the J. C. Penny's, where he told a clerk that he had "just got a great load off my chest and I'm going out and get married." A short time later Ben was on Holly Street near Cornwall Avenue, when he was apprehended by Detective Elmer LaPlant, the same detective punched by Worstell in 1929.

LaPlant simply walked up to the passenger side of the car as it was stopped, opened the passenger door and slid into the front seat next to Ben, calmly asking Ben to pull over. The smiling driver said, "Sure, Elmer," and pulled over.

The body of Elsie Worstell was removed to the Bingham-Dahlquist funeral home and mortuary, where coroner Hood held an official postmortem. Those assisting him included Dr. William A. Hulbush and Dr. Charles V. Farrell. Their findings concluded that death was due to a crushed larynx from the strangulation and a hemorrhage at the base of the brain caused by Ben slamming his mother's head against the floor. The physicians stated that Mrs. Worstell's neck was not broken, as was first believed. Once the autopsy was complete, Hood took his findings to Keplinger. Both decided to try and talk with Ben.

At the city jail, the barber had recovered from a deep slumber. Exhausted, the young man slept the afternoon away. His jailers claimed he had not stirred all day. Ben was being held in the jail's canvas-padded cell for his own protection. The cell was only five and a half feet deep, and seven and a half feet in length. It had a double-layered, two and a half inch wooden door with eleven peepholes bored into it, each the size of a quarter. These holes allowed the jailers to observe the prisoner inside. If for any reason the inmate within had superhuman strength, there was a steel cell door outside the wooden enclosure, which was held by a set of heavy steel hasps embedded into the brick and mortar wall.

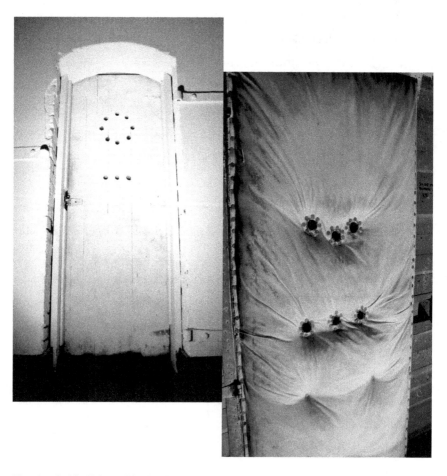

"Boy, I socked her!" Ben told a friend through the padded cell door. The city jail was located beneath the old city hall. Today, the building is better known as the Whatcom Museum. The padded cell door still hangs on its hinges, and the only padding is on the back of the door. Photo taken by the author.

It was late afternoon when the prosecutor and Dr. Hood arrived at the jail. Worstell had yet to be formally arrested, but was held pending charges.

Keplinger wasn't going to interrogate Ben, but had hoped he would volunteer to talk to him about what had happened that morning, and that Dr. Hood could evaluate his competency. Ben was taken into the office of Chief of Police, Reuben N. Fredeen, where Keplinger sought to piece together the details. He was welcoming and friendly to Ben, offering something to drink and speaking calmly as to a friend.

Bursting into uncontrolled sobbing when the prosecutor asked him when he had last seen his mother, Worstell shouted, "She never liked me. She was a good mother, but did not understand me. I like to go out and have a good time and enjoy life."

The breakdown of the "alleged" slayer of his mother occurred faster than expected. As Ben crumbled, Keplinger, Hood and Fredeen were taken aback by Worstell's willingness to cooperate. Her continual nagging on the evils of late night hours and a good time drove her son to murder.

After his first fits of sobbing, Worstell grew calmer, and with only a few irrational statements reconstructed the scene in the kitchen of his mother's apartment. He told the prosecutor he had been out late Sunday night and arose Monday morning to face bitter criticism from his mother. She argued with him, criticized his attention to girls rather than attending church with her. Worstell then stated that his mother left the house soon after their first argument, and that she took up the argument immediately upon her return home from downtown. She told Ben that she had had enough of him letting the devil into her home and was prepared to send him back to the hospital; she said that she was going to make some tea, go meet with an attorney, and take him back. Ben said he suddenly lost his temper and struck her in the nose with his fist, and she dropped to the floor. He then sat on his mother while she was down, and choked her with his hands with all his strength, while simultaneously beating her head against the floor.

The police chief, prosecutor and Dr. Hood listened until Keplinger finally stopped the dialogue, stating at this point a written confession was in order before going any further. Ben complied, and with the help of another officer dictated the confession. In his statement for the prosecutor, Worstell described how he killed his mother by strangulation after knocking her down with a blow from his fist. The attack followed after a bitter argument over "girls and dancing." Afterwards, gauging his response, Keplinger asked Ben if he liked his father, and would he mind if they contacted him. Ben was thrilled, responding that, his father was his pal.

After their talk, Dr. Hood told the prosecutor he was convinced that the man was not mentally sound. Pondering his options, Keplinger made a firm decision not to file murder charges against Worstell until he had an opportunity to speak with Ben's father, Dr. Gaylord Worstell, of Big Sandy, Montana. The senior Worstell was expected to arrive in Bellingham either late Tuesday night or Wednesday. It was a bit of an unusual step for Keplinger, but then the case was unusual. He felt he needed to converse with Dr. Worstell about Ben's past history before progressing further.

Photo of the Worstell home and insert of Ben published in the Bellingham Herald the day following the murder. Bellingham Herald.

The front page of the Monday evening *Bellingham Herald* featured the two-line headline, which read, "MRS. ELSIE WORSTELL STRANGLED; SON ARRESTED AS KILLER SUSPECT. Body Found In Kitchen By Neighbors, Mrs. Elsie Worstell Strangled to Death and Badly Beaten in Forest Street Apartment, Officers Capture Son, Barber, Former Inmate of State Hospital, Accused."

Having been told that his father was coming, Ben was anxiously awaiting the arrival of "his pal." Confined in the city jail's padded cell, Worstell declared he was "feeling fine" to his jailers, and speaking through the peepholes of his cell door, he asked about the weather outside. He told anyone who would listen that his father had always been his pal and was on his way to see him. "Although ready and willing to discuss the slaying of his mother," Worstell worried because his girl had yet to visit him at the jail. He said he planned to marry her at once and stated that the first thing he would do when he left the jail was to go to her. No girl is known to have visited Worstell in jail, or during his trial. He may have known of a girl in his group of friends and imagined a relationship that never existed. Witnesses and visitors claimed that Ben was more jubilant than at any time they had ever seen him before. As if a great weight had been lifted from him. His jailers said Ben spent most of his time "talking to himself, singing, whistling, and brief periods of sleep rounded out the hours." One friend of Worstell's, who chatted with him through the door of the padded cell, claimed that Worstell suddenly shouted, "Boy, I socked her!" And then added, "It's great to have so many friends."

Since Ben was more accommodating than expected, police turned the case over to prosecutor Keplinger and prepared the written confession for release to his office. If Worstell entered a plea of guilty to a charge of murder, a Superior Court jury would be impaneled to hear the evidence and determine the severity of his crime. Just what charge would be filed against him, Keplinger had not decided.

Digging into Worstell's records, Keplinger noted that Ben had been committed to the Northern State Hospital at Sedro-Woolley on June 6, 1929, according to hospital superintendent Dr. Edward C. Ruge. While confined at the hospital, Worstell was found to have epilepsy, according to a letter from a Dr. J. W. Doughty to Mrs. Worstell. No mention of this malady was made either in Ben's commitment or Elsie's letters. Dr. Doughty wrote, "After these spells, he seemed quite confused and talked in a rambling manner."

Ben was paroled on September 8, 1931. Keplinger noted that hospital parole officer Gunnar Apenese had visited Worstell on November 19, 1932, finding him at his barbershop. He was living with his mother on High Street and appeared, according to the officer's report, to be normal. When he returned a few months later on January 21, Apenese this time called at Worstell's home, where he found Ben talking with his mother. Elsie made it clear to Ben's horrified parole officer that she had been "beating the fear of God into her son," literally beating. She felt it was her personal mission to steer her son into serving God's will. Ben sat in a chair smiling at the parole officer, while his mother did all the talking. "Mrs. Worstell," the report added, declared she was engaged in "getting seven devils out of her son." She told the officer that she already had "cured Ben of the devil of drink, of the devil of reading newspapers, and the tobacco devil," and that she was presently striving to cure him of the "devil of desire." Worstell himself, however, was reported to be apparently in "normal condition," but the parole officer must have suspected Ben would find his way back to the hospital soon.

"Worstell," said Apenese, "was suffering from what we term a manic depression. Every hospital for the insane has many of these cases who have been discharged for years and who are now perfectly normal. Worstell was one of this type."

Local reporters, also digging into Worstell's past, were quick on the scent of a story about a madman living amongst the people of Bellingham. They discovered local authorities had unsuccessfully attempted two years earlier to prohibit Worstell from working with the sharp objects of a barbers trade within the city. The files of City Attorney Glenn Madison contained a copy of a letter addressed to Charles Maybury, director of licenses, on December 30, 1931, urging that some action be taken to prohibit Ben Worstell from receiving a business license. This letter was written after Detective Elmer LaPlant had completed an investigation of Worstell's first release from the Northern State Hospital. Madison said he had never received a reply to the letter and, as far as he knew, the state had taken no step to prevent Worstell, who could frequently become quarrelsome, from continuing as a barber.

Ben had a small business called the "Home Market Barbershop" located in the Home Market at the corner of Magnolia and Commercial Streets, in the downtown business district. Circa: 1930s. Wilbur J. Sandison Collection, Whatcom Museum.

The *Bellingham Herald* obtained a file released from Superior Court records regarding Ben Worstell's commitment to the Northern State Hospital. They showed that, according to examining physicians, Worstell at that time was suffering from "religious mania" and believed "he has been chosen to deliver Satan from men" and that "he has left this world and is living in a spiritual world."

Reporters asked Keplinger, if he intended to fight against an insanity plea. "Any plea of insanity under criminal procedure must be filed by the defense," said Keplinger, "if attorneys for Worstell decide to enter such a plea as an excuse for the slaying." Insanity, premeditated or not premeditated, Keplinger knew Worstell was going away for good this time around, and that was all he cared. He had a firm understanding of Ben Worstell's difficulties and wasn't keen about the circumstances of trying him. He sympathized with Ben to the extent of realizing he was mentally challenged, raised by a domineering mother who had him in and out of hospitals, and he may have felt that the system, as it was, had failed Ben. He also knew Ben Worstell was a ticking time bomb, ready to go off, and it was only for the good of society that he be put away.

Dr. Gaylord Worstell arrived in Bellingham at noon, Wednesday, March 8, with his eldest son, Richard Allen. Ben's two sisters Grace Mauerhan and Fern Worstell (Ben's twin, of Berkley, California) would arrive later in the week. It was the first time Gaylord had set foot in Bellingham. Prosecutor Lawrence Keplinger escorted the men to police headquarters below the city hall. When advised that his father was coming to see him today, Ben was ecstatic and repeated again that his father had always been his pal.

After a short discussion, both father and brother readily agreed that Ben should be placed in an institution "and kept there." Richard recalled correspondence from his father in 1930 during Ben's parole, stating that it "seems Ben is quite a trial." Shortly afterwards, he was back in the hospital. The two men added that Ben had been a "problem" since childhood, but they had not believed him to be dangerous until the past few years. Dr. Worstell said he had not seen his younger son or his wife in years, although he had been sending financial support. With all parties in agreement, Chief of Police Reuben Fredeen and Inspector LeVerne McMurtrie made out an official arrest warrant. Keplinger stated he would be filing a first-degree murder charge, but that a plea of insanity would undoubtedly be filed by the defense.

Trial

Prosecutor Lawrence Keplinger filed first-degree murder charges in Superior Court on Wednesday afternoon after his meeting with Dr. Worstell. Ben was arraigned later that very afternoon before the Honorable Judge Ed E. Hardin. The information filed against Worstell charged the accused of killing his mother with premeditated design by striking and strangling her. It was a foul case of matricide.

Attired in a baggy gray suit and gray shirt, Ben Worstell appeared calm, though suppressed emotion was clearly evident in his eyes. Judge Hardin looked out over his bench at the prisoner and asked if he had an attorney present.

"No, I have none, but I plead not guilty," said the prisoner crisply. "I did the only thing I could, didn't I? I had to do it, to save my own life. It was in self-defense. She was a wonderful mother, but I couldn't do anything else."

When asked by Judge Hardin if he had the means to engage a lawyer, the prisoner replied, "I have friends who can help me out. I haven't any funds myself, but my father will get one for me."

Dr. Worstell rose to explain that he could not afford to employ counsel. Ben turned, staring coldly at his father, and shouted in rage, "What's the reason you won't get an attorney for me?"

"I don't care to hear any controversy," declared Hardin, slamming his gavel down.

Ben's demeanor abruptly changed as he turned back facing Judge Hardin. Smilingly, Ben replied with a simple, "All right." He then attempted to explain that he committed the murder "in self defense," but again Hardin cut Ben off, reminding him that evidence should be stated at the trial, not during arraignment.

"Okay," said Ben.

The court appointed Attorney Earle D. Kenyon of Baldrey & Kenyon to defend the accused. Worstell was remanded to the custody of the sheriff's department and placed in the Whatcom County jail. Russ Brock, a local boxer, who was awaiting a sanity hearing, occupied the only padded cell, so Worstell was confined to a steel cell, and would be closely monitored until Brock was removed.

On the morning of Friday March 10, Earle Kenyon entered a written and signed plea of "not guilty by reason of insanity and mental irresponsibility" in Superior Court before Judge Hardin for the accused. Worstell had orally pleaded not guilty, but the court directed that the plea be withheld from the record pending the new one. Kenyon stated that he would ask the court to appoint two physicians to examine the accused in preparation for the introduction of expert testimony substantiating the defense of insanity. At the request of the defense, the court appointed Dr. Solon Boynton, and Dr. Orville E. Beebe of Everson to reexamine Worstell before the trial, which was to begin Tuesday, March 14th at 9:30 am. Prosecutor Keplinger amended his first degree murder information to read that Worstell struck and strangled his mother "with his hands," not using any weapon. The state will aid in a showing of insanity through the testimony of Dr. Fielding H. Wilkinson, a psychiatrist who had observed Worstell at the prosecutor's request.

Funeral services for Elsie Worstell were planned for Friday, but were postponed until Saturday the 11th at 2 pm, as Fern could not arrive before Friday night. Her sister Grace decided not to attend either funeral or the trial, wishing not to attach herself to the family tragedy. A small service was held at the Bingham-Dahlquist funeral polar on 210 Prospect Street, where Hood had performed the post-mortem. The Rev. John Robertson Macartney, pastor of the First Presbyterian Church, officiated. The service was followed by interment in Greenacres Memorial cemetery. Elsie Worstell had been a resident of Bellingham for eight years.

Tuesday, March 14

With the courtroom packed with curious spectators, the first-degree murder trial of Benjamin D. Worstell, the barber of Bellingham, accused of slaying his mother, opened in Superior Court. Judge Ed E. Hardin presided over the proceedings. Prosecutor Lawrence Keplinger and Defense Attorney Earle Kenyon had agreed on the jury of nine men and three women in less than an hour after court convened. Keplinger immediately made his opening statement, which was brief:

> "On the morning of March 6th, 1933, Ben Worstell, who was then living with his mother caused her death by hitting her on the head and choking her. He had previously been in the insane asylum and at the time of taking the life of his mother he was showing distinct signs of the mental trouble returning."

Keplinger continued, elaborating in depth on the horrific circumstances related to the case. He related that a religious conflict between mother and son climaxed into the early hours over issues of morality, and how Ben had opened the door of her home to Satan. "Ben returned from a dance that night," stated the prosecution, "with the wretched smell of tobacco smoke and drink on his clothes." Mother Worstell berated him on the sins of alcohol, dancing, and smoking and for being out all night with a girl. After calling on Dr. Boynton that very morning, Mrs. Worstell, the prosecutor continued, returned to her home at 1323 Forest Street and confronted her son. She started to reprimand him for a second time that morning and told him she planned to send him back to the Northern State Hospital at Sedro-Woolley, from which he was discharged and paroled on January 29. This threat, the state contends, brought about a fit of rage, in which Ben Worstell knocked his mother down with a single ruthless blow of his fist, striking her face. This violent attack against the woman who bore him, was immediately followed by the son leaping onto her defenseless body, applying a strangulation hold with his own hands around her throat, while slamming his poor mother's head against the floor until she was dead.

"This poor woman suffered a crushed larynx by the bare hands of her own son. So enraged was Ben Worstell, that he slammed his mother's head into the floor with such powerful and brutal strength, it caused the blood vessels of her brain to hemorrhage into her skull." Keplinger told the jury, "There is little dispute as to the murder," but that the jury must decide as to his guilt or innocence and whether first degree murder, or a different homicide charge would be determined.

Kenyon also made a brief statement that the defense would show that Mrs. Worstell was a crazed religious fanatic, and that Ben "was about the only one that could live with her." It will be shown, he added, that Ben was "mentally irresponsible at the time of the crime and has been so ever since, hence he is not responsible for the act and should be found not guilty by reason of insanity," in accordance with his written plea entered in court the previous week. Kenyon readily agreed with the state's opening statement, as it obviously proved that his client snapped under the ruthless control of his domineering mother. Kenyon disagreed that Ben Worstell was a cold-blooded killer, with premeditated intent, but did agree that the accused was criminally insane, and should be tried as such.

The accused, wearing a dark blue suit and gray shirt, sat smiling inside the court railing beside his father, Dr. Gaylord Worstell. As Keplinger reconstructed the slaying of his mother, Ben lowered his head, his elbows on his knees, remaining motionless. Mrs. Margaret Hansell, who occupied the lower apartment at 1323 Forest Street, was the first state witness. Hansell recalled waking at 3 o'clock to hearing Ben singing and reciting bible passages and walking about upstairs, and then all fell silent for several hours. Then she described overhearing an argument starting about 7:00 o'clock, followed by

Mrs. Worstell going out into the rain and driving off between 8:30 and 8:45. A little while later she was making the bed, and her husband preparing breakfast, when an intense argument ensued upstairs. Then she heard "thumping noises" followed by a stifled scream. Ben's mother, she added, had told her if she ever heard them argue, that she must never come upstairs or interfere in any way, no matter what she might hear. "She said that God would take care of her," the witness stated. Hansell added on cross-examination that she had never been present when Ben and his mother were in conversation on religious matters or other controversial topics.

Day Two

Taking the witness stand in his own defense Wednesday morning, Ben Worstell told the jury that he did not kill his mother because he wanted to, but because he could stand no more abuse from her. "God knows I tried to help that woman as much as I could," he exclaimed. "I was practically the only friend she had in this town. But after taking it and taking it, I finally could take no more. When it was all over, I realized I had done wrong." He added that he never intended to slay his mother and that such a thought never entered his mind.

Under questioning by Defense Attorney Kenyon, Worstell described how his mother, prayed for him continually, and "harped" on religious subjects.

"My mother was very religiously inclined. I wanted to enjoy myself, but my mother accused me of bringing devils home. I was brought up in a very contentious home. I got so I could not sleep. I broke down and was sent to Sedro-Woolley. I got over it and returned home. The same thing occurred again – finally I went all to pieces and struck my mother, killing her."

Ben corroborated his earlier statement to police, in which he told how he had beaten and strangled his mother to death when she told him that she had arranged to have him sent back to the Northern State Hospital, from which he was discharged two months earlier.

Prosecutor Keplinger, on cross-examination, asked him repeatedly if he were not sorry he had slain his mother. It appeared for a moment that the accused would break down, but he did not. When the prosecutor asked if he was not sorry about it all or sorry that he could not attend his mother's funeral, Worstell replied emphatically, "You had a mother. I never had a real mother."

"Why didn't you leave her, then?" asked Keplinger.

"I asked Dad," Worstell replied. "But he said I should stay with her."

As Keplinger drew out again in detail Worstell's account of the slaying, Worstell's attitude changed. And when the prosecutor showed him a police photograph of his mother's body, lying on the floor of the kitchen, he declared, "All I remember now is striking her. I don't remember hearing her scream." Ben became quite emotional, covering his eyes and rubbing his forehead. He rocked back and forth slightly. Keplinger wasn't sure if the accused was going to fall to pieces or strike out.

Settling down, Worstell then testified that he felt that he "had to do it" for his peace of mind. Nothing, he added, worried him now that the "spell has been broken."

Defense witnesses called included: Rev. John Robertson Macartney, pastor of the First Presbyterian Church, Harlin B. Talbott, manager, and Ray F. Baker, assistant manager of the J. C. Penney store, Dr. Orville E. Beebe and Mrs. Mildred Wimbush, a neighbor of the Elsie Worstell. All testified they believed Ben to be abnormal, if not actually insane.

Reverend Macartney testified that the mother appeared "very fervid and emotional" in her religious views. On the Sunday morning before the murder, Ben attended his Bible class he recalled, and "seemed unusually active in mind," the pastor added. "His mind seemed to be like an electric light just before it burns out," he said.

Talbott and Baker recounted the many times Worstell came into the store and talked to customers, never terrorizing them, but surely annoying them by citing scripture. But over the past few weeks he seemed more threatening and declared on cross-examination they believed Worstell to be insane and not safe to be at large.

"Mrs. Worstell said," according to testimony by neighbor Mildred Wimbush, "last month she felt she was going to be a martyr, but was willing in order to save her son's soul."

Further evidence that Mrs. Worstell had an alleged premonition of tragedy was introduced by the defense in a letter she wrote to her estranged husband four days before the fatal attack. In this letter, she said that she "might go down a martyr" and that "this may be my last letter." She also said that "there is a terrible spiritual conflict in the spiritual world for Ben's soul," adding that "I am telling you this in case something should happen to me." Dr. Worstell took the stand to assert that his wife "was inclined to go to extremes in her religious devotions." For this reason, Gaylord Worstell disregarded any substance to the letter.

Other witnesses included Fern and Richard Worstell, who told about Ben's childhood. Dr. Boynton described to the court his last conversation with the deceased, begging her to contact the prosecutor to reinstate her son. Her physician was possibly the last person she met and talked with before her death.

Both sides rested shortly before noon. After a recess was called, Judge Hardin read his instructions to the jury. The case was placed in the hands of the jury at 2:21 pm, who went directly behind closed doors.

"Slayer Committed"

"Insanity Verdict Is Voted By Jury In Murder Case, Ben Worstell Is Found Not Guilty By Reason Of Insanity In Death Of Mother," announced the headlines of the *Bellingham Herald* in bold print. The evening edition headline had been held to the last minute awaiting the verdict. The court read the decision at 3:10 in the afternoon when the jury returned its verdict after deliberating less than forty-five minutes.

"Not guilty by reason of insanity," was the verdict read aloud in the courtroom; Ben Worstell stood by his attorney, smiling in his usual friendly way. Under normal circumstances Ben may have been able to walk out a free man, but jurors held, however, that Worstell was insane and dangerous to be at large. He would have to be committed to the insane ward of the state penitentiary at Walla Walla until pronounced, and proven cured. Ben Worstell was just eight days shy of his twenty-eighth birthday. Instead of a party, four days later a set of steel doors slammed shut behind him in his new home.

The following day, Ben appeared in the nearly empty courtroom to hear Judge Harden commit him to the state prison ward for the insane. Gone was the big crowd of curious spectators that attended the two-day trial. Only a court reporter, the two attorneys, Keplinger and Kenyon, Ben's older brother Richard, his twin-sister Fern, and his "Pal" Dad heard the sentencing the Judge read: essentially life in prison.

Epilogue

Besides being one of the shortest murder trials ever heard in Whatcom County at the time, it was also one of the least expensive, according to County Clerk Archie B. Stewart. The trial, including the sentencing of Worstell, lasting only two and one-half days, cost the taxpayers of Whatcom County only $324.45. It was a strange way at finding an upside to such a grievous tragedy.

Ben Worstell was received into the insane ward of the state penitentiary at Walla Walla on March 28, 1933, becoming prisoner #14854. His prison record states that he was involved in only one infraction during his incarceration, occurring on August 6, 1933, which earned him sixty-days in solitary confinement. Ben's medial records are still sealed as confidential at the time of this writing, but it appears his mental heath was deteriorating. He was transferred to Eastern State Hospital, at Medical Lake, near Spokane, on August 15, 1934, where he lived out another eleven years in that institution. Ben Worstell committed suicide by hanging himself on September 16, 1945. In the end, Elsie Worstell got her religiously fanatical wish that her son be kept from drinking and associating with women.

Name WORSTELL, Ben   No. 14854

Prosecutor's Statement

On the morning of March 6th, 1933 Ben Wrstell who was then living with his mother caused her death by hitting her on the head and choking her. He had previously been in the insane asylum and at the time of taking life of his mother he was showing distinct signs of the mental trouble returning.

Being criminally - Until
Crime Insane.   Term rel.by crt.
County Whatcom   Age 26
Rec'd 3-28-33   H'ght70
M. Exp.   Eyes Blue
Nat'vty Iowa.   Hair Brn,& bald,
Occup. Barber   Blood Negative
Record

Released *Trans. to E. State Hosp. 8-15-34*
Death fr. suicidal by hanging at E.S. hospital

Sentenced 3-16-33

W.S.P.
14854

Inmate's Statement

My mother was very religiously inclined. I wanted to enjoy myself, but my mother accused me of bringing devils home. I was brought up in a very contentious home. I got so I could not sleep. I broke down and was sent to Sedro Wooley. I got over it and returned home. The same thing occured - finally I went all to pieces and struck my mother, killing her.

Hans and Margaret Hansell, with their two daughters, had had enough, and refused to live in a house where a vile murder had taken place. Even in the depths of the Depression, and with money as tight as it was, the family relocated to 705 Halleck Street.

The property at 1323 Forest Street is a vacant lot today. At some point the house caught fire, but was saved, only to catch fire again. Once again, a fast response from the fire department saved much of the structure. However, the city determined it unfit for habitation, condemned it, and had it torn down.

There was an interesting turn of events during the final stages of research into this sad case. Dr. Gaylord Worstell, while overseeing the trial of his son Ben, paid for the burial of his estranged wife, Elise. He wouldn't pay for a headstone; she now lies in an unmarked grave, which in itself is interesting, as Elise had assets of her own.

An interesting twist in the final days of the Worstell tragedy comes to us after the death of poor Ben. Five days after his suicide, Gaylord had Ben's body transferred from Medical Lake to be laid to rest next to his mother. Was this an act of compassion on Gaylord's' part, the arbitrator of peace between the divided mother and son in death? Or was it the final slap in the face of his dead wife, for the treatment of her son? The sentiment is worth exploring, if we had the answers, but we only have the question to ponder. Gaylord, on his own initiative saw to his son's interment, but refused to mark the grave with any inscription or stone bearing his name, just as he left his wife.

SOURCES

www.ancestry.com

Bellingham Herald: 3/6/1933, 3/7/33, 3/8/33,3/9/33, 3/10/33.

Bellingham Police Records, Washington State Regional Archives.

Cloona- Worstell, Ann Jean, *Happiness Was Born a Twin: A Biography of Dr. Gaylord Worstell*. Hp PSC, Los Osos, California, 2004.

Heritage Quest

State of Washington State Archives Penitentiary, 14854 Commitment Records.

State of Washington State Archives Probate Records 32, page 242, No. 7130.

State of Washington Archives Penitentiary Admission Register Index: patient 5667.

Washington State Penitentiary, Penitentiary Inmate Register.

Sate of Washington Archives Penitentiary Washington State Archives: Clemency files

U.S. Census. Whatcom County, Washington. 1920.

Washington State Digital Archives.

Whatcom Criminal Index, Washington State Regional Archives.

Whatcom County Courthouse: Criminal Case Files, No. 5136 3/9/33 Book 2.

Chapter 11
Headless in Bellingham

Guisseppe Stumpo. Washington State Archives, Olympia.

Guisseppe Stumpo appeared on the job at his customary time of 8 o'clock on the morning of Wednesday, November 4, 1914. He was a member of a Bellingham & Northern Railway (Milwaukee Railroad) section crew, with six fellow Italians. He wasn't very motivated this morning, walking about in a daze; his mind was off somewhere else in some distant trance. His appearance was all the more noticeable, as he normally walked with a stoop, but today his bend was even more pronounced. His fellow countrymen noticed a cut on one cheek with smears of dried blood that had undoubtedly been inflicted a short time previously. "That couldn't be good," thought his co-workers. Stumpo was forever fighting with his wife, Dominica.

His foreman, Jay S. Williams, was not on site yet, and Stumpo apparently became nervous. He decided not to follow the work crew out to North Street, where they had been repairing track. He walked up to his good friend Antonio Vitulli of Mola, Italy, shook his hand, gave him a hug, kissed his cheeks, said good-bye, and started walking aimlessly southward along the tracks. Antonio hollered out to Guisseppe several times, but he continued on, deaf to his friend's calls, his heavy shoes stumbling on the rail ties.

Stumpo's strange behavior aroused suspicion in his crew, who knew of his family troubles. An hour later the men stopped working and talked it over, deciding to tell their foreman Jay Williams, who had just arrived. Williams had known of the continuous trouble in the Stumpo home. Guisseppe had been arrested for family desertion recently, and Williams at once became suspicious that the fellow had had another quarrel with his wife. He decided to go to the laborer's home and see if things were all right there.

Jay Williams held little regard for the way Stumpo treated his wife and family. He probably would have fired Stumpo long ago, but that would have only hurt the three young children. Some of the non-Italians on the work gang suggested giving the "wop" a going-over, but Williams said no. Guisseppe had a good job and saved his money like a miser, but spent little on his family, and spent even less time at home with them. Dominica, desperate to feed her children, found it necessary to beg for food in the neighborhood. As a last resort, she finally went to the police and reported that her husband had deserted his family, leaving no money to provide for the little ones. Driven to despair, she had her husband arrested. In doing so, Dominica feared her husband might attempt to kill her for the humiliation.

Police nabbed the Italian on September 29, too him to police headquarters and found $818.60 stashed inside his clothing. Guisseppe refused to pay the bond for his release. Knowing he would have to return home to his wife, he chose to remain in the city jail. After two weeks his jailers tired of him and turned Stumpo over to the Whatcom County jail. During his confinement, Dominica would periodically appear at the police department where sympathetic officers handed over cash taken from their prisoner. Stumpo, possibly fearing the loss of all his stash to his wife, posted the $150.00 bond for his release, agreeing to go home to his family.

An aerial-balloon photograph taken in 1912 showing the Ohio Street area of Bellingham. The Stumpo home is visible as indicated with white arrow. Wilbur J. Sandison Collection, Whatcom Museum.

Jay Williams had a gut feeling that something was wrong. He told his crew to keep on working, that he would return shortly. On reaching the Stumpo home at 506 Ohio Street, he knocked on the front door several times. No one answered and the door was locked. Williams walked around to the back of the house, stepping over some detritus along the side yard and walking further past Mrs. Stumpo's dead garden. She had harvested the small vegetable patch the week prior and canned what she could for the coming winter. But most of the produce was eaten off the vine, as she had nothing else to eat and her children were starving.

506 Ohio Street today. Photo taken by the author.

Before reaching the rear of the house, Williams could hear children crying. He thought to himself, no wonder Dominica hadn't answered his knocking, she had her hands full with a wailing child. Once around the corner, he headed for the back door. Passing the kitchen window first, Williams glanced over his shoulder through the glass pane, halting suddenly in his tracks. Peering through the window, he saw a woman's body lying on the floor in a large pool of blood. The youngest of the children, an eleven-month-old girl, was bawling her eyes out from a cradle near the kitchen woodstove. Williams looked over to see another boy of two years old sitting naked on a chair, banging away contentedly with a wooden spoon in his hand. The tot's clothes were tossed close by on the floor, as if the mother was about to dress the child when she was attacked. The eldest of the children, a twelve-year-old boy, stood barefoot in his mother's blood, watching her in silence.

The Stumpos had no telephone, having been disconnected some long time ago, so Williams ran from house to house before finding one to use. He called the police station, catching police chief Alexander Callahan at his desk. Callahan quickly responded, arriving with coroner Henry Thompson. Williams was back on the scene before authorities arrived, doing his best to remove the children to a nearby neighbor's home.

The news of "murder" spread like wildfire; a gathered throng of ghoul-ish spectators was already well formed in front of the Stumpo home when Callahan arrived. He quickly ordered his men to disperse them from the crime scene as he and coroner Thompson entered the house. The children were gone, but evidence of their presence was still visible in the kitchen. Baby clothes were tossed about the kitchen. A few bowls of cold oatmeal were upturned and spilled across the table and floor. There was a pound of bacon partially sliced with a knife on a cutting board. The room was entirely a shambles, partially due to the Stumpo's a lack of orderliness, but a greater disruption due to a desperate struggle that took place hours before.

The murder of Dominica Stumpo was one of the most heinous crimes Alexander Callahan had witnessed since James K. Thomas killed his wife back in 1908, burying her in her own potato patch. The killer's weapon of choice was a badly nicked double-bitted axe. Smeared in dark, clotted blood, the axe lay next to the shattered body where the woman fell to its blows.

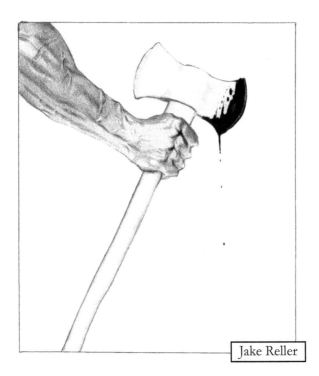

Jake Reller

Callahan told reporters that all clues indicated that the victim had prepared breakfast and was probably dressing her children the moment her life was taken. Mrs. Stumpo had been struck multiple times in the neck from behind, claimed the coroner. The head was nearly severed, but for a strap of skin that still connected it to the torso. If the blade had been sharp and fresh, her head would surely have been taken clean off in a single swing. Dominica Stumpo was a frail, small-framed woman, and claimed not to be in the best of health. She wasn't more than five feet five inches in height. Coroner Thompson ordered her stricken corpse to be removed to the Wickerman undertaking parlors.

Manhunt

Chief Callahan began his manhunt soon after his study of the crime scene, and following the body's removal. Deputy Sheriffs Wilson Stewart, Emery Hess, L. A. Thomas, and patrolman Patrick Jessup joined in the hunt for Guisseppe Stumpo. Callahan calculated that in the time between the slaying and when the alleged killer Stumpo left his job site, there were no scheduled departures by either train or boat. The fugitive would have to escape by foot. Callahan wrote a description for his men provided by Jay Williams. They were looking for a man of Italian origin, 37 years of age, 140 pounds, five-foot, four inches in height, with dark, well-groomed brown hair, brown eyes and a clean and well-trimmed beard. He walked with a limp and probably was still wearing his greasy railroad work clothes. Williams noted Stumpo was last seen heading south along the tracks. He knew of another section crew working the tracks out of Blanchard, near the Skagit County line, and would warn them to be on the lookout.

Telephone messages were flashed to all parts of the county regarding the manhunt in progress. Officer Charles Schysler thought it wise to notify the Huntoon Oyster Company at Clayton Bay. The company had a commanding view of the road leading south. Schysler was informed that a man fitting the warrant's description had already walked through the area. Jay Williams, who was still with Callahan, placed a call to Harvey C. Gowey, the section boss for the interurban line south of Clayton Bay. Gowey, carrying his double-barreled shotgun, set out after the "alleged" killer on foot, taking his bulldog in tow. After the manhunt, he told Williams that his "bull-pup was just as good as a second man." By 2 o'clock he spotted Stumpo making his way toward Blanchard.

After following the track for some distance, Gowey decided to cut cross-country to head off suspect Guisseppe Stumpo, catching up with him at Samish Bay. It wasn't long before Gowey and his bulldog caught up with a bedraggled little man with a distinct foreign accent. The man was slowly meandering along, with no apparent destination. He put up no resistance when Gowey stopped him.

Gowey searched the man, but found no weapon on his person. He asked Stumpo how he came by the scratched cheek. Stumpo wiped away some dried blood with the back of his hand, claiming to have been struck by a branch. The Italian made no attempt to flee Gowey, but kept repeating that he was not the Italian he was looking for. He even claimed never to have been in Bellingham. Gowey, however, would not listen to the story, but marched his prisoner to Clayton Bay.

Upon their arrival, loggers and fisherman working in the area overwhelmed Gowey, chanting, "String the little wop up." A rope was slung over an extending tree branch above the front of the Clayton Bay beach.

Gowey, with his shotgun pointed toward the crowd held the unruly mob back. To Gowey's relief, a few of the rabble soon voiced concerns that the "wop" might not even be the right man. After all, claimed some cooler heads, they had little information to go on. That caused the rowdy men to hesitate long enough for Gowey to get a call out to Callahan to get there before a lynching ensued.

Samish Bay mill above Blanchard, near Clayton beach, running south toward the Skagit flats where Stumpo was taken by Harvey C. Gowey, the section boss for the interurban line. The lumbermen cried, "Hang the Wop" and it was all that Gowey could do to protect his prisoner. Whatcom Museum.

Taking the interurban trolley, Alexander Callahan arrived on the scene. He saw a desperate Harvey Gowey protecting his prisoner. Stumpo was cowering behind the foreman, suffering from a few kicks and punches that Gowey couldn't prevent. Stumpo pled to the constable that there had been some mistake, as he wasn't the fugitive they were looking for and that he had never been in Bellingham before. Callahan searched the man's pockets turning them out. Slipping a hand inside the suspect's coat, he drew forth a letter addressed to a "G. Stumpo" of Ohio Street, Bellingham, on the envelope. Callahan waved the letter in front of Stumpo's face. He then reached for the ragged man's hat. Inside the band was a label of a Bellingham haberdasher. "Never been in Bellingham before?" Callahan waved the two objects in front of Stumpo. Guisseppe put his head down, and Callahan slapped a set of bracelets on his wrists.

The men walked toward Blanchard. Gowey followed close behind with his shotgun and bulldog. At the Blanchard depot, Chief Callahan packed his prisoner into an interurban trolley car. Callahan next called ahead for a taxi to meet them at the depot to swiftly take them away to the city jail. As the chief suspected, a large crowd had gathered to greet them. Several threats on Stumpo's life were shouted from the crowd, along with insults to his Italian heritage. "Hang the Wop" was hollered, and ignored by Callahan as he pushed through the throng. On seeing the mob steadily crushing in around them, Stumpo completely broke down. Police officers rushed through the crowd, opened a corridor, lifted the terrified prisoner to his feet, and carried him to the taxi.

At the city jail, two Italians were asked by Callahan to occupy the cell with Stumpo, hoping he would talk freely to them. But he remained silent, refusing to speak to the men. He was then taken from his cell to make a statement in regard to the events leading to the death of his wife. Present were Chief Callahan, County Prosecutor Frank Bixby, and a reporter. The Italian shrugged, claiming ignorance of the English language. Callahan next decided to enlist the services of a reliable interpreter. A Holly Street merchant named Julius D'Aprile, from Valenzono, Italy was his choice. Valenzono readily accepted the assignment.

This time around, with a fellow countryman in the room, Stumpo seemed to relax a little. At first the Italian's talk was disjointed. Stumpo was clinging against the wall, hiding his hands beneath his armpits, and panting heavily. Callahan spoke softly to Stumpo and asked him to tell them what happened that morning. Slumping into a chair, Stumpo told his story:

"We had a little quarrel last night. This morning I get up, she tell me I not go to work today-that she have me 'pinched' again and I must go to court. (Apparently Stumpo decided not to support his family again.) Last night I split the wood outside the door, and I go out there. She tell me again that I must go to court today again and I get so mad I don't know what I do. I go inside with the hatchet and hit her. She fall down, and I go out to work. I don't think she's dead because she cry and shake when I go out.

The children are asleep, I think, and I go. After I get to work I get afraid…I go away. I don't know where I go. The scratch I get on my eye I get somewhere in the woods, I don't know."

Authorities said that Stumpo was in no condition to give all the material facts and incidents of the killing, but his statements served the purpose of branding him beyond doubt as the murderer. He insisted upon calling the double-bitted axe a "hatchet," but otherwise his confession was full and complete. He admitted to both the crime and the facts upon which the officers effected his capture. After Guisseppe Stumpo finished his disjointed story, he broke down, losing all control. He was led, manacled, to the county jail, and placed under a suicide watch.

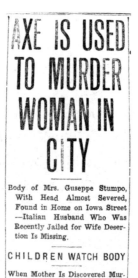

AXE IS USED TO MURDER WOMAN IN CITY

Body of Mrs. Guseppe Stumpo, With Head Almost Severed, Found in Home on Iowa Street —Italian Husband Who Was Recently Jailed for Wife Desertion Is Missing.

CHILDREN WATCH BODY

When Mother Is Discovered Murdered Little Ones Are Found Watching Corpse—Police Fail to Find Trace of Missing Man.

Guisseppe Stumpo

Eight years earlier Guisseppe Stumpo was living in Concrete, Washington on the Upper Skagit River. He arrived in America in 1904, spending his first years in the Pittsburgh steel mills. He left three brothers and two sisters behind in his native land. He could not read or write, but worked hard at building a pleasant home, and was proud of his prized rose gardens. Never during that time did he bother applying for citizenship. Once established, he sent for his betrothed, Dominica Mario, from Rugliano, Cosenza, Italy, who arrived in America with her father. The Concrete justice of the peace married the couple in 1910, and her father returned to the old country. "The agreement," said Stumpo, "was that I was to give all the money I made to her."

Stumpo claimed trouble began soon after their marriage. The modest home Stumpo built, and his little garden was his pride. He worked hard, giving his new wife every dime he made to stash away, soon accumulating five hundred dollars in savings. Then one day, Dominica ran away to Seattle with all their money, leaving him ignorant of her whereabouts. A week later she returned on her own accord, to an embarrassed Guisseppe Stumpo. She had spent $265 having fun in the big city. "I forgave her," so claimed Guisseppe, "but after that I kept the money, for I did not want her to run away again. Her act humbled me and I could not face my friends at Concrete anymore, so we moved to Bellingham."

Relocating, Guisseppe found work on a section gang for the railroad. By this time the Stumpos had three children in their household, two boys and a girl. "We were saving money again" he said, "but she wanted to keep the money, and I would not let her. Then she had me arrested. I promised to forget the past and try to get along with her."

Then in March 1914, Dominica and her babies were neglected by her husband, left to rely on charity. Mrs. Stumpo was often seen begging for food and other necessities from her neighbors, dragging the children to their doorsteps. A few weeks earlier, following threats upon her life by her husband, and in an attempt to force her husband to provide for her children, Dominica had Guisseppe arrested on grounds of family desertion. Stumpo simply shrugged his shoulders when arrested and said he had no money to give his family. $800 in bills was discovered hidden in his coat upon his arrest.

Stumpo maintained that after his release "I went home, kissed her and the babies and said I was going to forget all about the past. I bought groceries and clothing for the kids and went to see the railway foreman and asked for my job back. I got it and started back to work again." But after his release neighbors complained that constant quarrels ensued nightly, and that Mrs. Stumpo expressed the belief that her life would be taken if something were not done. Neighbors asserted that Dominica would take her children to their houses and sit upon the steps at night, afraid to go home when her husband was there.

Continuing his story of the events leading to the crime:

"On the evening of November 3, about three weeks after I had been released from jail (a second time for desertion), the owner of the house came to collect the rent. I drew my money out and paid four months' rent in advance. This made my wife mad and she started to swear at him, so that he had to leave. We had been eating supper when the landlord came and I told the babies to keep on eating. To save further trouble I went to bed."

"In the morning I called for her to get up and make breakfast. She said she was not my servant and would not do so. I got up and cooked breakfast myself. I was ready to go to work when she got up. She told me I could not go to work, but must go to court again instead. I told her I had no call to go to court. She said she would have me arrested if I tried to go to work. She jumped me and tried to take my dinner bucket away. I grabbed a piece of (fire) wood and struck her. I just meant to hurt her. Then I went out to work. I got to the tool house and then realized I would be arrested, so I started to walk."

The Road to Trial

Shaky, but attempting to stand bravely on his own in the Superior Court, Guisseppe Stumpo pled guilty to the charge first degree murder. Standing next to him was his interpreter, Julius D'Aprile, who translated a few of the judge's words for clarity. Stumpo stated that he did not need an attorney, that he was ready to plea. He didn't care any longer what became of him. Judge William Pemberton asked the Italian if he cared what became of his three young children, but his only answer was that "someone would take care of them." Again, Stumpo expressed that he was guilty and to go right on ahead and charge him for his crimes.

STUMPO ENTERS GUILTY PLEA TO MURDER CHARGE

Italian Who Was Caught at Blanchard Yesterday After Severing Wife's Head With Axe Confesses and Pleads Guilty When Arraigned in Court—Sentence Not Passed.

WANTS TO END HIS LIFE

Murderer Kept in Close Confinement—Does Not Care What Becomes of Him—Says ''Someone'' Will Care for Children.

Judge Pemberton would not pronounce sentence immediately, preferring to look up the law on the question of whether he had the right to deliver the sentence. He expressed his doubt as to whether he ought to go ahead and sentence Stumpo, as capital punishment had been abolished in the State of Washington the previous year. The harshest sentence he could hand down would be to send him to the state penitentiary for life. An old law on the statute books read in part: "But if the defendant pleads guilty a jury shall be impaneled to hear testimony and determine the degree of murder."

This law, however, was followed when prisoners were sentenced to death for their crimes. Now that that form of punishment had been abandoned it was believed that the judge held the right to go ahead and pass sentence. However, in this particular case it was decided to look carefully into the law and if it was determined that evidence shall be taken, Stumpo probably would be brought before a jury.

While awaiting determination, Stumpo was sent to a cell in the county jail. He was kept in confinement, as he had threatened to kill himself. Jailer Bink Byland took every precaution to prevent a suicide on his watch. All articles potentially dangerous enough to end his life were stripped from Stumpo. Depressed as he was, Byland said, his prisoner still "eats and sleeps as though his conscience is not troubling him."

On Saturday, November 7, Stumpo sat with his interpreter Julius D'Aprile to officially write a full confession. In his statement, Stumpo declared he did not mean to kill his wife, but truly believed, as he remembered it, striking her with a piece of firewood while in a rage. How the axe got into his hands, he did not know. D'Aprile told Stumpo that an attorney had been secured to defend him. Stumpo in turn said he should not be charged with murder in the first-degree, as he didn't intentionally kill his wife. He said it was a matter of self-defense, maintaining that his wife had him imprisoned unjustly and that she had threatened to send him back to jail once again on a trumped-up charge, just before he attacked. Stumpo now claimed he was only concerned with the welfare of his children.

"I pray to God to come down and defend me at the trial. I care only for the children. My heart bleeds day and night for the babies. I pray to the Virgin Mary to see that the babies are taken care of."

By Monday, November 9, Stumpo's panic and fears began to settle down, and he started to think clearly. Shaken by the prospect of a life sentence behind bars, he withdrew his plea of guilty in the hopes of a shorter term in the penitentiary. Attorney Jerome W. Romaine was appointed by the court to defend Stumpo. Romaine's first act was to beg the court for a continuance of November 30, as defense hadn't sufficient time to prepare a case for trial.

Meanwhile, Stumpo was beginning to act strangely, giving rise to suspicions that Romaine was setting in motion an insanity plea. According to Jailer Byland, Stumpo was either feigning insanity or was really losing his mind. He was mumbling strangely to himself, and his fellow prisoners understood enough Italian to learn that Stumpo was talking of killing his three children by boiling them to death. Judge William Pemberton made it clear that if Romaine wanted to pursue this kind of defense, his client would undoubtedly be sent to the insane ward of the state prison for life.

Next, Romaine dropped hints to reporters that maybe Stumpo wasn't insane. Perhaps he didn't premeditate the slaying of his wife, but committed the act in a fit of passion. Puzzled, reporters believed if this defense were used, it would be necessary for jurors to determine the length of time a murderer should have before it were considered premeditated. If it is found that Stumpo did not premeditate the killing, then he cannot be tried for first-degree murder, which would be life in prison.

On Monday, November 30, Guisseppe Stumpo sat passively in Superior Court as jurors were being selected, not understanding a word of the legal jargon being spoken during the proceedings. After twelve men and women had been thoroughly examined, County Prosecutor Bixby accepted the jury. Then Stumpo was asked through his interpreter Julius D'Aprile if he was satisfied with the jury selection. Stumpo said he did not understand the question. His attorney Jerome Romaine then declared that they would accept the jury, as his client had no objection.

In his opening statement to the court at 11:45 am, Whatcom County Prosecuting Attorney Frank W. Bixby argued that evidence would show that Stumpo had first beaten his wife with a length of stove wood, inflicting severe wounds to her scalp and eye. Having beaten his wife onto the kitchen floor, he then went outside and picked up a double-bitted axe, with which he struck two fatal blows, severing her jugular artery and nearly removing his wife's head. The axe was one of the exhibits in the courtroom now being shown to the jury. "All they did was quarrel," said Bixby. "No cause was assigned to such brutality, except that he would have been arrested for nonsupport of his wife and children, had his wife lived."

Jerome Romaine for the defense argued for over an hour in his opening statement to save Guisseppe Stumpo. Directing his testimony to the jury, Romaine told how Dominica had ran away from him earlier, taking her husband's hard earned wealth and humiliating him. Humiliating him so much, he was forced to leave the community of Concrete, his job and his home. The morning of the crime, she had the audacity to threaten his client, to put her husband in jail for nonsupport. And then, his wife, "goaded the accused on to the murder, which he says he does not remember having done, (Dominica) was more to blame for the heinous murder than the Italian himself."

Twelve witnesses for the state took the stand, each being cross-examined. The first witness, Anders G. Wickman, undertaker, described the condition of Dominica's body when he received it. Antonio Vitulli, section hand, gave his account of the accused that morning when he walked away from his job. Harvey Gowey, the Blanchard agent who apprehended Stumpo, told his account of the capture. Neighbors Carrie Helgeson and a Mrs. Smith gave testimony regarding the verbal and physical arguments at the Stumpo household, and how Dominica and her children were always begging for food. Others on the stand included police officers Nugent, Callahan, Lasse, section hands Harland Helgeson, and Eston Tarkston and foreman Jay Williams.

The defendant's counsel held that there was no malice of forethought in the crime and that Stumpo did not strike to kill, and should not be convicted for any greater degree than that of manslaughter. Hearing that the defendant was going into the witness box, a much larger crowd of spectators filled the courtroom, overflowing the court on Tuesday, December 1. Stumpo went on the stand at 11 am, and told his story in answer to questions put forward by a new court interpreter, Angelo Visintainer. The Italian denied the confession he purportedly made to Chief Alexander Callahan after his capture on November 4 at the city jail. He further declared, through his interpreter, that he had never told anyone he killed his wife with an axe.

Prompted by Romaine, Stumpo gave a short history of his life, having come to the America ten years before to start a new life. He had never been to school. His first job was in the steel mills of Pennsylvania. Later, after saving money, he traveled to Seattle, eventually finding a home in the town of Concrete, Washington, where he worked in the cement factory. He told of sending back to Italy for the girl who would become his bride.

On the morning of November 4, Stumpo claimed his wife threatened to have him rearrested for non-support. She had caused his arrest a few days before, but there was a settlement agreement that prevented his incarceration in the city jail again. Tensions increased once again. That morning, Guisseppe said, Dominica was in a foul mood, complaining about their home life, feeling like his servant and not having as much money as she wanted. Stumpo responded with his fears of her running away again if she had more money, saddling him with the children to raise himself. With fits of anger, she told her husband not to bother with work today, as she was going to have him rearrested. At that point, Stumpo told the court that he "became angry and my mind went blank for a long while afterward."

Stumpo declared on the stand that he did not know what happened next, that "he didn't kill his wife, but that the Devil did it." In answer to direct questioning as to whether he struck his wife with a stick of firewood or with an axe, he declared he did not know what he had done. He said he did not know he had killed her until arrested late that afternoon at Blanchard. Cross-examination continued late into the afternoon and evening. There was testimony drawn from questioning that the defendant had intended to kill his wife. Stumpo stated that if he did not support her, he would have to go to jail just the same. The defense, having little more evidence to offer, rested their case.

The jury heard last agreements at 10:30 pm. Judge Pemberton, being patient throughout the proceedings, allowed much time and leeway in the presentation of both prosecution and defense. But at this late hour Pemberton was waning, and he saw it in the eyes of jurors as well. He announced that they should go home and they would continue with deliberations in the morning. Pemberton decided to go over his instructions with the jury, so that they could go straight into deliberations come morning.

At 10:00 am, Wednesday morning, December 2, the jury came back into the courtroom asking for more explicit instruction on "premeditation." The theory of the defense was that Stumpo had not premeditated the killing of his wife, and therefore should not be punished for first degree murder. Judge Pemberton informed the jurors that his instructions fully covered this point the previous evening and told them to carefully reread his instructions. Just before noon the jurors announced that there was no hope of reaching a verdict at that time, and they were taken to lunch. At no time during their deliberations was there any chance of Stumpo being acquitted of the murder charge, but one juror believed that the conviction should be second degree murder. It was this juror who kept the rest of the jury divided throughout the day.

The dilemma was that the Stumpo case had brought attention to authorities of a defect in the penal code of the state, which, it is said, should have been remedied. Earlier, Stumpo was ready to plead guilty to first degree murder, and in fact did so. Then it was discovered that the judge could not impose sentence in a first degree murder case in which the defendant pleads guilty, without a jury hearing evidence and fixing the degree of murder. State attorneys claimed that this law was intended to apply when capital punishment was "in vogue" in the state. The intention of the law was that no one man could sentence another to die for a crime. Capital punishment had since been abolished, but the law still read that when a man pleads guilty to first-degree murder, evidence must be taken and the degree of murder fixed by a jury of twelve persons.

In the Stumpo case, the defendant changed his mind about pleading guilty while the judge and prosecutor were getting ready to take evidence in the case. Under the second degree murder charge the judge has the right to sentence the prisoner from ten years to life. But under first degree, the law makes it mandatory that a life sentence be imposed.

At 3:30 in the afternoon, the jury returned from deliberation. The jury foreman handed over the verdict, which found Guisseppe Stumpo guilty of murder in the first degree, for which Judge William Pemberton immediately made his decision to declare a sentence of life in the state penitentiary in Walla Walla. Stumpo was also required to pay court costs amounting to $93.50. He asked that the accused be removed from the city jail as soon as arrangements could be secured. Stumpo wiped tears from his eyes with a bandanna handkerchief. "He cried for but a moment," said the *American-Reveille*, "then regained his stoical and unperturbed manner..." The prisoner was taken to his cell. His face became ashen as he was thrust into his steel cage, and he appeared as if he was going to be sick, said his jailers. Later in the afternoon Stumpo regained his composure. He laid on his cot and his voice, when questioned, was of a lower pitch than usual. He said, "Can no help now." When asked if he felt badly he replied with half a smile: "Oh! Sometime." A reporter in the courtroom asked defense attorney Romaine if he intended to appeal the decision. His response was that no trial would be asked for.

Applications were soon made in juvenile court for the adoption of two of the children. The two-year-old boy, it was claimed, found a home with a prominent family, and would probably be adopted. The youngest, an eleven-month-old girl, was expected to find a good home, claimed the *Bellingham Herald.* In addition to the petitions from private citizens, the Sacred Heart Home of Seattle, a Catholic institution, applied to be given custody of the children. They reasoned it was the role of the Catholic Church to protect the children of their faith. However, Stumpo's convict entrance and medical examination records indicated a penciled notation claiming the "Sisters of Charity have children" in their custody.

Walla Walla

Guisseppe Stumpo was received on December 12, 1914, as prisoner #7502. His medical examination (paraphrased) states his thoughts to be coherent, emotions diminished, and his memory fair. His tonsils were enlarged and his teeth rotting with pyorrhea. They were loose from his head, and pus oozed from the tooth sockets, but he was passed by the prison doctor as "able to do hard work."

Judge William Pemberton sent a letter on December 19, 1914, to Henry Drum, warden and superintendent of the Washington State Penitentiary at Walla Walla, introducing the new prisoner now in his care. Pemberton made a dismal impression of himself, first by misspelling Drum's name as Drunkle. The judge then went on to explain how he came by the decision for Stumpo's life sentence, blaming the new state law regarding first-degree murder. This was followed by an overview of the heinous case he had overseen. He told how Stumpo nearly severed his wife's head from her body with an axe…failure to support his family…and those poor children. "I thought it best to let you know something about the facts of this particular case."

Pemberton confused the warden further by adding, "I am of the opinion that the usual treatment given to a life prisoner will disclose the fact that the defendant will be of services to you." Drum answered the letter on December 23, asking the judge in the first paragraph what he was talking about regarding "the usual treatment." Pemberton quickly responded back that he had "made the statement hastily and it was made without knowledge of your method in treatment of the prisoners." Pemberton admitted that he had yet to visit a prison, but assumed when prisoners were committed for a period of their natural lives, the warden in charge usually endeavored to treat them in such a manner that would be of service to the institution. He assumed, that if Stumpo were given such treatment, he might develop into a useful helper.

The judge continued writing in what amounts to be an embarrassing ramble of words, until an awkward pause is sensed in the tone of his explanation. Pemberton next stated that he should visit the state's institutions to know something of their conditions. "Since it is my duty to commit persons to these Institutions. If I am mistaken as to your methods I certainly request your pardon." Pemberton continued to ramble on, repeating himself before giving up and concluding his letter, "I would be glad to hear from you if you would have the time and if you have any information that you could give me on the prison life…"

The prison doors slammed on Guisseppe, and he was nearly forgotten. At some point during his incarnation, Stumpo learned to write. A letter written by him was found in his prison record file; on the top is a notation "Sample of Writing" dated August 19, 1918. It was addressed to the Honorable Henry Drum, Prison superintendent:

Dear Sir:

Will you please place my name in the State list for tobacco? I have no funds and no friends. And I need Tobacco. I am working hard in the mill. And expect to be here for some time yet, so please grant me this favor.

Very Respectfully
Joe Stumpo 7502 – 9E4

As time slowly passed for Guisseppe, he wasn't entirely forgotten by the outside world. The Italian Counsel would occasionally check in on the national, inquiring on his condition and health. And after years of no personal contact, his family searched him out.

On March 1, 1925 a letter from Frank Stumpo, Guisseppe's brother arrived. He was newly arrived in America and took up residence in Chicago. Frank wrote in longhand to the new warden, Clarence E. Long, wanting to know how his brother was getting along. "I sincerely hope that you or somebody may inform me about him. I would like to know if I have any way of writing to him, telling him news." Warden Long notified the brother on March 13 that Guisseppe was still confined and is in good heath and spirits, and that he could indeed write to him.

It appears the brothers either didn't correspond, or perhaps Guisseppe ignored his brother's letters, as Frank wrote the prison warden again on September 21, 1934: "Warden: Can you tell me if Joe Stumpo is still in the penitentiary? He has been sentenced there some time ago, and we were just wondering if he is still alive."

This time Frank was advised that "our number 7502 was transferred to the Eastern State Hospital at Medical Lake, Washington, on April 5, 1931." And referred Frank to a new address.

After a decade and a half behind prison bars, Guisseppe's mental state began to decline. His only reported infraction was an inability to keep quiet. At one point, he was confided to eat alone in his cell for 60 days for constant talking in the dining hall. On March 24, 1931, warden Long, agreed with prison physician J. W. Ingram that Guisseppe Stumpo needed adequate care at the Eastern State Hospital. Ingram reported that after fifteen months of observation, it was his opinion that inmate #7502 was suffering from delusional paranoia, and must be removed from the population to a hospital for the insane for treatment. The following day, Guisseppe's documents were being processed. He would be removed with inmates, Carl Carlson and Floyd Bullock to Spokane for further care. His travel documents claimed he had no property to transport with him.

The Italian, Guisseppe Stumpo died on March 7, 1943 at Medical Lake in the Eastern State Hospital, Spokane at 49 years of age. He had gone mad.

SOURCES

Bellingham Herald: 11/4/14, 11/5/14, 11/6/14, 11/7/14, 11/9/14, 11/10/14, 11/17/14, 12/1/14, 12/2/14, 12/3/14.

Bellingham Police Records, Washington State Regional Archives.

Correspondence related to Guisseppe Stumpo held at the Washington State Archives.

State of Washington Penitentiary Records Walla Walla Inmate No. 7502.

State of Washington Penitentiary Inmate Registers.

U.S. Census. Whatcom County, Washington. 1910.

Washington State Digital Archives.

Washington State Penitentiary, Penitentiary Inmate Register.

Chapter 12
Murder at the Lone Jack

The murder at the Lone Jack mine is an old, unsolved cold case, but law enforcement and the folks living in the town of Glacier at the time firmly believed that they had their man. Because the murderer was never apprehended, no court records or inquests exist to tell the account. Still, there is enough circumstantial evidence to draw conclusions. Fortunately for us, there is just enough information to (pardon the pun) mine from, to tell the story.

What is known of the murder at the Lone Jack comes to us from a few articles written in Bellingham newspapers, after the discovery of a corpse in a mine shaft, and from the writings of local historian Percival Jeffcott in his 1963 book, *Chechaco and Sourdough*. Fortunately, Mr. Jeffcott interviewed some of the old-timers directly involved in the search at the time of discovery. The case was then followed up decades later in Mike Impero's history of the Lone Jack.

Mr. Jeffcott gives most of the story's credit to H. E. Barnes, an old sourdough of the early prospecting days in the Mt. Baker District. Barnes claimed to have joined the gold rush in 1898, and spent a considerable amount of time in search of the elusive rich ore on Mount Baker. In telling the story, Barnes said he personally knew the parties involved in the incident.

Jeffcott also interviewed the elderly Mrs. Hazel Bottiger, a lifelong resident of Glacier. Her husband Frank Bottiger was a personal friend of the victim, and the "alleged" perpetrator. This is the story as related by all parties.

A Little Background First

August 23, 1897, is the date that inaugurated what was then known as the Mount Baker Gold Rush. Late that Monday afternoon, Jack Post was prospecting on the east side of Bear Mountain when he spotted a large outcrop of quartz. Working his way up a steep incline, he reached a wide vein and followed it beyond the ridgeline. Dropping down in elevation below some small cliffs, he continued his journey until regaining the lost elevation, then slowly moved closer toward the quartz vein. The hillside grew so steep that footing became difficult to find purchase. Post soon found himself forced to scramble tightly up against the walled terrain. Before long, the prospector reached the vein he was so desperately pursuing. Post looked over the seam with a grin, and broke away a piece with his trusty hammer. Holding the quartz up to the light, he discovered his sample was rich in gold flake.

Jack Post hurried back to the Twin Lakes campsite where he and his partners Russ Lambert and Luman Van Valkenburg had been based the past two weeks. No doubt that evening was one hell of a party.

Their patented claims would become the Lone Jack, Lulu, Whist, Jennie and Sidney mines. By September 1899, English & Son of Baker City, Oregon, bought out the Lone Jack claim. The new owners were outfitted to start building the necessary cliffside stamp mills, bunk and cookhouses, tramways, and the means of hauling the needed heavy equipment up the mountainside. Not being familiar with the landscape, the owners had a complete lack of knowledge of the severity of the winters and deep snows in the North Cascades, which set them back years in developing the mines. Regardless, the Lone Jack eventually proved to be the most successful gold mine in the region, producing a half-million dollars' worth of gold between 1898 and 1907.

The two tunnels of the Lulu shaft. Photos above and below courtesy of Michael Impero.

The Italian and the Swede

During the winter of 1915, the Boundary Gold Company (The Lone Jack) ceased operations for the winter months. This was an annual occurrence due to inaccessibility, extremely deep snowfall, freezing temperatures and the fear of avalanche carrying the mining structures off the face of the mountain. Usually the first sign of winter's approach was enough to shut down the mines before miners and prospectors would be snowed in. With winter's closing of the facilities, it was time for workers to return to civilization and spend their hard-won earnings on drink and women, until spring's warm thaw reopened the mountain once again.

Jack Post hurried back to the Twin Lakes campsite to inform his partners, Russ Lambert and Luman Van Valkenburg that he discovered a rich vein. Courtesy of Michael Impero.

The winter months also proved to be a time when hardy bandits would enter the shafts to chip away at the ore and steal a fair share of wealth. Because of this expected annoyance, the Boundary Gold Company would employ a man to stay behind and guard the shafts, preventing thievery.

Martin Orner, said to be a likable Swede, had been employed at the Lone Jack for several years. He was favorably known for his friendly nature and honest dealings. When not at the mine, he spent his time in the town of Glacier, getting to know folks in that community, including the well known Bottiger family. He was easygoing and trusted by the men with whom he worked, as well as management. He had worked around the Lone Jack and knew it well...a perfect match for the company's need for a watchman. It must have been quite an honor when he was asked if he would care to winter-over to watch the mine.

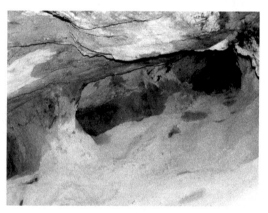

A mined out vein of the Lulu shaft. This gap in the rock was once filled with ore rich quartz crystal. The rock pillars remain to support the ceiling, but are ore rich themselves. Courtesy of Michael Impero.

By mutual agreement, Martin would draw no salary; in lieu of payment, he was free to work out as much gold by hand as he wished during the long winter months. He also had free access to the company stores in the cook-house. Orner must have thought over the prospects of a lonely winter with no one to talk or play cards with, as he requested that another man on "like terms" be sent to winter-over with him. He anticipated the hardships and monotony of the short winter days and long nights. The mining company agreed to the Swede's terms. There was a man that Orner had in mind, a friend he had made at the mines, Tony Copan. Copan was a short Italian, known at the mines and in Glacier as "the Dago." (It is this author's opinion that Copan's real name may have been Antonio Capannetto or Capannirre.)

Jeffcott would recall, "The arrangement was, we would say, conducive to future trouble, for if ever a setup would lead to 'cabin fever' and mutual disagreement, this was it – at least in our opinion..."

The agreement and terms were very generous. The two men were free to mine, and mill as much gold by hand as possible during the winter months. They worked away at pounding out the gold from the ore of the mine, as their pay depended on their efforts. With winter fast approaching, the two said their farewells to all their friends in Glacier, and headed to the Lone Jack to establish housekeeping for the coming six months of winter.

To winter-over at the mine was to endure great hardships. The short winter days and long freezing nights pushed many of men over the edge. This may seem a poor image of the bunkhouse, but think of the time of year, harsh conditions, and primitive camera of that day. Courtesy of Michael Impero.

During the harsh winter months that followed the "two foreign men with contrasting blood, features and language" had to "pass the long winter by themselves, with only the gold in the mine to act as keepers of the peace." We can only assume they got on well together during their self-imposed in-carceration. After all, Orner did choose Copan as his over-winter partner, which would indicate a good rapport existed between the two men. As the snows buried the mountain, so it closed the curtain on the men until spring.

The old sourdough H. E. Banes and Frank Bottiger were together that night near the end of winter, when a tired and bedraggled character slowly plodded his weary way into Glacier, carrying a heavy sack over his shoulder and "well nigh out." It was growing dark as he entered McDonald's Store. He threw his heavy burden down by the friendly, warm stove. The few patrons at the bar looked in surprise at the unknown stranger in long black facial hair growth, until one of them recognized the Italian and spoke up.

"Hello, Tony! Where did you come from?"

The Italian kept his eyes mostly on the floor, as all waited for his an-swer. Hesitatingly Copan answered slowly in his strongly Italian-accented and garbled English, "Ah gotta da mine back," he said without raising his eyes.

"You came back without Martin?" interposed another bystander. "Where is he?"

Tony shifted nervously at the question asked of him, and hedged for a time to formulate an obfuscating answer. Then, when he realized further hesitation would create suspicion, he answered, "Ah nota know where da Martina iss. He go bya da gun, he hunta da deer, not coma da mine back. Ah, coma by da gold, getta da help find da Martina."

Where is Orner?

Copan told the men that Orner had gone off hunting for deer a few weeks earlier and had yet to return to the mine. Copan related that he had gone out searching for Orner over the next few days, but was unsuccessful in finding any trace of him. After a lapse of considerable time and giving up all hope, Copan knew he needed to notify the authorities so he returned to Glacier with his story, personal gear and the bag of gold milled by both men.

The small mountain hamlet of Glacier was the jumping off point to the goldfields. Laura Jacoby's Galen Biery Collection.

As the men at MacDonald's Store pressed home their questioning, it rapidly turned into a harsh interrogation. Arno Hauptfeisch, standing over Copan with fists clenched, wanted to know where his friend Martin was. Tony's answers became more evasive and labored, as he tried to find the words to explain himself. Martin's friends were convinced Copan was hiding something, and as the evening wore on, they became more suspicious that the Italian was lying. The witnesses, in recounting the story to Jeffcott, claimed Tony "freely" showed the gold he had brought out of the Lone Jack, some $1500 worth. With tensions growing, it was more likely Copan was seriously roughed up and his belongings ransacked.

Unsatisfied with their results, Frank Bottiger demanded that Copan return with them to the Lone Jack Mine, to investigate conditions left behind up there. If a dastardly deed had transpired at the mine, they would find evidence to that affect. The law was not called, nor was Orner's disappearance reported to authorities, as a form of vigilante justice took hold.

291

"In those days," say Glacier's old-timers, "the law wasn't wanted this side of the Warnick Bridge." And the law knew it, leaving the mountain community alone, unless called upon.

Frank Bottiger, circa 1910-1920. Bottiger family photo.

Needless to say, Tony Copan was terrified and reluctant to go anywhere with the men. There was no doubt in his mind that he would be lynched, whether or not evidence of foul play was discovered. After all, he was only "the Dago" to the mountain folk. Copan clearly indicated that he wasn't going back, but Bottiger forcefully persuaded him to return with the group, most likely at gunpoint.

The hike to the Lone Jack was twenty-three miles from Glacier, and the tunnel and stamp mill were well up the face of a mountain, in extremely steep terrain. Snow still lay deep in most areas as the men began their search. Upon looking for several days, the vigilantes found nothing that indicated any type of foul play had taken place. The disgruntled group returned to Glacier and surprisingly released Tony Copan to his freedom. Within two days, Copan slipped out of Glacier with the two shares of gold, never to be seen again.

Nothing more was ever heard of Martin Orner. Maybe it was true, and he had an unfortunate accident while hunting. This wouldn't have been unusual in the mountains during winter. Orner could very easily have fallen, broken a leg and frozen to death. If so, it was possible that a prospector or hunter might at some point find his remains. Then the mystery would be solved.

Approach onto the Lone Jack. Courtesy of Michael Impero.

Discovery in the Lulu Shaft

In August of 1919, Bert Lowery, a trapper and longtime prospector, arrived in Glacier from tromping around the Twin Lakes. He reported that while on his routine trap-line rounds, he had "casually entered one of the Lone Jack tunnels." Entering what is known as the Lulu shaft, his light shone on a strange looking object floating in a mined-out winze, which was shallow in seepage water. (A winze is an abandoned prospect shaft within a mine, no ore having been found.)

293

Lowery's curiosity got the best of him, and he entered the water to see what he had found. With his light raised high, he moved toward the floating object on the surface. Upon closer inspection, he recognized what looked to be a tattered cloth bag. As he gave it a roll toward him with his hand, a mass of rotted clothing and flesh peeled away, revealing the body of a man underneath. A startled Lowery stumbled away from the winze, falling, crawling and scrambling as fast as he could move. Collecting his wits after the shocking discovery, Lowery reentered the winze to figure out who it might be.

Dramatization. Photo credit Jake Reller.

The body Lowery discovered had been bound by wire and sunk to the bottom of the winze by means of a rope tied to a heavy rock. Over a period of time, the rotting rope gave way and the body partially rose to the surface. Further exposed to air, the body was rapidly decaying.

After a closer look, Lowery determined that the body might be that of the missing Martin Orner. Lowery returned to Glacier with his news. Frank Bottiger, Arno Hauptfeisch and Orner's friends returned to the mine shaft with Lowery to confirm his suspicions. This time Deputy Sheriff Alfred Medhurst and coroner Dr. N. Whitney Wear accompanied them.

Bert Lowery. Courtesy of Michael Impero.

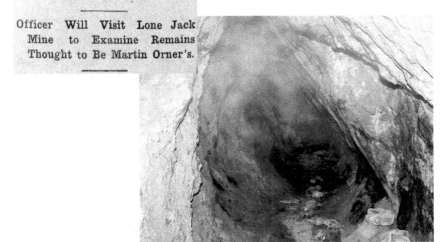

DEATH MYSTERY WILL BE INVESTIGATED BY WEAR

Officer Will Visit Lone Jack Mine to Examine Remains Thought to Be Martin Orner's.

Inside the Lulu shaft. Courtesy of Michael Impero.

Dr. Wear and Deputy Sheriff Medhurst found the fleshy skeleton floating on the surface of a deep pool, less than a hundred feet from the mouth the shaft. The men were soon looking down at the body in the winze. They attempted to carefully remove the decaying carcass from the water.

Dr. Wear claimed that owing to the long lapse of time and decomposition, identification was impossible, and it would be difficult to say whether it was a suicide or murder. There was evidence that the rope was wrapped around the neck, as well as the thicker portions of the body. Bottiger, Hauptfeisch, Lowery and all of the Swede's friends present had no difficulty in identifying the decomposed corpse as that of Martin Orner.

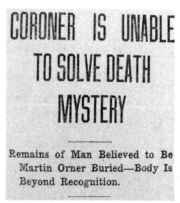

CORONER IS UNABLE TO SOLVE DEATH MYSTERY

Remains of Man Believed to Be Martin Orner Buried—Body Is Beyond Recognition.

The men recovered the body, took the remains from the shaft, and gave Orner the best burial possible in almost solid rock soil on the hillside of Bear Mountain. They placed a rough wooden headboard to mark the placement of the Swede.

The Whatcom County sheriff started a statewide search for Tony Copan and followed his trail to Seattle, where he had deposited the gold into the United States Assay Office for $1,500. After that, the trail ran cold, and no trace of Copan was ever found beyond Seattle.

How the big Swede was taken down is a question of conjecture. There was no sign of blood or a struggle of any sort at the Lone Jack. And you can be sure that if there were, justice would have been served on the spot.

Another important observation is that no mention was made of any visible defensive wounds on Tony Copan when he returned to Glacier. If Copan indeed killed Martin Orner, it must have been committed with the greatest degree of surprise and precision to overcome the man and leave no evidence, or receive no wounds on his person.

Closing Thoughts

When the body of Martin Orner was recovered, Dr. Wear made no mention of an obvious gunshot or knife wound, which would have been apparent to the keen eye of a physician. This leaves only a few hypotheses as to what occurred at the Lone Jack. Were the two men in route along the trail to or from the mine when Copan jumped the Swede? Another possibility was that the slaying was committed within the Lulu shaft, making it easy for Copan, not having to drag the body far, but to simply sink it. That would have accounted for the lack of finding a crime scene, but the Italian would surely have received some infliction. The only way it could have happened is if Martin was not aware of any pending danger, taken by surprise.

I believe the best-case scenario was that Martin Orner was poisoned, then while in a weakened state strangled by his friend Copan. That leaves the open-ended question: did Copan find some poison in the bunk or cookhouse? Possibly in the storeroom, where varmints and rats would have found a rich winter's food supply, thereby becoming a crime of opportunity. Or did Copan premeditate the murder, bringing a lethal substance with him? After the two worked and milled their gold, Tony Copan may have found the time ripe to administer the fatal dosage and be off with his friend's share. I would further suggest that Copan may have even prepared the meals, and slowly administered a poison over time to weaken his partner. Martin would likely believe he was sick from the cold winter in the mountains. He would have been an easy kill for Copan if that were the case.

Years later, Loran Nace, a friend of Percival Jeffcott, was camping with his wife at Twin Lakes, and came across the outline of an old grave. The inscription on the headboard was weather-beaten and illegible. Nace later asked Bert Lowery about the grave. An old man now, Lowery confirmed it was the grave of Martin Orner.

SOURCES

Bellingham Herald: 8/25/1919, 8/28/19.

www.geneologybank.com

Impero, Michael G. *The Lone Jack: King of the Mount Baker Mining District*, 2007. Murder at the Lone Jack Pages 99-100.

Jeffcott, Percival R., *Chechaco and Sourdough: or The Mount Baker Gold Rush: Pioneer Printing Co.*, Bellingham, WA. 1963. P. 135-139.

The Leader: 6/23/1916, 8/11/16, 8/25/16. 1/26/17.

U.S. Census. Whatcom County, Washington. 1910 and 1920.

Chapter 13
Foul Play at White Horn

"Lifeless Body Of Pete Hannesson, Farmer, Found Near Home
With Bullet In Head, Suicide Not Likely"

Bellingham Herald: Tuesday April 5, 1927

A mystery shrouds the death of Pete Hannesson (Teitur Hannesson), an Icelandic White Horn farmer living just south of Birch Bay. His lifeless body was found at his home, about two miles southeast of Pleasant Valley, with a bullet hole drilled neatly through the back of his head. There were no witnesses and few clues.

Dave Shore, a Bellingham junk dealer, was driving past Hannesson's farm at one o'clock in the afternoon on Tuesday April 5, 1927, when he decided to visit his old friend Pete. He was driving around the back county roads that day looking for items to purchase and resell in town. "One man's junk is another's treasure." And that's how Dave Shore made his living. He decided to stop by to see if Pete had anything to get rid of. Pulling up into the farmer's drive, Shore was startled to discover Hannesson laid out on his side in his driveway. Shore didn't know what to make of it at first. Had Pete passed out drunk? Was he ill? Pete was known to be sickly with a long-term illness. Shore leapt from his truck calling out his friend's name, then froze in his tracks as he approached. Pete Hannesson was sick all right, but it was too late for Shore to offer any help. Pete was dead!

Making a hasty examination of the body and determining that Hannesson was truly lifeless, Shore drove to notify Dr. Carl Clifford Hills of nearby Custer, who made an immediate investigation. Shore nervously told Doc Hills that he had seen neither a murder nor suicide in his life, but Pete Hannesson's death was the strangest thing he'd ever seen. Arriving at the crime scene, Dr. Hills looked over the corpse and agreed with Shore that the scene was indeed the strangest he'd ever seen too. Hills summoned County Coroner N. Whitney Wear and Sheriff Tom C. Fraser of Bellingham. Hills told the men on the telephone that he believed some hand other than his own had killed Hannesson. "It looks like murder to me."

Dr. Wear and Sheriff Fraser left for the site of the shooting shortly after 2 pm and were met in Pleasant Valley by Dr. Hills, in whose company the investigation was made. Pulling up the drive in their cars, the men got out and walked over to the corpse of Pete Hannesson. It was indeed an unusual position for a body, which lay on the gravel, on its right side in a fetal position. A bullet hole entered squarely in the back-center of Hannesson's skull. There was a small puddle of blood spread out beneath his head. The strange part was the location of a .38-caliber pistol used in the killing. It was found gripped tightly between Hannesson's knees with the muzzle pointing outward in front of his legs toward his forehead, with the pistol's grip behind his knees pointed downward.

"If this were a suicide," claimed Hills, "it would be impossible for the victim, even lying on his side, to contort his body completely around and place the muzzle to the upper back of his head, discharge the weapon, then place the gun between his knees in the opposite direction." Furthermore, he would have to use both hands to fire the gun, and then reposition the handgun in his hand to place the grip downward behind his knees, and the muzzle frontward. Then Hannesson would have to move his arms upward away from the weapon, stretching them outward, all while dying, if not already dead. Dr. Hills pointed out powder burns in the hair at the base of

Hannesson's skull, indicating that the shot had been fired at very close range. A concentrated ring of residue around the rim of the bullet hole and the heat from the muzzle flash singed Hannesson's hair, making a small ring of residue burnt into the flesh.

Hills and Wear next pointed out to Sheriff Fraser what he already knew. Hannesson's blood had started to settle with the force of gravity, draining from the capillaries and pooling in lower-lying portions of the body, creating a pale appearance in some places and a darker appearance in others. Hills moved one of the limbs, noting that the muscles had begun to stiffen into a state of rigor mortis. It was a cool April morning, and the body's temperature had dropped.

Both doctors agreed that death was five to seven hours earlier. Hills declared, however, that he could not account for the fact that the gun, no part of which was touching the ground, was found jammed between Hannesson's knees. Such positioning was mute evidence of what some were led to believe had been murder.

The shooting of Hannesson recalled the glare of publicity reflected upon the White Horn District a year earlier, when Harold Carlson, an eighteen-year-old deaf mute, three times within as many weeks became the purported victim of attackers. The alleged attacks on Carlson included shooting, strangulation, assault and throwing him into a well from which he was pulled out nearer dead than alive. The improbability of Carlson surviving this list of assaults led then Sheriff Alexander Callahan to the conclusion that the whole affair was a hoax. The death of Hannesson might throw some doubt into the theory that young Carlson was a "victim" of his own conniving. The youth repeatedly insisted that he had been ambushed in an attack. This was a prospect, that Fraser did not wish to repeat in the White Horn District.

Neighbors in the vicinity related to the sheriff and Dr. Hills that they believed they heard a gunshot between eight and nine in the morning. The sound seemed to emanate from the direction of the Hannesson farm. Hans

Haukinstead, a neighbor residing directly opposite the Hannesson farm, said he heard the shot at about 9 am and looked over toward Hannesson's. He said he saw no one, and did not investigate. No one claimed to have seen anyone or anything unusual all morning; however, Hannesson's body was found about forty feet from his home within full view of the Whitehorn Road. Any passerby could not help seeing the dead man's body. Sheriff Fraser's questioning seemed to indicate the sixty-year-old Hannesson had no known enemies. He was a bachelor, and for twenty-six years peacefully resided on his farm in the White Horn District.

Farmer Ends Life?

The following day, April 6, recorded on page three of the *Bellingham Herald*, Doctor Carl Hills was astonished to read "Farmer Ends Life." Pete (Teitur) Hannesson, 60, met death by his own hands, claimed County Coroner N. Whitney Wear and Sheriff Tom Fraser, thereby concluding the investigation of the White Horn farmer. Suicide was the conclusion drawn notwithstanding the fact that the gun, which was believed to have snuffed out Hannesson's life by a shot through the back of the head, was found firmly held in an unusual position between the dead man's knees, where he lay. Just how Hannesson managed to send a bullet, from the rear, and therefore managed, as it was supposed he did, to place the .38-caliber pistol between his knees, where it was held in the grip of lifeless limbs, neither Coroner Wear nor Sheriff Fraser ventured to explain.

Dr. Wear was perfectly satisfied with his conclusion "that Hannesson took his own life as a sequel to eight years of illness from which there appeared to be no relief, declared that he believed someone had picked up his gun and placed it between Hannesson's knees sometime between the hours of death," estimated at 9 am by neighbors who reported hearing a shot, and the time when the sheriff and coroner arrived at the scene approximately five hours later.

In his investigation, Coroner Wear said residents of the district advised him that Hannesson had been in poor health for many years, that it might have prompted him to take his own life. Neighbors said he had lived a solitary life, rarely mixing with the community.

"There were numerous footprints around the body," admitted Dr. Wear. "Of course, after the body had been discovered and before we arrived, several people had been there. It is possible that someone picked up the gun and placed it where it was found."

Sheriff Tom Fraser believed "that so far as his office was concerned, unless requested, no further investigation would be made." Fraser told papers that his officers followed a murder theory when they searched Hannesson's home for clues. About $200 was found in the house, and this was believed to preclude the theory that robbery may have prompted murder. A small box of revolver bullets matching the gun found between Hannesson's knees was found located in the house. Even Sheriff Fraser agreed with Wear as to the plausibility that some passerby had seen the body and after investigating had placed the gun between Hannesson's knees and departed, not wishing to be implicated in the shooting.

Something Stinks in Iceland!

The farmer's body was removed to the Blaine mortuary, pending funeral arrangements. Reverend H. E. Johnson of the Icelandic Church arranged an April 7 funeral for Teiter Hannesson. It was to be held at the mortuary, before internment within the Blaine cemetery just outside the town.

Less than 24 hours after Hannesson's body had been found, two petitions for letters of administration of his estate were on record in probate at the Whatcom County Superior Court, and a third petition was in the offing.

Dr. N. Whitney Wear was the first petitioner, his request indicating that Hanneson had left seven cows, two horses and other farm animals, all in immediate need of attention. The deceased was said to have had $208.08 in cash. The estate was estimated to be valued at $5448.80.

Shortly after the petition of Dr. Wear was filed, a petition belonging to Ralph P. Duxbury was entered. Duxbury said he believed he was more qualified to act as administrator, as he was a farmer. Thorgier Simonarson of Blaine considered the advisability of filing a petition. But Simonarson stepped up, claiming Hannesson had left a Will written in 1919, which was on deposit in a vault at a bank in Blaine. Judge Brown took no action on any of the petitions until the Will was searched for and presented.

Sure enough, a Will by Hannesson was produced, assigning his friend and fellow Icelander, John Stephenson of Blaine, as his executor. It was Hannesson's wish that all his property be liquidated, and all monies to be delivered to the "Chief Doctor of Iceland," Gudmundur Bjornson. His wishes were followed to the letter; his assets were transferred to Reykjavík to be "held by Bjornson and his successors forever in a fund to be known as the Gudrun Teitsdotter Memorial Fund."

Gudrun Teitsdotter was Hannesson's mother. The fund was to help "alleviate suffering in the vicinity of my mother's home." This would be "Fra Hvetarose Andakelshrapp Borgorfjardorayvlu, Iceland, Kena Homeaar Johansson fra Kvenneiryn, Daim 1875." The interest of the fund would support women and children in need. Hannesson mentions in his Will that funds would also help those afflicted with tuberculosis, shedding light on the fact that his mother had the disease, or perhaps it was his own longtime illness. In fact, Stephenson forwarded all of his friend's funds (totaling $4833) to Bjornson, which was received February 17, 1928.

The case was closed as fast as it opened. Hannesson's body was quickly disposed of, and no further questions appeared on the subject thereafter. The only person questioning the case was Dr. Carl Clifford Hills, of Custer. Hills strongly pointed out that no note or letter was written to clarify Hannesson's reasoning for taking his life, the location of his Will, nor his intentions. Some indications suggest that Hannesson, being sickly, with no wife or heirs and having substantial assets, could die and no one would question his demise. Was Hannesson murdered? It certainly appears that something strange was at work for Sheriff Frasier to "wrap up" the investigation within 24 hours and change the death from a murder to a suicide, all under the strangest of circumstances.

Head stone of Teitur Hannesson, interred at the Blaine Cemetery. Photo taken by the author.

SOURCES

www.ancestry.com

Bellingham Herald: 4/5/1927, 4/6/27.

www.geneologybank.com

Heritage Quest

U.S. Census. Whatcom County, Washington. 1890, 1910, 1920.

Whatcom County Assessor & Treasurer – Property Details.

Whatcom County Auditor Grantor Indirect and Grantee Direct Records, 1927-1929.

Whatcom County Probate Case Files, No 6318, 1927.

Whatcom County Superior Court Case Files, No. 6318, 1927.

Maps

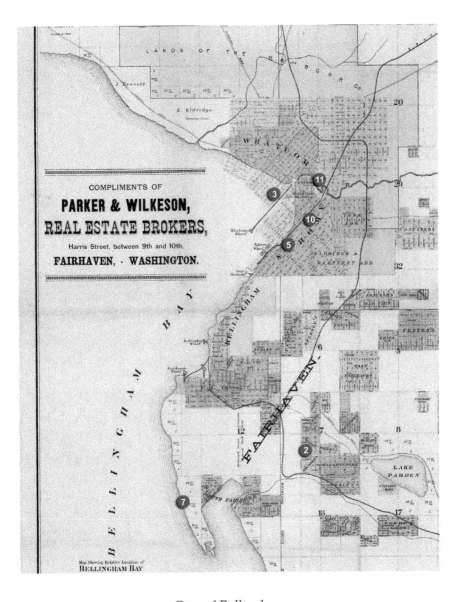

City of Bellingham

2 - Padden murder

3 - Snowball Wallace murder

5 - Frederick Dames murder

7 - Tunnel 21

10) Elsie Worstell murder

11) Dominica Stumpo murder

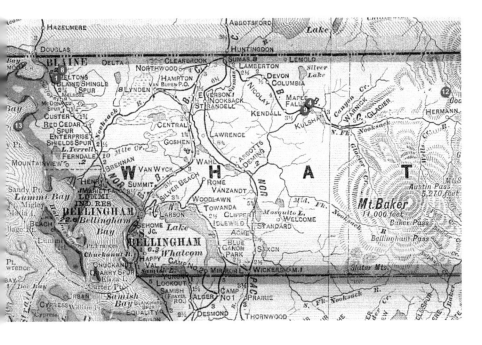

Whatcom County

1 ~ Josephine Thomson murder   9 ~ Sam Thompson murder

4 ~ James Logan murder   12 ~ Martin Orner murder

8 ~ Gaultier & Thurston murders   13 ~ Teitur Hannesson murder

T. A. Warger is an historian based in Bellingham, Washington. As a film-maker, Warger is the recipient of the 2009 Washington State Historical Society's David Douglas Award for the documentary film, *Shipyard*. His latest documentary, *The Mountain Runners* (2012) is an award-winning and Emmy nominated film about the 1911-1913 Mount Baker Marathon. Warger is the co-author of *Images of America: Mount Baker*, writes for the Whatcom County Historical Society's Journal, and has written for the Journal of the Puget Sound Maritime Historical Society's Sea Chest. He received his BA from University of Nevada and graduate studies from Western Washington University. Warger is on staff at the Whatcom Museum.

Artist and illustrator **Jake Reller** received his BFA from Western Washington University in 2013 as Distinguished Scholar for his department. He is currently pursuing his masters at Virginia Commonwealth University and is represented by the Robert Fontaine Gallery in Miami, FL.

Printed in the USA
CPSIA information can be obtained
at www.ICGtesting.com
JSHW011744240324
59708JS00010B/69

9 780989 289122